THE HISTORY OF
FINSBAY LODGE, HARRIS
LIFE AND FISHING ON A HEBRIDEAN ISLE

THE HISTORY OF
FINSBAY LODGE, HARRIS
LIFE AND FISHING ON A HEBRIDEAN ISLE

Michael L.G. Gardner DSc FIBiol

Professor Emeritus, University of Bradford

Front cover: Norman Jamieson FRCS of Horsacleit, Harris with fish; Finsbay Lodge, based on a postcard by A.A. Chisholm, ca 1903.
Back cover: Oil painting of Finsbay Lodge, © R.A. MacLeod, Quidinish, Harris; Sunset at The Obbe, Leverburgh, © Michael Gardner

Published by:
Michael Gardner
Hazelhurst Brow Farm
Malvern Road, Bradford
West Yorkshire BD9 6AR U.K.
ISBN: 978-0-9559284-0-6
British Library Cataloguing-in-Publication Data
A catalogue record for this book is available from the British Library

Designed & originated by Carnegie Book Production, Lancaster
Printed by the Cromwell Press, Trowbridge

CONTENTS

Fishing on The Obbe at Leverburgh at sunset
© Michael Gardner

PREFACE BY DAVID CAMERON

This book will appeal to a wide variety of readers. Within its pages there are glimpses of unique Hebridean life experiences for both local and visitor at the beginning of the 20th century. When this is combined with the meticulously researched detail not of just the fishing but also of the characters that were drawn to the Isle of Harris, here you have a volume which must be of interest to any student of island life or to any enthusiast of the art of angling for wild fish.

I was brought up in a Hebridean angling hotel just before the decline both in the richness of fishing and in the number of colourful individuals who made the Isle of Harris their summer retreat. Professor Gardner's book brings back vivid memories of coming downstairs in the morning and finding the marble table covered in sea trout as a result of night fishing in July, then the evening ritual of weighing and recording the day's catch, and finally the late night conversations in the bar with a huge variety of fascinating people. Finsbay Lodge would have been no different.

This book fills a major knowledge gap in not only the astonishingly vivid and short-lived life of the Lodge and its guests, but also in the contribution which a Hebridean Island and its people made at a very particular and perhaps a very peculiar time in our history.

Finsbay Lodge is not treated in isolation, but its relationship with other features in the history of Harris is examined. The hotel at Rodel, the lodge at Borve, the fishing at Leverburgh and Horsacleit, and the school at Finsbay all play their part. The contributions of Leverhulme and Dunmore find their place along with Thomas Wilson, Archie Chisholm, the Lodge staff and the local children. It also shows that land reform and fish hatcheries are not just a late twentieth century feature but were happening almost 100 years ago!

The illustrations of the Finsbay Lodge building convey a sense almost of unreality of the Hebridean Sporting Association project and, although the photographic quality is excellent, sadly few pictures of the time have been discovered. However, each time this book is re-read, as it will be, the picture drawn by the words more than fills the gap. Each reading also leaves a feeling of wanting to know more.

The book will raise awareness of the Finsbay story and has the potential to attract further nuggets of information before they are lost for all times. I know that this is one of Professor Gardner's hopes.

It has been a privilege to write this preface, but it is well past time that you should be left to discover the book's delights for yourself.

David Cameron
Tarbert
Isle of Harris
May 2008

Acknowledgements

I am most grateful to the numerous people who have assisted me, contributed information, suggested sources or who have given permission to reproduce material. These include: Bath Archives, Bath Local Studies Library, the British Medical Journal; Charterhouse Archive and Ann Wheeler (Archivist), John Dewar & Sons Ltd and Jacqui Seargeant (Archivist); the Diageo Archive and Jennifer Birnie (Archivist); the Dunfermline Carnegie Library and Chris Neale; Edinburgh University Library (Salvesen Archive) and Tricia Boyd; Glasgow City Libraries; the Harris Community Trust and Gillian Scott-Forest; the Harris Historical Society and John Murdo Morrison; the Inverness Field Club and Gwneth Cameron (Hon. Secretary); Inverness Reference Library and Edwina Burridge; the Leverhulme Family Archive and Gavin Hunter (Honorary Archivist); the Moffat Museum Trust and John B. Murray; the National Archives of Scotland; the Ordnance Survey; the Royal Society; Rugby School Archives and Rusty MacLean (Archivist); St Andrews University, Christine Gascoigne, Rachel Hart and Dr Norman Reid; the Unilever Archives at Port Sunlight and Claire Tunstall (Archivist); the Western Isles Library (Stornoway) and David Fowler; Dr Jan Abel; Douglas Bertram; Gillian Bertram; Dr Helen Bilsby; the late R. Niall Campbell; Alastair Chisholm; Anne Costigan; Gordon Cumming; Jack Davis; Sir Tom Dunlop; Donald Ferguson; John Gifford; the late Lady Gubbins; Captain Donald Gunn; John B. Hill; Iain Hope; Tom Jourdan; Chris Lawson; Jonathan Lucas; John Macdonald; Joina Macdonald; John and Mimi MacKay; John MacKay; John Norman MacKay; David Maclennan; John Maclennan; Murdo MacLeod; Pat Mackreth; Prof. Donald Meek; Julia Melvin and Dr George Gandy; Dr Harold Mills; the late Nigel Nicolson; Dr Katherine Ross; Vince Taylor; Dr Ronald Weir; Fiona Whyte; and the late Eddie Young. The National Archives of Scotland, the Unilever Archives and Julia Melvin have been donors of particularly valuable archival information.

Particular debts of gratitude are due to Tony and Heather Scherr of Borve, Roddy MacLeod of Quidinish, John Angus Macleod of Largs (and formerly Tarbert), and my wife, Dr Marjorie Gardner, who have played key roles in my enquiries and have constantly delved into my queries and greatly encouraged me to uncover the story which had been *"a fugitive mystery for too long"* in the words of another correspondent. Without their endless help, this book would not have come to fruition. All care has been taken to ensure the accuracy of facts and the good faith of interpretations: the responsibility for these is mine, but it must be noted that the passage of time makes it impossible to verify all facts.

Last, but not least, I am very grateful to David Cameron of Tarbert for generously contributing the Preface and to Anna Goddard and Lucy Day of Carnegie Book Production for great assistance and commitment in producing this book.

CHAPTER ONE
INTRODUCTION

Ever since my first fishing visit to the Isle of Harris in 1970 I have been intrigued by the number of artificial lochs, dams, sluices, and other waterworks. It was obvious that these had been created many years ago for the benefit of angling. Harris has long had a reputation for excellent salmon and sea trout fishing, once highly exclusive, but now fairly accessible to anglers and a delight to those who enjoy fishing amidst wild Hebridean scenery. Even more perplexing was my subsequent finding that hardly anything is known about the history or origin of these works. The one exception to this is Loch Fincastle near Luskentyre, part of the Laxdale river system on the west side of the island, which is well known to have been built by Lord Dunmore, the proprietor of South Harris, in 1897/8. Loch Fincastle, now part of the Borve Lodge Estate, has been described in very positive terms by Hamish Stuart whose two books on fishing, *Lochs and Loch Fishing* in 1899 and *The Book of the Sea Trout*, published posthumously in 1917, have become regarded as classic angling literature.

It was astonishing to learn that there had been some sort of fishing hotel near Finsbay; although the ruined foundations of a very substantial building were still visible, nobody could tell me anything about this mysterious place!

I subsequently determined to delve into the history of Finsbay Lodge and the development of the fishing lochs in South Harris, and this book is the outcome of my research over a 7–year period. Initially I was reluctant to publish the findings, remarkable as they turned out to be, until I could answer all the important questions that remained enigmatic. However, recognising that these answers and the complete story may never be provided and with the fear that the existing historical knowledge could easily be lost, I am now telling the story of the extraordinary Finsbay Lodge, at Quidinish in South Harris, and the people who built it. These were a group of Glasgow businessmen who formed a limited company, the Hebridean Sporting Association, Ltd., in 1903. Information has now come to light about them and other key people associated with this innovative venture. The company also leased Rodel Lodge, now Rodel Hotel, opening up more accommodation and sporting opportunities until the First World War and a serious financial crisis interrupted their activities. It could be fairly said that there has never since been a similar large-scale and imaginative development for sporting fishing in the UK, let alone in the Outer Hebrides! The venture also had major benefits for men and women in the local community by way of provision of employment as ghillies and domestic staff.

In the course of investigating the history of this venture, the pioneering activities of the 7th and 8th Earls of Dunmore, the proprietors of South Harris, in developing the freshwater fishings of South Harris have come to light, and these are explained. Lord Dunmore's successor as owner of South Harris was the famous and charismatic Lord Leverhulme (later Viscount Leverhulme), who had founded Lever Brothers which eventually became the multi-national giant Unilever Plc. Lord Leverhulme's ownership of Harris and whose great efforts, not always appreciated, to bring industrial activity with new wealth and welfare to the island were extremely interesting matters for social history. Lord Leverhulme becomes especially relevant in the present context because it now turns out that the final fate – dereliction – of Finsbay Lodge was in his hands. However, he must not be blamed for its demise, as the First World War and the very nature of the Hebridean Sporting Association, its ambitious plans, and the financial burden of the whole venture had all contributed to set the scene for the end of the Association and their fine building. All these aspects are described in this book.

The Scottish Office, the fore-runner of the present devolved Scottish Parliament, was also of great influence in Harris. Because of its involvement, even then, in Land Reform and in subsidising transport to and in the Western Isles, it was closely involved in providing subsidies to aid the crofting counties of Scotland and in the Hebridean Sporting Association's bids to obtain a publicly subsidised shipping call at Loch Finsbay for the benefit of visitors to Finsbay Lodge. It also recognised that it had to attempt the near-impossible task of reconciling the conflicting interests of the crofting community and their returning servicemen with those of land proprietors; the attitudes and behaviour of proprietors in the Highlands and Islands ranged from benevolent to malevolent. While subsequent analysis strongly makes the case that Lord Leverhulme's intentions were wholly benevolent, this certainly was not clear to all parties at the time. Doubtless, there remain some people who question his motives, but they probably have considered only one side of the complex issues.

Over a hundred years have elapsed since the building of Finsbay Lodge. As well as lapses of memory and no particular desire by people to record local history, various fires and the ravages of two world wars have taken their toll on both private and public records. This seems to be even more true for Harris than for other parts of the country. Additionally, the fragmentation of estates in Harris since 1925 has contributed to the loss of records and other written information. Nevertheless, very informative archival information has been found, so that it has been possible to identify all the members of the Hebridean Sporting Association, to describe the angling results, to reproduce letters from an angling visitor who spent a week at Finsbay Lodge immediately before the outbreak of the First World War, and to quote an architect's report on the decaying structure of Finsbay Lodge in the early 1920s.

The whole story is remarkable. However, it is also particularly noteworthy, and alarming to anyone interested in heritage and local or sporting history, to see the extent to which details have been lost from knowledge, and it is hoped that this book will partially redress this. There remain enigmatic gaps in our knowledge of the story and, if any readers can explain these, I shall be very grateful to hear from them.

I should explain that I am not a professional historian. My professional background has been in medical biochemistry and physiology, but I also have long-standing interests in fishing and fish biology and in the Western Isles. Curiously, it turns out that several extremely distinguished characters in academic chemistry, world famous scientists, have had important links with the fishings of Finsbay Lodge and South Harris, and these will be explained below.

CHAPTER TWO

THE HEBRIDEAN SPORTING ASSOCIATION, 1903 TO 1920

In February 1903 a small group of Glasgow businessmen, solicitors and merchants, all keen anglers, formed a limited company, registered in Edinburgh, the Hebridean Sporting Association Ltd. Figs. 2.1 & 2.2 show the company's Certificate of Incorporation and the front page of the Prospectus; Appendix 1 reproduces the company's Prospectus issued to prospective shareholders. The company's stated aims were not financial, but to provide top class salmon and sea trout fishing on the Isle of Harris. The fishings there had hitherto been highly exclusive, accessible only to tenants who took year-long leases of shooting, stalking and fishing. The sea trout fishing, in particular, was reputed to be among the best in Scotland and perhaps equal to the best in the world.

The initial subscribers founding the company were:

- **John Malcolm** (1858–1929) Ship Broker from Glasgow – he styled himself and signed as "Jno. Malcolm" – who almost certainly was the prime mover in the venture and who remained deeply involved throughout its existence. His enthusiasm for fishing was almost certainly generated by his grandfather, William Tough, who had been for many years the Inn Keeper at Scourie in Sutherland (see p. 195). See Fig. 2.3; also Fig 13.6 in Chapter 13 below;
- **John Dempster** (~1848–1914) Produce Merchant from Carmunnock near Glasgow;
- **William Fergusson** (~1853–1916) Solicitor[1], Glasgow who became Chairman;

---

[1] Scottish solicitors at this time often were described as "Writers", a term now reserved for Writers to the Signet. It is possible that Mr Fergusson was a distant cousin of John Malcolm, but any family relationship was not a close one

- **James Anderson** Manufacturer, Glasgow;
- **David Strathie** Chartered Accountant, Glasgow;
- **Charles Robert Murray** (~1857–1917) Iron & Steel Merchant, Glasgow; and
- **Thomas James Gilchrist Boyes** (~1848–1925) Solicitor, Bonnybridge.

The initial company Directors were: John Malcolm, John Dempster (until his death in 1914), William Fergusson (until his death in 1916), and James Anderson (until his resignation in 1907).

David Strathie was appointed as the Auditor, and Boyes & Fergusson (116 Hope Street, Glasgow)[2] acted as the company's

---

[2] Boyes & Fergusson became Boyes & Cameron until the death of J. Burns Cameron in 1953 after which the business was amalgamated with Andrew Howard McFarlane and later subsumed into Bannatyne, Kirkwood, France & Co.

This Prospectus has been filed with the Registrar of Joint Stock Companies, in terms of the Companies Acts, 1862 to 1900.

The Hebridean Sporting Association,
LIMITED.

Incorporated under the Companies Acts, 1862 to 1900, under which the liability of Shareholders is limited to the amount unpaid on their Shares.

SHARE CAPITAL, - - - £10,000.
In 1000 Shares of £10 each.
(Present Issue 600 Shares of £10 each).

Payable £1 on application, £2 on Allotment, and the balance as may be required.

A considerable number of Gentlemen have promised their support, and should the present Issue be over applied for, they will have a preference in the allotment.

Directors :—

JOHN DEMPSTER, Produce Merchant, Craigmiln, Carmunnock, *near Glasgow*.
JOHN MALCOLM, Ship Broker, 3 Kensington Gate, Kelvinside, Glasgow.
WILLIAM FERGUSSON, Solicitor, Veremont, Park Gardens N., Partick, *Glasgow*.
JAMES ANDERSON, Manufacturer, 4 Kingsborough Gardens, Kelvinside, Glasgow.
An additional Director may be appointed at the first Statutory Meeting of the Company.

Bankers ;—

UNION BANK OF SCOTLAND, LIMITED, St. Vincent Street Branch, Glasgow.

Auditor :—

DAVID STRATHIE, Chartered Accountant, Glasgow.

Solicitors :—

BOYES & FERGUSSON, 116 Hope Street, Glasgow.

Secretary and Registered Office :—

GEORGE DUKE STIRLING, Chartered Accountant, 154 St. Vincent Street, Glasgow.

EXCHEQUER
EXCHEQUER 11 FEB. 1903 EDINBURGH
10 FEB. 1903

REGISTERED
11 FEB. 1903

M John Malcolm,
Hon Secretary

Fig. 2.3 John Malcolm, founding Director of the Hebridean Sporting Association. From *The Bailie* 1913 [1].

Solicitors. Both Mr Boyes and Mr Fergusson were founding subscribers. The company Secretary was George Duke Stirling CA[3] at their registered office at 154 St. Vincent Street, Glasgow until he resigned due to ill health in 1907, after which he was succeeded by W.B. Mackie at 116 Hope Street, Glasgow, the address of the Association's solicitors. In 1907, Thomas Binnie Jr (1867–1937: Land Valuator, Glasgow) and in 1918 Samuel Stevenson (1871–1937: Timber Merchant, Newlands, Glasgow) became Directors.

Initially the Company had an authorised capital of £10,000, divided into 1000 shares of £10 each, though to raise further funds this authorised capital was increased to £13,000 in 1905 to include 300 preference shares of £10 each. To raise even more capital when it became clear that the Association's financial situation was difficult, debentures were issued (£890), but the debenture holders waived their interest. The company also took out a number of loans which became an increasing burden. The Company's Prospectus never provided for the issue of a dividend, so this form of return cannot have been the motive for membership. The possibility of the investment making a capital gain on the eventual disposal of Finsbay Lodge was not explicitly mentioned, but a finite lifetime for the venture may have been envisaged. Some shareholders may have been anticipating this and may have regarded the venture as an interesting speculative investment.

The Company quickly attracted 75 shareholders, each person initially putting in the minimum investment of £100 (except for one, John Collins, a master at Rugby school, who managed to join with a smaller investment of £50!). The sum of £100 would be the equivalent of about £10,000 invested by each member at today's rates[4].

---

[3] George Duke Stirling was a brother-in-law of John Dempster

[4] It is convenient to use a multiplier of 100 x to estimate the current cost, but a slightly more accurate estimate would be £7,700, based on the composite price indices in 1903 and 2007.

Surname.	Christian Name.	Address.	Description.	Number of Shares allotted.
Names, Addresses, and Descriptions of the Allottees.				
Dempster	John	Craigmilar, Larmannoch	Merchant	10
Malcolm	John	70 Wellington Street, Glasgow	Shipbroker	10
Fergusson	William	Tennant Park Dowanhill Partick, Glasgow	Solicitor	10
Anderson	James	1 Kingsborough Gardens, Glasgow	Manufacturer	10
Strathie	David	162 St. Vincent Street, Glasgow	Chartered Accountant	10
Murray	Charles R	Westbank, Parkhill, Glasgow	Merchant	10
Boyes	Thomas James Gilchrist	Thorn, Bearsden, Stirlingshire	Solicitor	10
Wilson	John	156 St Vincent Street, Glasgow	Chartered Accountant	10
Stirling	George Duke	156 St Vincent Street, Glasgow	Chartered Accountant	10
Huslop	William	162 St. Vincent Street, Glasgow	Solicitor	10
Reid	William Loudon	7 Royal Crescent, Glasgow W	Physician	10
Stevenson	Samuel	Polmadie Saw Mills, Rutherglen Road, Glasgow	Timber Merchant	10
Kennedy	Moses Hunter	23 Kingsborough Gardens, Glasgow	Contractor	10
Dunlop	Thomas	70 Wellington Street, Glasgow	Shipowner	10
Brown	Albert Richard	36 West George Street, Glasgow	Merchant	10
Macleod	Dugald Brodie	11 Belhaven Terrace, Glasgow	Retired	10
Cochran	Reginald Purves	Buntings, Uxbridge, Middlesex, England	Captain Royal Clergy	15
Nevill	Hugh	4 Corbet Court, Gracechurch Street, London E C	J.P	10
Bond	E Morton	Groylands, Surbiton, Surrey	Gentleman	10
Bond	Richard Shaw	Groylands, Surbiton, Surrey	Gentleman	10

Fig. 2.4 The first page of the first annual return of shareholders in the Hebridean Sporting Association Ltd. Each year a similar register was prepared. Reproduced by kind permission of the National Archives of Scotland [BT2/5276].

The surviving Company's House records [2] [5] preserved by the National Archives of Scotland in Edinburgh include the names and addresses of the shareholders as part of the annual returns required by the Companies Act (1900), and Fig. 2.4 shows the first page of the first return; but the archive contains only two Directors' reports (those for the 1903 and 1908 Annual General Meetings) and an incomplete set of annual financial accounts. The Association's own files of correspondence and folios of members' details have

---

[5]   Numbers in square brackets refer to citations in the Bibliography at the end of this book

unfortunately not been preserved. Appendix 2 lists details of the shareholders, and Chapter 13 gives brief biographical snapshots of some of them: it is clear that there were many interesting characters among them.

Several people, writers and local Hebrideans, have assumed that the founders were an *English* fishing club, but this is not the case. This mistake may have been because "incomers", especially non-Highland and non-Gaelic-speaking ones, and landed proprietors were often colloquially given the euphemism "English", the Hebrideans being naturally an insular population.

The 75 shareholders in the new company came from all over the UK, though there was a distinct predominance of Glaswegians (33), many living in the Kelvinside area. There were 11 solicitors, but other professions featured among the membership: 4 chartered accountants, 2 clergymen, 3 coal merchants or coal masters, 5 merchants, 3 ship owners or ship brokers, 1 physician and 2 surgeons, and 4 describing themselves as manufacturers. There was only one lady subscriber, and she was the sole Harris resident among the shareholders – Mrs Christina Wilson (née Christina Paterson from Bernera) who was the 2nd wife of the Lochmaddy solicitor, Thomas Wilson, also a member, discussed below. Between them, the two Wilsons had 35 shares (including the Preference Shares that were later issued), a greater investment than any other member.

Many of the Subscribers to the Company were highly prominent men in Scottish civic and commercial positions. It is clear, though, that use of Finsbay Lodge or Rodel Lodge and the fishings was not confined to Company shareholders, though the stated intention was that priority for accommodation at Rodel Lodge would be given to shareholders. Newspaper reports of fishing results often included anglers who were not shareholders; Professor and Mrs Purdie, also Professor and Mrs Henderson, were regular visitors, but not shareholders. (Professor Henderson eventually became a shareholder in 1919, by which time the Association was about to go into liquidation).

We suspect that at least a few of the shareholders who invested in the Association did so to give their support to the novel Hebridean development, rather than from any desire to fish or to benefit eventually from any monetary gain. It is likely that there was a wide spectrum of motives of shareholders; some wanted access to the famed fishing, others wanted a capital return in due course, while others simply wanted to support the venture and the community. Some may have seen the potential for the opening up of the Harris fishings to visitors and the potential benefits of such developments.

Harris had been owned by Alexander Norman Macleod until 1834 when he sold it to the 5th Earl of Dunmore for £60,000. In about 1890 Charles Adolphus Murray[6], the 7th Earl of Dunmore transferred the whole estate to his son, Alexander Edward Murray, Viscount Fincastle VC who later succeeded as the 8th Earl of Dunmore in 1907. The Hebridean Sporting Association entered in 1903 into two separate leases with Viscount Fincastle. Regrettably, the Dunmore's legal records, including probably these Leases, appear to have been lost in a fire at their London solicitors in World War II. Neither are there any records remaining at the successors to the Dunmore family's Edinburgh solicitors.

One lease was for 5 years in the first instance, but was subsequently extended, for the Lodge at Rodel (see Chapter 4) which provided accommodation for about 10 to 15 guests and also its fishings at the Obbe which encompassed a major system close to the village of An t-Ob. In December 1920 An t-Ob was renamed Leverburgh after the Bolton soap magnate Lord Leverhulme[7], founder of Lever Bros (which became Unilever in 1929), bought Harris from the 8th Earl of Dunmore in 1919 and tried to establish a major sea-fishing industry and other commercial enterprises there (see Chapter 11).

The second lease entered into by the Hebridean Sporting Association with Viscount Fincastle was a 15 year lease[8] for the Finsbay and Grosebay fishings on the East coast of South Harris together with land at Quidinish. The Association was to use this land for building their magnificent Finsbay Lodge (see Chapter 3). Fig. 2.5 shows a painting of Finsbay Lodge by a retired engineer and amateur artist, Roddy A. MacLeod, a native of Quidinish less than a mile from the Lodge, who based it on the Archie Chisholm

---

[6] He was renowned as an amateur explorer, having walked and ridden 2,500 miles, traversing 41 mountain passes and 69 rivers through Kashmir and Tibet

[7] Leverville in the Congo was created by Lord Leverhulme, one of the centres of his palm-oil enterprises

[8] This was subsequently revised to be a 20–year lease from June 1905 with a break at 10 years

picture postcard (the picture on the back cover of this book is based on this painting). The lochs in the fishings leased comprised almost all the lochs in South Harris, and they are detailed in Chapter 5. It eventually turned out that the end of this lease was to coincide with the accumulation of debts by the Association and the sale of Harris by Lord Dunmore to Lord Leverhulme, all of which marked the beginning of the demise of the Association. Together, the two leases comprised over 38,000 acres in addition to the extensive fishings and the Lodge at Rodel.

The rents payable to Viscount Fincastle were quite substantial[9]: £350 per annum for Rodel (House plus fishings) and £500 per annum for Finsbay and Grosebay (fishings, land, and shootings) – say a total of about £85,000 p.a. in current terms! (Later, in the 1925 sale particulars after Lord Leverhulme's death, see below, the rentals for Rodel Hotel and fishings and for Finsbay fishings were estimated at £200 and £150 respectively.) These rents were obviously going to be a major financial burden on the Association with its 75 members, especially as there was no surplus capital to invest and apparently no strong income stream, so the Company was not self-financing. The published accounts (see Appendix 3) do not show any income from visiting anglers, apart from board and lodging, even for non-shareholders. As far as we can see, the Company functioned on its capital. The working capital was substantially depleted by the extravagance of the building costs for Finsbay Lodge and the furnishing costs for both lodges, both of which greatly exceeded the Directors' initial estimates. However, their investment did give the members the use of an enormous variety of outstanding fishing in dramatic remote surroundings – 38 named lochs were included (see Chapter 5) – together with the use of about 30 boats. It remains speculative as to whether the lack of provision for income to meet the rents and taxes was deliberate and connected with a plan for a limited lifetime for the venture.

Appendix 3 shows extracts from the existing financial records, and it is clear that the Association's non-capital expenditure exceeded the income in all except three years over the period 1906 to 1916 (Data for 1903 to 1905 are not available). By 1908,

[9] These accounted partly for the downfall of the Association. With hindsight, Viscount Fincastle's charges were steep but he, in turn, was at that time investing much capital in developing the fishings – see Chapter 7.

the cumulative loss had amounted to £3,596, and the Directors reported to an annual general meeting that they were taking steps to curb expenditure. This was just their first financial crisis!

Though the rents paid to Viscount Fincastle totalled £850 per annum for the initial two leases, the accounts show that these were substantially reduced from at least 1906. New 20–year leases with Viscount Fincastle were effected in 1906[10], with a break to be allowed after 10 years from 1905. It seems probable that, in order to ameliorate their financial situation, the Association agreed with Viscount Fincastle to reduce the extent of fishings leased by removing the Horsacleit and Grosebay fishings from the lease. The Association's advertisements in Watson Lyall's *Sportsman's and Tourist's Guide* ceased to mention the Grosebay fishings from the issue of Summer 1906 onwards. From 1908 onwards, their advertisements in that Guide were smaller and lacked a picture of Finsbay Lodge, presumably as part of the economy measures.

Fig. 2.5 Painting of Finsbay Lodge by Roddy A. MacLeod, a native of Quidinish, Harris, who based it on the 1903 postcard picture taken by Archie Chisholm. A.A. Chisholm was a member of the Hebridean Sporting Association, Procurator Fiscal at Lochmaddy, and an accomplished photographer who took many postcard scenes in the Long Island (see Chapter 12). Reproduced by kind permission of R.A. MacLeod.

---

10   There is some uncertainty of the date of the revised leases as the Feu Charter issued in 1916 refers to the date of these 2 leases as 1908.

The Association had also bought some guns, and its Memorandum of Association had included the laying down of grouse and other game as one of their possible objectives, though it appears that shooting was never significantly among its real agenda. It advertised the grouse and winter shootings in *The Scotsman* newspaper in August 1904, but no income from this ever appeared in the accounts. They purchased for £40 a wagonette and harness, presumably to provide transport to the more distant fishings or between Finsbay and Rodel and the sum of £100 was budgeted for horses "if required". There was no evidence that these were ever required!

The extent of sporting opportunities available to members and other guests was far greater than any other syndicate fishings currently known to the author. Initially at least in the existence of the Association, quality and quantity were sought, regardless of cost. Facilities for canoeing, mountain climbing, sea excursions and fishing, and camping out also were advertised in the 1903 Prospectus which was imaginative and innovative (see Appendix 1).

It is clear that fishery improvement was prominent in the Association's ambitious plans. However we believe that they, unlike Lord Dunmore (see Chapter 7), never operated a fish hatchery. In the early years of existence, the Association spent £412 on "improvement of lochs" (including £200 spent by June 1903 at the very start of their operations), though the available records give no details of the actual works undertaken. However, for comparison, one can note that Hamish Stuart, in *Lochs and Loch Fishing* (1899) [3, p.345], states that the creation of Loch Fincastle (then and now an important fishery on the Borve Lodge Estate) at the outlet of the River Laxdale into the sea near Luskentyre by Lord Dunmore had cost about £200 in about 1898[11]. One may suppose that the success of creating Loch Fincastle provided the stimulus to dam the Mill Pool which appears to have been a tidal pond, part of the Obbe, until after 1903. So obviously a lot of work could have been done for the Association's £412.

It is interesting that the terms of lease and the Association's

---

[11]   However, this figure of £200 may include the other fishery improvement work undertaken by Lord Dunmore and his factor, Thomas Wilson, on the Laxdale system – see Chapter 7.

Prospectus did not mention the Mill Pool between the Obbe and L. Steisevat, and the large scale Ordnance Survey 1903 maps show only a tidal basin, an arm of the Obbe, where the Mill Pool is now. There was a mill on the shore of L. Steisevat, near where the Church of Scotland at Leverburgh currently stands, but no dam was shown on the map. Hence, it seems that either Viscount Fincastle or the Association were responsible for construction of the dam at An Clachan to create the Mill Pool, a brackish pond, effectively at the head of tide, in the first decade of the 1900s. Watson Lyall's *Sportsman's and Tourist's Guide* first mentioned the Mill Pool in the issue for Summer 1910, though one cannot be confident that the earlier issues of the *Guide* were reliably up to date. They do, however, prove that the Mill Pool was created before 1910, and it is almost certain that it was created after February 1903. We do not, though, know definitely whether this was the work of the Hebridean Sporting Association or Viscount Fincastle – see Chapter 5. It is perfectly possible that the Mill Pool was created between February 1903, when the Company was formed, and June 1903, when the first Annual General Meeting was told that £200 had already been spent on loch improvement.

With such a plethora of successful business people and accountants, it is clear that the Hebridean Sporting Association was not being run by a bunch of enthusiastic but amateur tyros making financial misjudgments, so this cannot be the reason for

Well-built sluices are still to be seen on the outlets from many of the other lochs, even in quite remote locations, and these too must have been the work of either Viscount Fincastle or the Association, though there is remarkable lack of knowledge about early developments on these fisheries in writing or in the hands of current or recent proprietors. Land Registry deeds in the Register of Sasines shed no light on these developments. A few of the fishing improvements, certainly those for removal of obstructions at the mouth of the Horsacleit River (near Meavag on the east coast), were to be financed by the Proprietor, Viscount Fincastle, according to the particulars given in the Association's Prospectus (1903). These were intended to make the Horsacleit system, including L. Mora and L. Uamadale, accessible to salmon and sea trout with the prospect that they would become excellent fisheries – at this time, Loch Horsacleit (also called House Loch) and the lodge on its shore did not exist – see Chapter 8.

With such a plethora of successful business people and accountants, it is clear that the Hebridean Sporting Association was not being run by a bunch of enthusiastic but amateur tyros making financial misjudgments, so this cannot be the reason for

Fig. 2.6 Advertisement from the Autumn 1914 Issue of Watson Lyall's *Sportsman's and Tourist's Guide to the Rivers, Lochs, Moors & Deer Forests of Scotland*, showing the Rodel Angling Club and the Finsbay Angling Club being run somewhat independently.

its financial fate. A pre-planned limited life, running on capital, together with the serious, but wholly unpredictable, problems caused by World War I offer a much more plausible explanation – see below. The expenditure greatly exceeded preliminary estimates, and it appears that use of the fishings and accommodation was less than anticipated – a matter of over ambitious planning and, perhaps, an attitude of passive acceptance by the shareholders who were mainly, but not exclusively, prosperous men. At this time, many successful businessmen were quietly philanthropic: the Hebridean Sporting Association may well have appealed to some as a worthy and novel cause. Its activities certainly provided significant employment among the community and opened up access to Harris to outsiders.

Despite the business experiences of the Directors, the number of accountants in the Company, and the fact that their auditor, David Strathie, was also a founder Subscriber, the financial record of the Association seems to have been a fiasco. The authorised capital for the Company was £13,000, but it was not fully taken up. There clearly was a serious underestimate of the capital cost of the lodge and its furnishings; furthermore, almost every year the Association ran at a financial loss, so that debts continued to build up.

In 1905, additional Preference Shares were issued, though it appears that interest on them was never paid. Eventually, 755 ordinary shares plus 115 preference shares of £10 had been taken up. Likewise, debentures were later sold (£890) in 1907, with a repayment date of 16 June 1925, but the 5% interest on them was always waived by the holders. The venture was running on ever-diminishing capital. It seems that no income provision had been made to meet the substantial rents. The charges to visiting anglers simply did not meet the regular outgoings, especially the rental.

As a response to their recognition of the ever-worsening financial situation, the Association formed two clubs, first the Rodel Angling Club in 1908, then shortly afterwards the Finsbay Angling Club, so that the running costs and board and lodging charges of Rodel Hotel and Finsbay Lodge could be accounted for separately. Shareholders were invited to pay extra, up to £10 per year, for membership of one of these clubs. Members were entitled to a 10% discount on their board and lodging costs. The plan was that only £5 of the fee would be called up unless the year's accounts showed a deficit, in which case the remaining £5 would be collected! The two clubs were run somewhat independently, at least with respect to making bookings (see Fig. 2.6), and their finances were independent of the Association whose accounts began to show payments received from the clubs for board and lodging. No shareholder ever sold or cashed-in their shares, though quite a number passed them on to executors or legatees[12]; and there is no record of any shareholders expressing concerns about the financial affairs of the venture. One Director, James Anderson, did resign from office, but appears to have continued his membership.

In 1911, 1912 and 1913 (no full financial data available for 1912) the accounts at last showed an annual profit, and it looked as though the financial situation was coming under control – see Appendix 3. However, the declaration of War inevitably damaged the business. The 1916 accounts, filed very late at Company's House, reported:

> "The War has interfered greatly to the Association's disadvantage with the lease of Finsbay (which expires in June 1918) there having been very few guests in the last 2 seasons, both seasons were very dry and sport suffered" [2]

By the end of 1916, the cumulative losses amounted to £4,807 (i.e. about £400,000 in modern terms) and considerable loans, both from the bank and from individual people especially two Directors, had been received. The Inventory of William Fergusson's Estate in 1917 recorded nil value for his Ordinary shares, Preference shares, and Debenture loan [4].

The Company's Prospectus, issued in 1903, had hinted that the Leases and the ownership of Finsbay Lodge might have a finite life:

---

[12] A considerable number of the shareholders died during the lifetime of the Association, but from natural causes rather than active service

"... At the termination of the Lease, this Lodge may be taken over by the proprietor at a valuation, but, if not, it will remain the property of the Association ... ". [2]

We can only guess whether this might have been a planned "exit" devised in the knowledge that the key founders would be beyond their prime and ready to demit from a good period of first class sport; also some of the shareholders may have hoped that their investment would have provided a capital gain. As matters turned out, this was very prescient. The year 1916 saw the deaths of two of the Founders and of quite a number of shareholders and the aftermath of a financial crisis that had resulted in the Company being sued in 1915 in the Court of Session, the most senior civil Court in Scotland, by their Proprietor and Feu Superior for arrears of rent [5]; further there was a collapse of tourist trade to the Western Isles and general dysfunction caused by World War I. This marked another financial crisis, which turned out to become an irretrievable situation!

In 1915 following the Court of Session proceedings against them for arrears of rent, the Association lost their tenancy of Rodel Lodge and its fishings; these were taken over by a new organisation *"The Rodel Syndicate"* (see Chapter 4 and Fig 4.4). However, as explained in Chapter 4, this Syndicate also was doomed to develop financial difficulties! The loss of Rodel Lodge caused serious extra financial losses to the Association in 1915, especially through depreciation of the assets, mainly furnishings and boats[13], associated with Rodel – see the extracts of the accounts in Appendix 3.

In 1916, Lord Dunmore (the 8th Earl) granted a Feu Charter [6] at a cost of £1 per annum to the Association in respect of 15 acres of land including the land on which Finsbay Lodge stood. This would enable the Association to sell Finsbay Lodge. In this Charter he explicitly stated that he did not wish to take over the Lodge, an option already written into the lease which had expired at the 10– year break on 16 June 1915.

The Feu Charter obliged the Association *"... to keep the Lodge in good tenantable order ... and, in the event of fire, to erect a new Lodge or dwelling of at least a value of £400 ... . To keep the fence enclosing the piece of land in good order ... and not to sell spirits,*

---

13 In fact the Association in liquidation subsequently recouped £149/1/6d in 1922 or 1923 from Lord Leverhulme for these assets

beer, ale or other intoxicating liquors ... " It further stipulated *"While not coming under any obligation to do so [they] shall protect the fishings in the sea coast or other waters on the Estate from injury by unauthorised persons but shall not be liable to appoint watchers or incur any expense beyond what they themselves consider necessary ... "* [6] It is curious that such a legal document stipulated this whilst not making the fishery protection a formal obligation. Nevertheless, it shows that watchers (or bailiffs) were then regarded as important to secure the safety of the fishery against poachers or unauthorised fishers. Most Harris estates with ongoing fishery interests have continued to see such protection as necessary.

Finally, the Association ceased their operation in 1918. The 15–year lease had ended in June 1918. Lord Dunmore had sold the whole of South Harris (except for Borve Lodge, which he retained for his personal use till 1923) to Lord Leverhulme in May 1919 for £36,000[14]. The founding Chairman of the Association, William Fergusson (Solicitor), had died in 1916, and another founding Director, John Dempster (Produce Merchant), had died in 1914. The financial situation was so serious that, despite all the loans, the Association could not meet its liabilities: obviously, fishing holidays had been significantly curtailed by the First World War with an additional knock-on effect on the financial returns. We know that latterly a member, strongly suspected to be John Malcolm, one of the founding Directors, and Honorary Secretary of the Finsbay Angling Club, was personally paying the rent for the Association[15]: at the time of the 1916 accounts the Association owed John Malcolm over £500 (equivalent to about £50,000 in modern terms) in 1916.

As the company's accounts were now regularly showing a deficit, voluntary liquidation was started after a general meeting in 1920 and completed in 1922 [2]. The liquidators were James Burns

---

[14] In December 1919, Lord Leverhulme transferred the South Harris estate to his Lewis and Harris Welfare and Development Company; he owned all the shares except one owned by his son and one by Sir Herbert Morgan who was a Director of Lever Bros and a personal aide to Lord Leverhulme.

[15] J. Burns Cameron, the Company secretary, wrote on 21 March 1919 to the Registrar of Joint Stock Companies stating *"... This Company has ceased carrying on business, having given up the fishing rights in Harris and no revenue is being received ... . I may say that all the disbursements in connection with the Company have been made recently by a private individual"* [2]

Cameron, Solicitor, 19 Blythswood Square and Arthur C. Strathie, 86 St Vincent Street, Glasgow[16]. One of the local myths about the Lodge was that the "English" [sic] members had all been killed in the 1st World War. This however is erroneous, though it is true that the War had badly damaged the financial situation and that several of the Directors and shareholders had died naturally during the period of the War, but not on active service. During the War, visitors could not come to fish[17], the ghillies were away on military service, yet the rents still had to be paid to Lord Dunmore – a cruelly impossible situation and one not conducive to continuing with the essential maintenance of a wooden building on an exposed site. Lack of exterior painting was later blamed for the structural condition of Finsbay Lodge.

Surprisingly, the Company's statutory records, at least the Company's House records retained by the National Archives of Scotland [2], of the dissolution of the limited company do not include any final accounts of the assets received or transferred by the liquidators and agreed at the final winding-up meeting on 23 November 1922 (see Fig. 2.7).

Despite the unique scale of the fishing venture, remarkably little appears in the old books on angling, presumably because it was a private venture: the name of the Hebridean Sporting Association is now largely unknown. W.L. Calderwood, who was Inspector of Salmon Fisheries for Scotland and normally a very reliable authority, refers to it in some detail (see below, page 87) in his wonderful encyclopaedic book *Salmon Rivers and Lochs of Scotland* published in 1909 [7], but unfortunately he failed to update the description for his second edition in 1921 [8] by which time the Hebridean Sporting Association had been disbanded and was in the process of liquidation. Some other literature quotations about the Harris fishings are included in Chapter 5 below.

Fairly regular reports of catches did appear in the angling columns of *The Scotsman* newspaper, and some are mentioned in

---

16   Modern company law would have probably forced liquidation at an earlier stage when the company was unable to meet its liabilities (though its ability to gain loans and interest through the generosity of some Directors and members gave it some protection) and would not have permitted the accounts to have been audited by a member of the company or the liquidator(s) to be members.

17   The Western Isles were a "restricted area"

Chapter 5 and in Appendix 4 below.

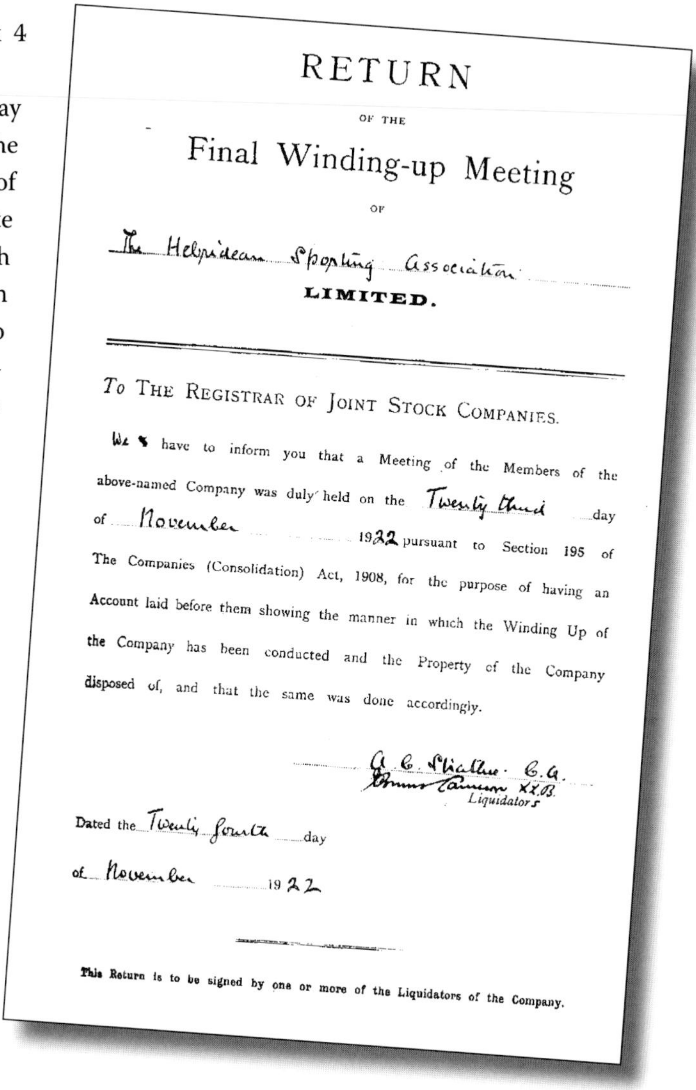

This whole venture may fairly be regarded as the immediate fore-runner of "time-share" or "syndicate ownership" in fishing, though shares in the Association did not entitle the holders to specified weeks' sport. It pre-dated the formation of the famous Grimersta syndicate in Lewis, and it was on a very much larger scale (both in terms of membership and extent of fishings) than the Grimersta operation. An excellent account of the Grimersta, marvellous for its accounts of both angling and social history, has been written by Michael Wigan (2000) *Grimersta: the story of a great fishery* [9]. According to that source, much of the history of the Grimersta, its lodge and its syndicate has been preserved only by remote chance coupled with smart action by the present housekeeper at Grimersta Lodge. Unfortunately, no similar papers giving insight into the inner workings of the Hebridean Sporting Association have yet been found (apart from the formal reports required under the Companies Act), and they are likely to have been destroyed: also the period is just too early to have fallen into the time when the local Historical Society was collecting oral tradition.

It is over 100 years since the Lodge was built, 85 years since the Association ceased fishing in Harris, and about 75 years since the Lodge was finally dismantled, so contemporary memories are

RETURN

OF THE

Final Winding-up Meeting

OF

The Hebridean Sporting Association
LIMITED.

To THE REGISTRAR OF JOINT STOCK COMPANIES.

We have to inform you that a Meeting of the Members of the above-named Company was duly held on the Twenty third day of November 1922 pursuant to Section 195 of The Companies (Consolidation) Act, 1908, for the purpose of having an Account laid before them showing the manner in which the Winding Up of the Company has been conducted and the Property of the Company disposed of, and that the same was done accordingly.

G. C. Strathie. C.A.
Thomas Cameron X.X.O.
Liquidators

Dated the Twenty fourth day of November 19 22

This Return is to be signed by one or more of the Liquidators of the Company.

Fig. 2.7
Formal report of the final winding-up meeting of the Hebridean Sporting Association signed by the joint liquidators in November 1922. Reproduced by kind permission of The National Archives of Scotland [BT2/5276].

not going to fill in the complex gaps! One correspondent, a Tarbert native, remembers spending a night as a child in 1924 at the Keeper's Cottage adjacent to the Lodge (he could identify the year, since he was sent away from home during his mother's confinement for his sister's birth!), and as our enquiries continue a few more people are unearthing dim family memories and even letters written from Finsbay Lodge. Perhaps long hidden or lost records will turn up to enlighten us!

Was the venture a success? While we cannot be certain about the original long-term motives of the founders, the whole business of building Finsbay Lodge in difficult terrain, staffing it, improving the fishings, and running the whole venture must have taken a tremendous amount of determination, enthusiasm, logistic acumen, organisation and skill. The financial collapse was due to a mixture of over-ambition and optimism[18] followed by external catastrophe in the form of World War. However, the scale and complexity of the whole operation and the accomplishments were quite dramatic, arguably without parallel nowadays anywhere in Great Britain, and should be credited as such in the historical record. The Directors and members had enjoyed some 15 years of remarkable fishing and must surely have created the momentum for the development of the Harris fishings and their subsequent opening up to a wider range of visitors and tenants.

Unfortunately we can only speculate about the final sentiments of any of the shareholders or of Thomas Wilson (the largest shareholder) or of John Malcolm (founding Director and ultimate financier) at the demise of the venture. Good employment opportunities had been provided, satisfying those with community benevolence motives; good angling had been provided, satisfying those wanting excellent sport in a splendid environment; a bad financial outcome had met those whose intentions had been financial.

The various artificial lochs together with their dams and sluices that benefit the Harris fishings nowadays for both local anglers and visitors, some the work of the Hebridean Sporting Association and some the work of Viscount Fincastle, are a monument – albeit almost wholly unrecognized – to these works.

---

[18] This could have been either careless or "care-free"!

CHAPTER THREE
FINSBAY LODGE, QUIDINISH

The first action by the new company, the Hebridean Sporting Association Ltd, was to arrange for the construction of their own fishing lodge or hotel which was to be ready for the opening of their fishing season on Saturday 1 August 1903. This was a most dramatic building, like a fairy-tale castle, with landscaped grounds on the Quidinish[19] peninsula on the east coast of Harris, just north of the village of Finsbay on the shore of the sea-loch, Loch Finsbay. *The Scotsman* newspaper of 8 August carried a brief report of the opening of the fishing (Fig. 3.1), though the quoted totals of sea trout caught do not add up sensibly!

Now, sadly only the foundations, substantial stone footings, remain (Fig. 3.2 & 3.3). The scale drawing of these foundations (Fig. 3.4) shows the size of the building, roughly 78 feet long by 56 feet deep, excluding a wing at the north-west rear of the building which is difficult to assess.

The building was said in the company's Prospectus (see Appendix 1) to be constructed in Norwegian style, and the four known photographs of it show that was a most charismatic, large structure with twin hexagonal turrets, totally unlike any other building in the Western Isles. It is perhaps little wonder that a local historian and writer, who had seen just one postcard picture, concluded that this picture must have been a fake or an artist's impression of what the lodge might have looked like [10] !

The building of the lodge cost £2,894 plus separate payments of £502 for the foundations, £604 for the water supply and £383 for the gardens, roads, piers, fences etc. The original estimate envisaged by the Directors in establishing the company and promoting it to potential subscribers had been just £2,000! To this must be added the cost of furnishings at £1,198 which had originally been estimated

---

[19] Also known as Quidnish and (Gaelic) Cuidhtinis

Fig. 3.1 Report in *The Scotsman* newspaper on Saturday 8 August 1903 of the opening day and week's catches at Finsbay Lodge.

HARRIS.—The fine new fishing lodge erected by the Hebridean Sporting Association, beautifully situated at the side of Loch Finsbay, Harris, in the Western Hebrides, was opened for anglers on Saturday. Well-known and of high repute as a sea trout resort, but until now strictly preserved, the Finsbay lochs have upheld their reputation, and some very good sport has been had. The following were the baskets: — August 1 — Mr Scott, Finsbay, 22; Mr Bulkeley, Finsbay, 113; Mr Scott, Strathmore, 27; Mr Bulkeley, Lingerbay, 27; Judge Bradbury and two Misses Bradbury, Finsbay, 20; Colonel Grant and Mr Sellar, Manish, 144; Judge Bradbury, Holmasaig, and Miss Bradbury, Finsbay, 3; Colonel Grant, Finsbay, 8; Mr Scott, Flodabay, 7; Mr Bulkeley, Flodabay, 45; Mr Scott, Finsbay, 20; Mr Blaine, Finsbay, 9; Mr Mackenzie, Holmasaig, 1; Colonel Grant and Mr Sellar, Lingerbay, 2; Judge Bradbury, Flodabay, 56; Mr Bulkeley, Lingerbay, 2 and 1 salmon; Mr Scott, Holmasaig, 36; Mr Sellar, Manish, 5; Mr Mackenzie, Huamarat, 5; Colonel Grant, Flodabay, 4. The total catch for five days has been 1 salmon, 6 lb., and 244 sea trout, the weight of the sea trout running from ½ lb. to 2 lb. The Association has acquired a fifteen years' lease of the Finsbay fishing from Viscount Fincastle, the proprietor, of South Harris, who is expected shortly to visit the lodge.

to cost £500. The company's optimism, or that of the founding Directors, was always greater than its commercial economics.

The location of Finsbay Lodge (sometimes called Finsbay Hotel; also Lodge a' Ghroba Dhuibh) was at National Grid reference NG 083 875, just about 25 yards from the shore of the sea-loch, with spectacular views. The aerial picture of the location (Fig. 3.5) shows how ideally it was placed for fishing the 3 systems that drain into the sea loch, Loch Finsbay, and which hold migratory fish.

The view to the east from the front door would show the Isle of Skye on a clear day; the view behind the Lodge would be of the rugged Lewissian Gneiss rocks of Roneval[20]. Just 100 yards away to

Figs. 3.2 & 3.3 The foundations of Finsbay Lodge still remaining. Note the proximity to the sea (Loch Finsbay) and the cliff face, presumably caused by blasting the Cnopa Dhubh. The modern building at the left of Fig. 3.3 is the fishing hut belonging to The Hundred Lochs' Fishery.

---

[20] *ROINEABHAL.*

Tha 'n t-uisge nochd air Ròineabhal	*There is rain tonight on Roneval*
's tha ceò air Beinn a' Chuailein	*and mist on Ben Cuailein*
's mo smuain air laithean m'òige	*and my thoughts are on the days of my childhood*
nuair a b'eòlach mi mu'm bruaichean:	*when I well knew your slopes:*
ar leam am bruadar oidhche	*I imagine in my night dreams*
mi bhi cluinntinn sailm 'nam mìlseachd;	*that I hear psalms in their sweetness;*
chi Ròineabhal 'na greadhneachas	*I see Roneval in its grandeur*
buan-mhaireannach mar Fhìrinn	*everlasting as Truth.*

[Verse by John Angus Macleod who was Bard at the 1971 Mod at Stirling]

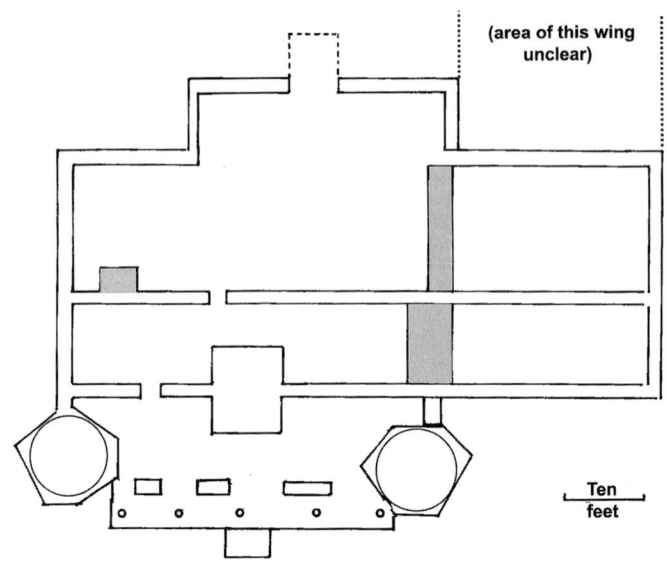

Fig. 3.4 Approximate scale drawing of the remaining foundations at Finsbay Lodge. It is not certain whether the towers were hexagonal or octagonal: they appear to be 6–sided, but Donald Cattanach's report to Lord Leverhulme (see page 44) describes them as octagonal. The area occupied by the back wing, at the north-west corner of the building, is unclear.

(area of this wing unclear)

Ten feet

the north-west was the tidal zone of the river below Loch Holmasaig with most attractive artificially created pools (Fig. 3.6).

Fig. 3.7 shows a general view of the Finsbay district inland from the Lodge's situation showing how the rocky landscape – sometimes described as a "moonscape" – dominated the local scenery. Most lovers of wild Hebridean scenery would be entranced by the location of Finsbay Lodge but, surprisingly, Miss Emily Paul (later Mrs Emily Macdonald), niece of Lord Leverhulme, wrote in her delightful little monograph "*Twenty Years of Hebridean Memories*" [11]:

> "*One day we went to look over another Lodge called Finsbay, on the east coast of Harris. A more desolate spot I never wish to see, and one wonders how anyone could ever have built a Lodge in such a stony barren place. Presumably the trout fishing was good*".

Her visit with her uncle was almost certainly in 1922 by which time Lord Leverhulme or, more correctly, his Lewis and Harris Welfare and Development Company owned the whole of South Harris including the Lodge; at this time he had not decided what he was going to do with it. Her harsh description was surprising as she was a considerable enthusiast for Harris and Lewis, eventually settling at Gisla in Lewis with her husband Dr Donald Macdonald, a native of Stornoway, who wrote *"Tales and Traditions of the Lews"* [12]. If she had been enthusiastic about Finsbay Lodge or its situation, the future of the Lodge might have been very different, as her uncle was disposed to give her a wedding present of property at the time when the fate of Finsbay Lodge was in the balance. He gave her Uig Estates in Lewis. In contrast, Professor Purdie, a regular summer visitor at Finsbay Lodge, wrote in private correspondence in the most glowing terms about the enchanting location of the Lodge (see page 160–161).

One can be confident that the location of the lodge was influenced by two key factors: (1) the proximity of the tidal pond and sea pools at Finsbay, the Abhainn na Ciste river and loch system, and lochs Holmasaig, Huamavat and the numerous neighbouring lochs; and (2) the good sea access into Loch Finsbay with regular shipping services from Glasgow for passengers and cargo on the *SS Dunara Castle*. This ship's wonderful service to Harris is discussed further below (Chapter 9). It would be wrong, though, to suggest that the ship's calling at Finsbay was instituted for the benefit of the Lodge, as this call had been made since about the late 1800s and was continued until the 1950s. It is important to realize that road transport on the East side of South Harris was almost non-existent in 1903 and was very poor until the mid-1950s: after then, it became possible to ship cargo into Tarbert, then continue south by road – an integrated transport service provided by MacBraynes.

At present, we know of only four pictures of the splendid building. The best known one (Fig. 3.8) is from a postcard which has been reproduced in the book by Bob Charnley (1993) *The Western Isles: A Postcard Tour – 2 Harris and Lewis* [13] and subsequently in Bill Lawson's (2002) *Harris in History and Legend* [10].

The photographer responsible for the postcard picture is not named on the postcard. However, a considerable number of postcards of identical style, with Gaelic wording *Ceud-sreath d'n Eilean-Fhad* (First Series of the Long Island) on the message side and with the title in red print on the face of the card, have been found in this Cairt Phostail series. The late Bob Charnley, a retired police detective who particularly enjoyed applying his detective skills to the identification of historical Highland photographs, reproduced a number of these postcards in his two admirable books of Hebridean postcard images [13, 14]. Eventually he concluded that the postcard had been printed by Philip Hunt in Manchester and

Labels on the aerial photograph:
L. Huamavat
L. Dempster
L. Holmasaig
road to Tarbert
site of old road
site of Keeper's House
L. Dubh Heillih
site of FINSBAY LODGE
L. Finsbay (sea loch)
Quidinish
road from Rodel

Fig. 3.5 Aerial view of the sea loch, Loch Finsbay, and the area around Finsbay Lodge. Reproduced under licence from Getmapping Plc.

that the photographer was Archibald (Archie) Alexander Chisholm (see Chapter 12), and he tracked down a cousin of Archie Chisholm who supported this. The identity of the photographer has now been confirmed to me by Archie Chisholm's grandson who possesses many of the original photographs and who has kindly supplied several pictures including the 2 portraits of Archie Chisholm – see Figs 12.1 & 12.2 below in Chapter 12.

This photographer is of special relevance here: Archie Chisholm was a member of the Hebridean Sporting Association. His official career was in the legal profession, as Procurator Fiscal in Lochmaddy. However, he was a most accomplished amateur photographer, and he produced many picture postcards of scenes throughout the Long Island. His obituary in the Inverness Courier stated that the quality of his photography was recognised in him being elected as President of the Photographic Society of Great Britain, the forerunner of the Royal Photographic Society, but this honour has not been confirmed by records at the Royal Photographic Society or the National Media Museum. He was a close friend of Thomas Wilson,

Fig. 3.6 The tidal river below Loch Holmasaig showing artificially made pools. The arrow shows the track leading to Finsbay Lodge. The viewpoint for this picture is about 50 yards from the site of the Lodge.

Fig. 3.7 The rocky landscape around the township of Finsbay between Roneval and Loch Finsbay. The site of Finsbay Lodge is just out of sight at the far right of the picture.

Figs. 3.8 & 3.9 Finsbay Lodge or Hotel. This picture postcard scene was photographed by Archie A. Chisholm, Procurator Fiscal at Lochmaddy. He was a member of the Hebridean Sporting Association and was responsible for a great number of picture postcard scenes throughout Lewis, Harris, the Uists, and Barra. Note that this particular postcard had been sent in the 1960s to John MacLeod, the son-in-law of Sam Morrison, the Finsbay Lodge Gamekeeper, and is addressed to "Groba Dhu" ("Black chunk"). The Keeper's cottage is clearly visible behind the Lodge. Postcard kindly loaned by Roddy and Murdo MacLeod.

solicitor and factor in Lochmaddy, who also was a member of the Hebridean Sporting Association. They were pioneers in the story of land settlement and reform in the Outer Hebrides, and more about this appears below (Chapter 12).

Though Bob Charnley was correct about Chisholm being the postcard photographer, he made two significant errors in his caption to the picture of Finsbay Lodge. First, he quoted a passage from a book by Hamish Stuart, but he stated that this came from *Lochs and Loch Fishing* which was published in 1899. In fact, there was nothing about Finsbay Lodge in *Lochs and Loch Fishing* [3]: the statements quoted were actually from Hamish Stuart's later book, *The Book of the Sea Trout* [15], which was not published till 1917. A simple mistake, but one that has mislead many people interested in the history of Finsbay Lodge to assume wrongly that Finsbay Lodge was built before 1899; the date of construction is unquestionably 1903. Charnley also stated that the Lodge had been destroyed by wind and fire. There is no evidence of any fire and no charring at the site, nor do the older local families know of any fire; also a great deal of woodwork was re-utilised elsewhere in the neighbourhood. The demise of the Lodge was gradual, due to neglect and decay, followed by intentional dismantling. There may well have been a modest fire to dispose of left-over rubbish, but it was not a fire that destroyed the building. It is true that a gale had damaged the building, but only to the extent of collapsing a chimney stack [16].

There are three other pictures known of Finsbay Lodge (Figs. 3.10, 3.12 & 3.18 below). Fig. 3.10 is a postcard view taken about 1905 from Ardvie, across the sea-loch, Loch Finsbay, and Fig. 3.11 shows the same view photographed recently. Fig. 3.12 is an advertisement used by the Association in each issue of Watson Lyall's *Sportsman's and Tourist's Guide* from Summer 1904 to Autumn 1907.

We have only two pictures of the interior of the Lodge (see Figs. 3.16 & 3.17 below). However, a brief description is provided in the Field Books of the Inland Revenue (Scotland) survey of 1911–12, and Professor Sir James Irvine described some of the daily routine in Finsbay Lodge in his letters to his wife (see Chapter 10). The Inland Revenue survey, popularly known as the New Domesday Book, covered the whole of Great Britain, its purpose being to establish baseline values for all properties so that Lloyd George could impose a tax based on the increase in land values – an early form of Capital Gains Taxation specific to land, part of the Finance

Fig. 3.10 Finsbay Lodge viewed from Ardvie, looking across Loch Finsbay. Postcard of ca 1905. Picture kindly supplied by Tony Scherr.

Fig. 3.11 The view from Ardvie nowadays, looking towards the site of Finsbay Lodge. The hut (with red roof) for "The Hundred Lochs Fishery" can be seen in the centre distance, just behind the site of the Lodge.

The Hebridean Sporting Association
LIMITED.

SALMON AND SEA TROUT FISHINGS
IN
SOUTH HARRIS, OUTER HEBRIDES.

RODEL HOUSE AND FINSBAY LODGE.
Obbe and Finsbay Fishings.

THIS ASSOCIATION has leased the Fishings of a large part of SOUTH HARRIS. The Lochs include the famous OBBE of Harris, and numerous other excellent Salmon and Sea Trout Lochs, which are now for the first time thrown open. The Lochs and Streams have been improved and new Lochs formed at considerable expense.

SEA FISHING AND BOATING.

Particulars, Terms, &c., from the Secretary,
GEO. D. STIRLING, C.A., 154 St. Vincent Street, Glasgow; or from
JAMES DOWELL, Land Agent, 'Lumley House,' 34 St. James's
Street, London, S.W.

Fig. 3.12 Advertisement for the Hebridean Sporting Association. This advertisement appeared in Watson Lyall's *Sportsman's and Tourist's Guide* from 1904 to 1907, after which only a half-page advertisement, without illustration, was published.

Act (1909) which was repealed in 1920. The Inland Revenue valuers placed a value of £1,500 on Finsbay Lodge, of which £1,480 was for the buildings – dramatically less than the actual cost in 1903. Finsbay Lodge was described as follows [17]:

> *"Wood and corrugated iron; comprising servants' hall, 2 servants' bedrooms, kitchen, 2 sculleries, pantry, butler's pantry, store, office, drawing room, 2 sitting rooms, dining room, smoking room, 21 bedrooms, 3 bathooms (hot & cold) and W.C.s. All in good repair. Also Keeper's house in brick and felt – very ??? 6 rooms over. Laundry (wood & corrugated iron); shed; henhouse. All in good state of repair."*

Donald Cattanach's later survey of the building for Lord Leverhulme in 1923, reproduced below, gives a much fuller description of the building's construction.

The water supply for Finsbay Lodge is worthy of comment. The Association created Loch Dempster (named after John Dempster, one of the founding Directors) with a substantial retaining dam about 140 yards long as both a fishing loch and a water reservoir for the Lodge (see Figs. 5.5 and 5.6 in Chapter 5). In the 1916 Feu Charter granted to the Association by Lord Dunmore, Loch Dempster was described as the Lodge's water supply [6]. The water supply was piped to a hydraulic ram system, a relatively advanced piece of water engineering for the period. Part of this can still be seen. This system uses the "water hammer" effect to drive water uphill – it in effect converts the kinetic energy in the moving water to potential energy. Unfortunately, it became clear in the correspondence about the eventual sale of the Lodge that the system had never operated satisfactorily! These ram systems are generally very simple and effective, provided they have been properly installed and adjusted, and have been popular in remote places. A further water supply for the Lodge (and probably also for the Keeper's Cottage) was provided by a small pond, known locally as Loch a Pump, at NG 084 877[21], where the remains of the steel pipework can be seen. The pond had been artificially enlarged, or even created from boggy ground, by earthworks.

In 1903 the Hebridean Sporting Association also built a house for a gamekeeper about 100 yards behind the Lodge. In the

---

[21] Ordnance Survey – National Grid reference

background of the Chisholm picture (Fig. 3.8) of the Lodge (and in the painting by Roddy MacLeod – Fig. 2.5) can be seen the Keeper's House. This is now in ruins (Fig. 3.13), its roof having blown down in a gale on (I am told) Tuesday 14 February 1989. Subsequently the brick walls were dismantled for re-use elsewhere. The present fishing hut built in the 1990s by the present fishing proprietors of the *"One Hundred Lochs Fishery"*, Dr Jan Abel and Mr Peter Brauchl, stands immediately to the rear of the Lodge site.

The Keeper for the Association was Sam Morrison (b. 1864, Manish; d. 1952 at the Keeper's Cottage, Finsbay Lodge), and the cottage was handed down to his son-in-law, John MacLeod (b. 1891), and it is interesting that the postcard reproduced as Figs. 3.8 & 3.9 above was actually sent in the 1960s to John MacLeod.

The Association also constructed a fishing hut at Grosebay. (see Fig. 5.16, page 106)

Though Professor Sir James Irvine described the bedroom furniture as simple (see Chapter 10), it is clear that the Lodge's public rooms were intended to operate on a grand and luxurious scale for its fishing guests. Little wonder, then, that Hamish Stuart [15, p.258] described the Lodge as:

> *"... unique among Hebridean residences, for it boasts trimly-kept grounds and one goes by garden paths to the nearer lochs ... To approach an otherwise typical Hebridean tarn of dark peat-stained water and wild rocky shores by a trimly-kept garden path, more suggestive of the fertile South than the most barren and rocky of all the outer isles, is a singular experience ... ." [15].*

Curiously, especially since two of the shareholders were senior members of the Scotch whisky industry, Sir John Dewar and Robin Duff Bell, the premises were never licensed to sell alcohol. When Lord Dunmore issued the subsequent Feu Charter in 1916, this stipulated that sales of alcoholic beverage would not be permitted without the prior permission of the Feu Superior [6]. Around this time, the temperance movement was strong in the Hebrides, and the previous Countess of Dunmore had established the Coffee House in An t-Ob as a temperance hotel. The Inverness-shire Valuation Rolls show that Rodel Lodge, though, was licensed throughout the Association's tenancy.

We do not know much about the original construction of the

Lodge[22]; however, it is likely that it was built from a "kit" of pre-fabricated components as this seems to have been common practice in these days for sporting lodges. This may have been supplied from Norway, hence the reference in the Association's 1903 Prospectus as "being built in Norwegian style", though it was stated in the Prospectus that several estimates for building had been sought. It is notable that the foundations were charged for separately from the building itself. Norwegians inhabited and had operated the whaling station at Bunavoneddar in North Harris until Lord Leverhulme took it over; also, Lord Leverhulme was said to have acquired Norwegian buildings for some of the houses that he built in Lady Lever Terrace at Leverburgh, and some houses in Scott Road, Tarbert were said to have been Norwegian. Norway had a thriving export market of wooden buildings which peaked around 1902, and Norwegian buildings' experts have confirmed that Finsbay Lodge appears as though it may have been of Norwegian origin. It has not been possible to confirm this[23], nor the suggested

---

22 The archived information of The Buildings of Scotland Trust show no record of the building, or of invitations to tender, in the contemporary architectural or building journals such as *The Builder* or *The Architect*

23 M. Thams of Trondheim was a major exporter of wooden goods to Great Britain, and he was a co-partner with Christian Salvesen of Leith. Tham's own substantial residence in Norway has, like the Lodge, unusual hexagonal turrets. Inspection of the Salvesen archives has not shed any light on this possible origin of building "kits" for sporting lodges in Scotland. Another prominent exporter was Strommen Varifabrikke, exporting via Kristiana (Oslo)

Norwegian origin of the nearby Horsacleit Lodge. John Mackay of Geocrab remembers his father, Roddy Mackay, telling him that his first job after leaving school had been at the construction of Finsbay Lodge.

The financial problems of the Association have already been discussed in Chapter 2. The mounting debts, the inability to continue payment of rent for Rodel Lodge and its fishings, the financial losses incurred by giving up Rodel Lodge, and the virtual extinction of the fishing activities due to the World War all conspired to terminate the venture. The financial consequences of all these adverse events are clearly visible in the extracts of accounts in Appendix 3. As previously explained, the lease of the land at Finsbay in 1903 had included a clause to permit Lord Dunmore to take over Finsbay Lodge at the end of the lease for a suitable sum. The Association invited Lord Dunmore to do this: however, he did not want the Lodge. In November 1916 he granted a Feu Charter[24] to the Association that would enable it to sell the Lodge, explicitly stating in this Charter that he did not wish to take over the Lodge. The Feu duty was set at £1 per annum [6].

We now know that the magnificent Finsbay Lodge became unoccupied in 1918, started to fall into serious disrepair, and was then sold in 1921 by the Association and its liquidators to Lord Leverhulme, who had become the new proprietor of South Harris in 1919.

By 1920, the Association recognized that its financial situation was legally untenable, with liabilities greatly exceeding the assets. Also, the lease on the Finsbay fishings had expired in 1918. It started negotiations with Lord Leverhulme, then an Extraordinary General Meeting in October 1920 resolved to wind-up the Company.

Following the sale of Finsbay Lodge to Lord Leverhulme, some furniture was moved to other of his properties on Harris and some other contents were sold off *in situ;* then after Lord Leverhulme's death the building, apparently by then regarded as uninhabitable, was auctioned by Knight, Frank & Rutley in London as part of the Rodel Lot (Lot 3) and mentioned simply as "the old Lodge of Finsbay" in October 1925. Subsequently it was allowed to fall into further rack and ruin with any remaining useful structural pieces being salvaged on an *ad hoc* basis by local residents and at a walk-

---

[24] See Chapter 2, p. 18–19

round sale. The date of this sale is unknown, but is suspected to be early 1930s or late 1920s – it could possibly have been in the mid 1920s, before Leverhulme's death, but this is less likely.

The correspondence between Lord Leverhulme, his factor Norman Robertson, and the Association is illuminating and sets the scene for the final demise of Finsbay Lodge. The architect's/surveyor's report from Donald Cattanach[25] reveals the true state of the building in 1923.

> **Lord Leverhulme to Norman Robertson, 23 September 1919:**
>
> *With reference to the Hotel at Finsbay I could only entertain the purchase of this hotel at what might one might call a break-up price. I consider the value of the hotel as property is very doubtful in its present condition, and in any case any possible income therefrom is still more doubtful. [18]*

> **Norman Robertson to Lord Leverhulme, 25 June 1920:**
>
> *I enclose a letter just received from Mr John Malcolm of the Finsbay Angling Club who own the Finsbay Lodge in which he indicates a figure of £2,000 at which they are prepared to sell Finsbay Lodge. I also enclose the balance sheet ... ..*
>
> *I do not know whether your Lordship would care to take over this building at any price or to what use you would put it to, but in any event I may give the following information which may be helpful if you do have in mind any proposals regarding Finsbay.*
>
> *The Lodge was erected by the present Company about 20 years ago and according to the balance sheet the cost was as follows:*

Lodge	*£4,382–17–3d*
Keeper's house	*£ 196–10–5d*
House furnishings	*£1,197–15–0d*
Carriages, boats, &c	*£ 222–11–4d*
TOTAL	*£5,999–14–0d*

> *The condition of the lodge, as you would have observed, is very bad indeed and for the want of paint the outside woodwork, doors and windows have been allowed to fall into decay to such an extent that a considerable expenditure would be required*

---

[25] Donald Cattanach (see Fig. 3.14) was the grandfather of Mrs Helen Morrison of the Harris Hotel, Tarbert and of David Cameron who kindly provided the Preface to this book.

before it would be put in tenantable order. The water supply would also require to be almost entirely renewed as the present system has never given satisfaction. I am unable to give an accurate estimate of what the cost would be to put the house in tenantable order but I could obtain this if you so desired.

The furniture is of quite a good class and the house is fully equipped. I have not been supplied with an inventory of the contents however, but I have been through the house on several occasions. There are 21 boats and, while some are in a state of disrepair, the majority are in good order.

So far as the fishing goes, it is good and I estimate that a rent of £250 would be got if the place were advertised along with the Lodge. The rent would be the gross rent and after deducting upkeep and keeper's wages the net return would be approx £100 per annum. This could be increased if the shooting ground which was attached to Kyles Lodge were included in the Finsbay let and the ground is within easy reach of Finsbay.

At the present time there is no return from the Kyles and Finsbay shootings and fishings, but with the acquisition of Finsbay

Fig. 3.14 Stalking party outside Borve Lodge. Donald Cattanach (architect and surveyor) is seen at the far right of the picture, and Norman Robertson (factor) is third from the right. The two Keepers, 2nd and 3rd from left, are believed to be Neil Morrison and Alexander MacLeod. Picture kindly supplied by Tony Scherr.

Lodge it would enable me to place those subjects in the hands of Shooting Agents. Kyles and Finsbay combined should bring in a rent of £500. At present there is no income from either place.

Finsbay Lodge is at the present moment worth nothing approaching £2,000 to the Club as they must remember that their house is lying derelict but I have also been looking at the matter from the point of view that it is not possible to get a tenant for either Kyles or Finsbay for the want of a house, and it has occurred to me that your Lordship might consider the question of making an offer to the Club for the purchase of the Lodge. In that event I shall be glad to know what figure you would wish me to offer. [19]

John Malcolm [at John Malcolm & Eadie, Steamship and Insurance Brokers, Glasgow] to Norman Robertson, 22 June 1920:

I duly received your note of 26 April. The delay in replying has been caused by the difficulty in getting the Directors together. I have now had the matter discussed with them, and as regards taking the fishings for this year, we are not disposed to do so.

As regards selling the Lodge, we duly note that you do not think that Lord Leverhulme will entertain such until knowing the lowest figure at which we are prepared to sell, and we also note that his Lordship is by no means anxious to buy the Lodge.

I sent you our last balance sheet a little ago but in case it has been mislaid I now hand you a fresh copy. You will see therefrom that the Finsbay Lodge stands at £4,382 – built at a time when such work was very cheap – while, as regards the furnishings, same were got under similar conditions, and have been well looked after, the material thereof having been specially selected for such a Lodge. There are also the boats etc.

In order to put the situation in a nut-shell at once, my friends today agreed that we would accept £2,000 for the Lodge, furnishings, boats etc. It, of course, has to be borne in mind that the cost of such today would not be less than 3 times what same cost us, and probably 4 times.

As mentioned previously, the house is in good repair, only requiring painting etc[26]. There is no doubt it has been very well constructed. [20]

---

[26] This statement is unduly optimistic in the light of Mr Cattanach's report to Lord Leverhulme in 1923 – see below

Lord Leverhulme to Norman Robertson, 28 June 1920:

I am obliged for yours of the 25th enclosing letter from Mr John Malcolm of the Finsbay Angling Club. Subject to your recommendation, it seems to me that we might bid £1,000 for boats, furniture and Lodge being all the property the Hebridean Sporting Association hold in the Island of Harris

I do not think we ought to go beyond £1,000. It is true the furniture may be worth more than the original cost but I doubt it if the wear of the Lodge is considered, and even so it would still be secondhand furniture and there would be all the cost of bringing it from Harris to some selling centre on the Mainland, which I think would exceed any bigger price that might thus be got. The lodge is a very doubtful asset. It is altogether too large for any possible use we could make of it, and in offering £1,000 I am doing so more with the idea of clearing the matter up than from any idea that £1,000 invested in this way would be a sound investment. [21]

Norman Robertson to Lord Leverhulme, 1 July 1920:

Finsbay Lodge: I have received your Lordship's letter of the 28th inst instructing me to offer £1,000 for Finsbay Lodge, boats and furniture and I have today communicated your offer to the Hebridean Sporting Association and shall keep you informed of the reply.

I agree that the Lodge is a doubtful asset and a substantial sum will be required to put the place in tenantable order, but I would be hopeful of receiving a fair revenue for the fishings if the Kyles and Finsbay shootings and fishings were rearranged. [22]

Lord Leverhulme to Norman Robertson, 8 September, 1920:

Here again I am quite agreeable for you to make the best bargain you can. The furniture seems to me to be the only item of value in Finsbay Lodge. If the Lodge is left as it is, it will all be down to the ground in a very short time. The furniture being at Finsbay can have little value because of the cost it would be to send a boat and take it to the mainland, say Glasgow, to sell. It seems to me that the tenants [sic] of Finsbay Lodge who own the furniture would really get very little for the furniture under these circumstances.

I am quite willing for you to purchase the remainder of the lease [sic] of Finsbay Lodge and the furniture contents from the *tenants [sic[27]] on the best terms you can. Perhaps if you offer another £300 or £400, the transaction might be closed.*

I cannot but think that the £1,000 offered under the circumstances was the full value but I am quite willing to go £300 or £400 more. [21]

On 31 January 1921, the Association and the liquidators formally completed the sale of Finsbay Lodge to Lord Leverhulme's Lewis and Harris Welfare and Development Company. The price stated in the Deeds was £500, but we can assume that the liquidators received at least £1,000 or £1,400 to include the furnishings and contents, the £500 being just for the building.

Norman Robertson to Lord Leverhulme, 2 February 1921:
Regarding Finsbay ... I am afraid the Lodge could not be occupied unless considerable repairs are carried out and I have the matter in hand and await Mr Pettigrew from Stornoway in order that the building may be examined at once and a report with estimate forwarded to your Lordship for consideration. Every endeavour would be made to push on repairs with a view to making the fishing available for the autumn. [23]

Lord Leverhulme to Norman Robertson, 7 February 1921:
I do not see how Finsbay Lodge could possibly be got ready for the coming season but I am writing to ask Mr Wall with reference thereto. It would seem to me that it would require altogether too big an expenditure on Finsbay Lodge for me to undertake it. [24]

Lord Leverhulme to Donald Cattanach, Architect and Surveyor, County Buildings, Lochmaddy, 3 September 1923:
I possess at Finsbay a building which was erected for accommodation of members of a Highland Fishing Society who, many years ago, leased from Lord Dunmore the fishings adjacent to Finsbay. This building, I think, has not been used since pre-war time. I purchased it mainly on account of the furniture which was wanted for other lodges and has been distributed but, with the construction of the new road from Leverburgh to Finsbay, I think that this building might be worth putting into thorough repair and furnishing with spare furniture I shall have from Ardvourlie Lodge, which since Sir Samuel Scott has taken

---

27 These words indicate that Lord Leverhulme was not fully aware of the Association's legal ownership or that his attention to detail was sometimes imperfect

the best of the shootings that used to be attached to Ardvourlie Lodge and added them to Ammhuinnsuidhe Castle, has not been lettable, and in my opinion has no prospect of being let.

If I remove the furniture from Ardvourlie Lodge to Finsbay after putting the building at Finsbay in thorough repair, then with the new road opened from Leverburgh to Finsbay, I think we should have a building that would be extremely useful for those who come in connection with work at Leverburgh and especially the Fisheries, and that it would justify the expense of repairs. I had an estimate prepared over 12 months ago by Mr Wall for dismantling the building and removing it to near Leverburgh, but the expense was practically as much as a new building, so that I had to disregard it.

It seems to me that perhaps repairs could be done economically and that it might be made serviceable at such an expense as would be reasonable. It must be a fairly substantial building, because it withstood many gales, especially the gale that blew down the entrance gates to Ammhuinsuidhe Castle and the trees at Lews Castle and which it withstood, so it seems to me it might perhaps pay for repairing. Could you pay a visit to Finsbay and report to me fully and completely, with estimate of your idea of cost of repair. Then when I am in Leverburgh in October perhaps we might find time to go together with others of the party to inspect the building at Finsbay and the repairs you had suggested with a view to adoption or otherwise. [25]

Donald Cattanach to Lord Leverhulme, 16 October 1923:
The building is of a good design and well planned.

Ground floor: Entrance hall, dining room, smoking room, reading room, manager's room, 7 bedrooms, kitchen, servants' hall, lavatories, 3 WCs, larder, pantry, scullery and fuel store.

First floor: 13 bedrooms, 2 bathrooms with WCs and lavatory basins, 4 bedrooms for servants leading from lobby at servants' entrance by separate stair. There is a verandah along the greater part of the SE elevation and there is direct access to smoking and dining rooms from same by means of French windows. Above verandah there is a balcony, access to which can be obtained from 4 bedrooms by means of French windows.

The building is a composite one, the foundations are of stone and lime, and the chimney stacks are of brick. The walls are framed

up with wood standards 4" x 2" and 4" x 4" posts at corners, a lining of felt is nailed thereon and the whole covered with weather boarding. The roof is framed with substantial timber trusses and purlins and is covered with sarking and corrugated iron.

There are 2 octagonal turrets rising above the main roofs and these are covered with lead. Water was supplied to the premises by means of a "RAM"[28] and the drainage discharged into the sea.

The inside walls and ceilings are of match boarding, all floors are of tongued and grooved timber except floors of kitchen offices which are of concrete.

There is an excellent wide stair of pitch pine leading to the first floor from Hall, and a stair 2' 9" wide of white wood leading to servants' bedrooms from back lobby.

Condition of premises: I made a very careful survey of buildings and paid particular attention to the framing for the following reasons:

1. The buildings are constructed mainly of white wood;

2. They cover a considerable extent in area;

Fig. 3.15 The Bays of Harris panel in the *Harris Millennium Tapestry*, which depicts Finsbay Lodge and the angling activities. Reproduced by kind permission of the Harris Community Trust.

3. The walls are high;

4. That if repairs are to be carried out, a large sum would be involved; and

5. That if the framing was in an advanced state of decay though the remainder of the material was fairly good, it would be wrong to suggest repairs.

---

28 Hydraulic ram

To come to the point at once, I give it as my frank opinion that the framing throughout the premises is in an advanced state of decay and to commence and tinker with the building in the way of repairs (though it would be a good job for the tradesmen) would be an absolute waste of money, if one were to expect a reasonably satisfactory building at completion.

I submit the following dilapidation which I am certain will justify my foregoing statement:-

All studs on standard posts and corner posts from sill upwards are completely decayed, south west wall of main block is loose and can be shaken out from 6" to 8", right up to past first floor. Ends of joists to walls for 2' 6" – 3' inwards are decayed. Flooring where examined in dining room, in one bedroom on ground floor and east bedroom on first floor is completely decayed for several feet from wall.

The outside boarding has become loose in many parts owing to the nails loosing hold of the standards. Bases at windows can be taken off by the fingers in many parts.

Several of the outer French windows are missing and generally the windows are jambed owing to the building being racked by gales.

The lead on both turrets is perished and water obtains access in several places.

One chimney stack was blown down by a gale and has not been rebuilt.

The railing on balcony is decayed, also snow cradles on roof of verandah.

The water supply is completely gone (I understand the piping was used for other works on the estate).

Several sinks, baths and lavatory basins are missing[29], likewise portion of the inside lead and copper piping (I understand that the foregoing was used in buildings in Leverburgh). Several stretches of cornice and picture moulding have also been removed. One grate is also missing.

Except for lining on outside walls and the deficiencies above stated, the interior woodwork of the building is in fairly good state of preservation.

---

[29]   Some may well have found their way into local crofts

The corrugated iron on roof, except for some minor defects, is in a fair state of preservation.

Proposals:

1. I recommend that no steps be taken to repair the existing premises;

2. If a lodge is required at Finsbay, a new building should be erected (probably one considerably less in size) when the greater portion of the internal lining, flooring, also wood work of roof, the best of the corrugated iron and internal fittings might be utilized;

3. If a lodge is not required or if it be decided to build a new lodge complete, the existing buildings should be demolished and the above mentioned material utilized in the works at Leverburgh.

In conclusion, I tender my regret that my report on the buildings is so unfavourable and that I have to refrain from giving an estimate for repairs to the building. I would be doing a wrong to myself and an injury to your Lordship if my report showed in any way that repairs could be satisfactorily carried out. [16]

Mr Cattanach's invoice for this detailed survey amounted to £10–10s-0d, and this survey can be seen to be the death knell for Finsbay Lodge.

The rateable value for Finsbay Lodge in the Inverness-shire Valuation Rolls fell from £40 p.a. to £25 in 1919, presumably reflecting its lack of occupancy; it ceased to be included in the Rolls from 1923 till 1927. Then in the Valuation Roll for 1927–28 it was recorded as *"Derelict – Proprietor is John Morrison"*.

In May 1925 Lord Leverhulme died, and his properties in Harris were auctioned by Knight, Frank and Rutley in a number of individual lots. Finsbay Lodge was referred to in the particulars of sale in October 1925 simply as "the old Lodge of Finsbay" as part of Lot 3 which contained Rodel estate (hotel and fishings). This telegraphically brief description, bereft of any details of number of rooms, character etc, makes it highly likely that the building was regarded as irredeemable due to its state of disrepair by that time. We cannot be sure whether any legitimate dismantling of the woodwork had occurred by this time. Unfortunately, the solicitors acting for Leverhulme's Trustees (Shepherd & Wedderburn, Edinburgh) no longer have records from that time. While Bob Charnley, in his book – see above, stated that the lodge had been destroyed by wind and fire and this story has often been repeated as an *ex cathedra* dogma, the story of a fire seems to be more mythical than real, though Mr Cattanach's report above does indicate that a chimney stack had been blown down in a gale. None of our contacts, though they would have been only children in the 1920s, remembers any fire; also, various bits of the structure especially wooden tongue-and-groove panelling and some fine wooden doors, found their way into numerous local crofts and houses. Windows and doors were said to have been used to create the old bar, demolished in the 1990s, at the back of Rodel Hotel. It seems implausible that these items would have survived if there really had been a fire. Two correspondents have mentioned dim memories of the Lodge existing as a part building and chimney stack. It is said, but not substantiated, that some of the furniture was taken to Rodel Hotel, for which the Association had also bought furniture (£241) during their tenancy.

Two people with local family reminiscences have independently said that there was a walk-through sale of furniture etc, where the entire contents of each room (furniture, floor boards, window frames) were sold off, and the best guess at present in that this was in the early 1930s. One family was said to have bought the total items from one room including windows, panelling, and flooring, and they made furniture from the wood. It has also been suggested that some of the wooden panelling was taken to Borve Lodge for the chauffeur's quarters, and there are numerous other anecdotal reports of woodwork being incorporated into more modern buildings. It is thought likely that the original verandah at Horsacleit was brought from Finsbay Lodge, and it is possible that this prospect was in Professor Henderson's mind when he acquired his shareholding in the Association as late as 1919. A substantial mahogany counter was taken to be used as the shop counter in the Obbe Stores. The old bar at Rodel Hotel (pre-1990s), including its exterior door, was said to have been constructed with many materials from Finsbay Lodge. One house in Leverburgh, that of the late General Sir Colin Gubbins, the famous wartime chief of the Special Operations Executive (SOE) [26], has a fine French inlaid rosewood table from the Lodge, a further sign of the fine taste in furnishings at Finsbay Lodge. Sir Colin had a part-share in the Obbe fishings, this being taken over by the Jourdan family who now have the major interest in the Obbe fishings.

Very pleasingly, the local community included a very attractive stylised image of Finsbay Lodge in one of the panels of the splendid Millennium Tapestry which is normally available for viewing during the summer months at An Clachan, Leverburgh which is adjacent to the Mill Pool – see Fig. 3.15.

Each of the 12 panels of the tapestry depicts historically significant events and activities in the various regions of Harris, and the South Harris Community Trust has marketed postcards of these.

The story of Finsbay Lodge can be summarised by the following verse which was very kindly translated into Gaelic for me by John Angus Macleod, a fine Gaelic scholar and the Royal National Mod Bard of 1971, who remembers the Lodge from his boyhood in Harris:

Seann Loidse Ghrinn Fhionnasbhaigh

Eadar Ròineabhal aosda is Loch seasgair Fhionnasbhaigh
laigh rùn-diomhair fuadain, seann Loidse eireachdail
 Fhionnasbhaigh.
Thainig fir Ghlaschu, agus thogadh an Loidse air a' Ghroba Dubh.
Chruthaicheadh lochan, rinneadh obair-cosnaidh, ghlacadh iasg,
 is chaitheadh airgead.
Ochòin, thraoigh na cistean-airgid, chaidh am màl gun
 phàigheadh, is dh'fhalbh na daoine.
Bha an Loidse bhochd gun iarrtas oirre, is dh'eug i.
Chaidh na pìosan breagha fiodha do thaighean eile anns na
 Hearadh.
Tha na daoine is an gillean 's an searbhantan air siubhal.
Tha ceòthan Tim an dèidh cur am falach gach cuimhneachan de'n
 t-seann Loidse ghrinn
agus, na clachan aosda an sud fhathast chan innis a chaoidh na
 sgeòil-rùin.

[Translation by John Angus Macleod]

The Fine Old Lodge of Finsbay

Between ancient Roneval and the sheltered Loch Finsbay
There lay a fugitive mystery, the fine old Lodge of Finsbay.
The men of Glasgow came, and the Lodge was born at the Groba
  Dubh.
Lochs were made, jobs were given, fish were caught, and money was
  spent.
Alas, the coffers dried up, and the men went away.
The poor Lodge was unwanted, and it passed away.
The fine wooden bits went to other homes in Harris.
The men and their ghillies and maids have passed away.
The mists of time have hidden the memories of the fine old Lodge,
And the old stones still there will never tell the secrets.

[MLGG]

Fig. 3.18. Finsbay Lodge photographed by A.A. Chisholm on 2 June 1904. Picture kindly supplied by Tony Scherr.

CHAPTER FOUR
RODEL LODGE, ALSO KNOWN AS RODEL HOUSE AND NOW AS RODEL HOTEL

Rodel House has a most delightful location at grid reference NG 048 828, a few yards from the fine natural harbour close to the southernmost part of Harris. This building has a venerable and interesting history from being a private residence, then a sporting lodge, and finally an hotel (Figs. 4.1 & 4.2). First built around 1781 for Captain Alexander Macleod shortly after he had become the owner of the Isle of Harris, this became one of the 5th Earl of Dunmore's sporting lodges after he bought Harris from the Macleods in 1834. Indeed, it was here that the Countess of Dunmore (Lady Catherine Herbert, wife of the 6th Earl) used to receive and pay for the locally woven Harris Tweed in the fledgling days of that industry. In 1876, the 7th Earl of Dunmore attempted to sell South Harris estate at the huge valuation of £155,000 and the advertisement referred to Rodel Lodge as "... *the residence of the present proprietor, the Earl of Dunmore, who has recently laid out a considerable sum on its improvement ... .*" [27]. In 1879, The Earl of Dunmore was awarded the Royal National Lifeboat Institution's silver medal, and 3 fishermen were awarded £5, for rescuing 7 people from a sunken yacht, the *Astarte*, after rowing 11 miles in heavy seas at 1 am and bringing the rescued people to Rodel House. There is a plaque on the outside wall at Rodel Hotel denoting the landing at the harbour there by HM Queen Elizabeth in 1952 from *HMY Britannia.*

The Inland Revenue valuation survey of around 1911–12 (see p. 31) described Rodel House as:

"*Stone & slate buildings – hotel, 3 storeys, 4 public rooms, 10 lettable bedrooms, & 4 servants rooms.*

Fig. 4.1 Rodel Hotel. Postcard picture, about 1903. Picture kindly supplied by Tony Scherr,

Kitchen, sculley & servants hall & pantry. Bath & WC. Conservatory & cellar.

Offices. Stone & slate. Coach house, washhouse, coal cellar. Old wood & felt building was used as sleeping rooms for servants: now ruinous (over)

Gamekeepers & gardeners houses. Stone & slate buildings of 3 storeys.

Ground floor used as stores.

1st & 2nd floors occupied by servants.

2 houses – one of 2 attics(?) & kitchen, other of 1 attic & 2 rooms – porch old & far through

Stone & slate lean to kennels

Stone & tile poultry house

Corrugated iron stable & harness room, stable for 6 horses – concrete floor.

Harness room with wood floor. WC"

The Inverness-shire Valuation Rolls indicated that the premises, unlike Finsbay Lodge, were licensed for the sale of alcohol.

The Dunmore family used this house themselves for at least some time. There is no record of it having been let to sporting visitors before 1903, though the sporting rights, probably for the whole of South Harris, were let during at least the 1890s to a Col. G.A. Percy[30]. In 1903 the Hebridean Sporting Association leased it furnished[31] from Viscount Fincastle for an initial period of 5 years[32] at an annual rent of £350, this including the Rodel and Obbe fishings which already had a very high reputation according to Watson Lyall's *Tourist's and Sportsman's Guide*. This was a separate lease, though arranged at the same time as the 15-year lease of the Finsbay and Grosebay fishings. As explained in Chapter 5, these constitute the vast majority of angling waters in South Harris. Rodel House is just over three miles from the Obbe system of lochs, and it remained as an ideal base for Obbe anglers until the 1970s.

The Inland Revenue survey mentioned above states that there was a Keeper's house at Rodel. The Gamekeeper from at least 1881 until about 1903 was John Finlayson (1849–1928), a native of Stirling. In 1881 he married Annie Morrison of Rodel, daughter of John Morrison, the tailor, and Effie Morrison (née Macdonald). Annie had been a Housekeeper, probably for the Dunmore family at Rodel Lodge. At the 1901 Census he was still Keeper at Rodel, but at his daughter's wedding in 1904 he was designated as "Retired Gamekeeper".

---

30   Col. Percy apparently stayed in Borve Lodge
31   The Association spent £241 on additional furniture
32   Subsequently renewed, though full details are unknown

Fig. 4.2 Rodel Hotel and Harbour. Valentine's postcard picture, about 1930.

HOTEL AND HARBOUR, RODEL   A.7783

Fig. 4.3 shows him fishing on Loch Steisevat in May 1904, the photograph being taken by Archie Chisholm who published it as a postcard with the caption *"A Favourite Cast, Outer Hebrides"* in his Gaelic Cairt Phostail series. It appears that John Finlayson's employment by Lord Dunmore may have ended when the Hebridean Sporting Association took up the lease of Rodel, though it is likely that he would have continued to act as a ghillie for the anglers.

After the Hebridean Sporting Association's financial situation had collapsed so badly that they fell into arrears with their rent to Lord Dunmore in 1915 and were sued in the Court of Session, the lease of Rodel House and its fishings was not renewed, though the Association continued to lease the Finsbay fishings from Lord Dunmore. At the termination of this lease, the building was suffering from lack of maintenance, as revealed in subsequent correspondence. A new and completely independent group – *The Rodel Syndicate* – took over the Rodel tenancy, both the House and its fishings on a 25 year lease, though we do not know all the terms of the lease.

Fig. 4.3 Photograph of John Finlayson, former Gamekeeper at Rodel, fishing at Loch Steisevat in May 1904. This picture was taken by Archie Chisholm (whose writing is seen below the picture), and published as a postcard. Reproduced by kind permission of Alastair Chisholm, grandson of Archie Chisholm.

Fig. 4.4 shows *The Rodel Syndicate's* advertisement in the 1915 issue of Watson Lyall's Shooting and Fishing Agency's catalogue. Their lease from Lord Dunmore obliged *The Rodel Syndicate* to make improvements to the house, including building an annexe. As matters turned out, the syndicate failed to do so and, worse, the property deteriorated, a fate that was set to recur 50 years later! Interestingly, the principal person in this syndicate was one of the partners in the London sporting estate agency of Watson Lyall & Co, a Mr William Murray of Hitwick Manor, Ampthill, Bedfordshire. Mr Murray had never been a shareholder of the Hebridean Sporting Association, but his firm had continually been reviewing (and advertising) the South Harris fishings in their biannual *Sportsman's and Tourist's Guide* – see Chapter 6, so he must have well recognised the attractive and productive nature of these fishings.

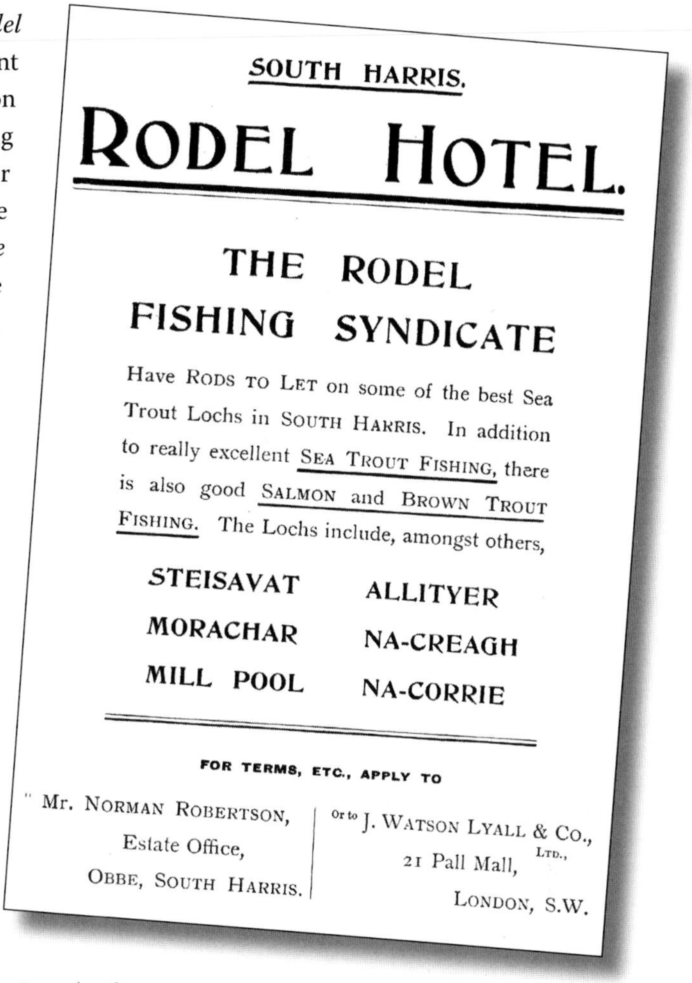

In 1919 Lord Leverhulme bought Harris from Lord Dunmore (see Chapter 11), and this included Rodel Hotel. We do not know who the other members of *The Rodel Syndicate* had been in 1915; however, by 1922 there were two partners in addition to William Murray. These were a Charles Collier of Bridge House, Culmstock in Devon and, rather remarkably, Lord Leverhulme himself. There was the rather strange situation of Lord Leverhulme paying rent from his personal funds to the Lewis and Harris Welfare and Development Company which was owned almost wholly by himself.

SOUTH HARRIS.

RODEL HOTEL.

THE RODEL FISHING SYNDICATE

Have RODS TO LET on some of the best Sea Trout Lochs in SOUTH HARRIS. In addition to really excellent SEA TROUT FISHING, there is also good SALMON and BROWN TROUT FISHING. The Lochs include, amongst others,

STEISAVAT	ALLITYER
MORACHAR	NA-CREAGH
MILL POOL	NA-CORRIE

FOR TERMS, ETC., APPLY TO

" Mr. NORMAN ROBERTSON, Estate Office, OBBE, SOUTH HARRIS. | Or to J. WATSON LYALL & CO., LTD., 21 Pall Mall, LONDON, S.W.

Fig. 4.4 Advertisement for The Rodel Syndicate in 1915 in Watson Lyall's Shooting and Fishing Agency's catalogue

The situation at Rodel grew serious in 1922 when *The Rodel Syndicate* fell into arrears with its rent (£125 per 6 months), obviously a potentially embarrassing situation for Lord Leverhulme personally: with hindsight, though, it emphasises the toll taken by World War on sporting ventures and that perhaps one should not be too harsh in condemning the Hebridean Sporting Association for their financial problems that had resulted in the Court of Session case brought by Lord Dunmore for rent arrears in 1915. Lettings of the fishings and of the Rodel Hotel accommodation had been remarkably poor, so income had been unexpectedly low. At least four factors appeared to influence this state of affairs:

(1) the post-war depression had serious repercussions on sporting and leisure expenditure;

(2) *The Rodel Syndicate* was charging what Norman Robertson, the factor for South Harris[33], described as "ridiculously high charges" at £35 to £60 per rod per month [28];

(3) some guests at the hotel had complained of poor fishing results and were thought to have spread this message around among other potential guests; and

(4) the manageress at the Rodel Hotel was felt to have been unwelcoming to the guests [29].

The post-war market depression was a real phenomenon, and the estate agents Knight Frank (later as Knight, Frank and Rutley) had reported similar difficulties in sporting lets all across Scotland. Knight Frank were well familiar with the Hebridean market, as Sir Howard Frank had acted for Lord Dunmore in the sale in 1919 to Lord Leverhulme; his firm subsequently were the main agents for the sales at auction of Harris after Lord Leverhulme's death in 1925.

The claims of poor fishing were not necessarily well founded. In 1921 Norman Robertson reported that *"the hotel was empty last season, not a single rod being let, although there were plenty of fish"* [30]. Mr Robertson urged Sir Edgar Sanders[34] to go and see Mr Murray of *The Rodel Syndicate* to persuade him of the importance of having good fishing records for the future. *"If we cannot show records, we cannot expect tenants"*. Some fishing guests had blamed

---

[33] Norman Robertson succeeded Thomas Wilson as factor in 1911
[34] Sir Edgar Sanders ran Lord Leverhulme's personal office at Lever Bros in London

Lord Leverhulme's works at Leverburgh pier as having a detrimental effect on the fishing: the frequent blasting and the carriage of stone from quarries by boat down Loch Steisevat were responsible, they claimed. Leverhulme denied this, but made an *ex gratia* payment of £70 to one guest [28, 31]. Norman Robertson, an angler himself, reported that he personally had had good fishing results on his relatively few fishing outings and he added that, although the blasting was still continuing, plenty of fish were present [28]. By September 1922 there were anglers, but the rent was still unpaid. Norman Robertson told Sir Edgar Sanders that "... *the hotel has been pretty well full up all season with anglers and there is no excuse whatever for failure to pay rent* ... "[32]. By now the rental arrears amounted to £375, and local tradesmen were owed £841.

The chaotic and *"exceedingly unsatisfactory"* situation at Rodel Hotel over the next few years is best described by the following quotations from written exchanges between Norman Robertson and Sir Edgar Sanders:-

Norman Robertson to Sir Edgar Sanders, 13 February 1922

Re Rodel Hotel, position is not at all satisfactory, and I have not yet received payment of the ½ years rent of £125 due on 1 September last. I have repeatedly written Mr Murray but he has been seriously ill and his partner Mr Davies of Watson Lyall & Co has been acknowledging his letters to say that the matter has been referred to Mr Murray but I have got no further satisfaction ... If their efforts to find tenants for their rods are on a par with their dilatoriness in other matters, it is not surprising that the rods should remain unlet.

... .Finsbay fishings: It is not much good advertising as there is no accommodation for a tenant, the present building being in such a state of disrepair that it was unfit for occupation without considerable repairs. I was in communication with a Mr FW Bennet recently and offered him Finsbay [fishings] provided he made his own arrangements as to accommodation at Rodel Hotel ... he has enquired but is unable to get accommodation at Rodel Hotel. Of course it would pay the Rodel Hotel Co[35] better to let their own rods ... they may be trying to let their rods first. [33]

---

[35] There is no trace of a Rodel Hotel Company being registered in Scotland at this time

Sir Edgar Sanders to Norman Robertson, 17 February 1922

The position with regard to Rodel is exceedingly unsatisfactory. Is our joint ownership of such a nature that we could take proceedings against the tenant in respect of his non-payment of rent … .

It is too bad of the Rodel Hotel people to refuse access for possible tenants of Finsbay if Rodel have no reasonable prospects of letting their own rods, and I hope you will be able to keep in touch with Mr Bennet in case the Rodel Hotel are able to accommodate him at a later date … [34]

Sir Edgar Sanders to Norman Robertson, 17 March 1922

The position with regard to the Rodel fishings is serious. Lord Leverhulme has asked me to see Mr Murray upon it in order that we may convey to him our view of the seriousness of the position and to urge him to let rods for this season [35].

Norman Robertson to Sir Edgar Sanders, 7 & 27 March 1923

Roof repairs are needed through defective sarking and some windows require renewing and others repairing. Flooring is bad in many places, and plastering is coming down … ..

I have received an offer from Thomas Campbell, Merchant, Tarbert offering £250 rent for the hotel and fishings. I showed it to Lord Leverhulme and he suggested letting hotel separately at £100 p.a. and keeping the fishing. No decision was made.

Kyles[36] is short of fishing and needs an extra rod and my idea is to attach a rod for Kyles on Loch na Moracha, this being the loch on which in the past almost every tenant of Kyles would have liked to fish.

Last year's tenant at Kyles caught 262 sea trout but no salmon.

The charges in the past per rod for Rodel Hotel was from £35 to £60 per month. Those charges were in my view ridiculously high and I repeatedly told Mr Murray so.

I feel certain that these high rents contributed to the failure of the Rodel Hotel Co as they were out of proportion to the number of fish expected.

Mr William Murray is a co-tenant, he died in September 1922.

---

36   Kyles Lodge, another sporting lodge formerly owned by Lord Dunmore, is on the coast at NF 998 878 currently owned by the Lomas family who are descended from Mr Venables who had been the long-term tenant of Luskentyre Lodge and deer forest. See Figs. 5.3 & 5.4.

Lord Leverhulme did pay £70 to one of the claimants re blasting at the mouth of the Obbe to make a pier – not admitting liability. The following year, blasting still proceeds and there are plenty of fish, so the previous year's complaint was groundless. [36, 37]

Detailed Memo in Lord Leverhulme's file on Rodel Hotel, March 1923

Summary: Leased by a syndicate, Lord Leverhulme (£915); Mr William Murray (£915); Mr Charles Collier (£865). Leased from LAHWAD[37] for 21 years from 15/5/1915 at £250 p.a. The Company has been unable to pay rent recently due to losses and at Martinmas[38] 1922 £375 was owing. Now a further £125 was due on 1/3/1923.

No satisfaction has been obtained due to the refusal of anyone to act during Mr Murray's illness. He died on 23/9/1922. Mr Collier, the other member, takes no interest in it whatsoever.

The lease required that lesees shall, not later than July 1916 or within 1 year from the end of War, build an annex at cost of £525. The annex has not been built.

Considerable repairs have been done, now in better state than at start of lease, but there is much to be done at present on painting and inside repairs. NR estimates the cost of this work at £250.

The lessees have spent £150/6/7d on loch improvements. [36, 37]

Lord Leverhulme, as a man of integrity, did not feel able to terminate the lease by LAHWAD to *The Rodel Syndicate* as this was legally binding for a 21 year period from 1915, even though the lessees (of which, ironically, he was one) had breached their contract by non-payment. Also, other breaches became apparent – the annex to Rodel House, which was contractually due to have been completed *"by July 1916 or within one year from the end of the war"*, had never been built; also, through lack of maintenance, the property was not in a good state though it was said to be in better condition than at the start of the lease. Matters were made worse by the fact that William Murray became seriously ill, and his partner at Watson Lyall & Co, Mr Davies, refused to deal with his affairs (being personal ones) relating to *The Rodel Syndicate*.

---

[37] Lord Leverhulme's Lewis and Harris Welfare and Development Company

[38] Martinmas is 11 November, a legal quarter-day in Scotland

Further, the third member of the Syndicate, Mr Collier, showed no interest whatsoever in its affairs and troubles! This dilemma was finally tackled by Norman Robertson, the factor, who drew up a scheme to terminate the lease by LAHWAD to *The Rodel Syndicate*, but to charge them the overdue rent plus £41 interest on the rent, a penalty fee of £100 for early termination and to charge £250 for the estimated dilapidation (sic) of the building.

Norman Robertson to Lord Leverhulme, 28 April 1923

Re surrender of the lease to the Rodel Syndicate, on payment of:

Valuation, rent in arrears, interest on rent £41, £100 penalty for breaking lease before the option date [1925], dilapidation valued at £250 = £1567 due. Less value of assets of £483, giving deficit of £809. [38]

Although Lord Leverhulme personally had to pay a third of these penalties, he was greatly relieved at this escape mechanism, and he annotated (in his characteristic blue coloured pencil) Norman Robertson's memo on this: *"I congratulate yourself, Mr Robertson, and all concerned on this settlement. Can we open the Hotel as an Estate Hotel for 1923 fishing?"* However, one can be sure that he did not forget the experience, as his Edinburgh solicitors (Shepherd and Wedderburn) later replied to an external suggestion that the various sporting lodges be turned into inns for anglers by writing that *"... this is somewhat similar to a similar venture in association with the Rodel Hotel and fishings in Harris in which Lord Leverhulme lost money, so he would not favour such a scheme ... ."* [39].

Sir Edgar Sanders to Shepherd & Wedderburn (Lord Leverhulme's Edinburgh solicitors), 1 May 1923

Rodel Hotel Co: There were debts of £275, in the hands of the late Mr Murray and was forthcoming.

Norman Robertson to Sir Edgar Sanders, 7 May 1923

Lord Leverhulme proposes that the [Rodel] Hotel and fishings should be managed by the Estate [S. Harris Estate]. I have told Sir Thomas Parkinson that an extra rod on Loch-na-Moracha will be available.

*Re Miss **** [the hotel manageress]: She manages the place well enough in a way, but I believe in the past she did not give much satisfaction to the guests as her manner was none too good ... . while she may be efficient, must also be pleasant.*

Repairs are needed ... quite a lot to be done .... reduced prices for rods. [29]

The complaints about the poor attitude of the hotel manageress were rather vague, but she did leave her position subsequently. These incidents do illustrate how many factors other than fishing catches can affect the success or failure of sporting lets.

HEBRIDES
THE ANGLER'S MECCA
Rodel Hotel, Leverburgh, Harris
Visit the Hebrides and behold Nature enshrined in all her seductive loveliness. Salmon and Sea-Trout and Shooting Facilities. Golf, Sea Bathing, Sea Fishing. Excellent Cuisine.
Telegrams—"HOTEL LEVERBURGH."

Fig. 4.5 Advertisement for Rodel Hotel in *The Scotsman* newspaper of 21 June 1930

The consequences of this debacle were that the South Harris Estate, c/o Norman Robertson, immediately took over responsibility for Rodel Hotel and letting the fishings. At Mr Robertson's instigation, fishing lets for relatively short periods would now be possible. Previously tenants had been expected to take their sporting leases for a month or, often, a whole season.

After the death of Lord Leverhulme in May 1925, Rodel Hotel and fishings were amongst the lots auctioned by Messrs Knight, Frank and Rutley in London in October 1925. This lot (Lot 3 in the auction), which included Rodel Hotel, the fishings (both the Finsbay system and a share in the Obbe system lochs, excluding Loch na Moracha which was sold exclusively to the buyer of Kyles Lodge in Lot 4), "the old Lodge of Finsbay" [sic], the Keeper's house at Finsbay and about 15 acres of land around Finsbay Lodge, was sold for a mere £3,600 to John (Johnny Archie) Morrison and Kenneth Campbell of Leverburgh, who then described themselves as Farmers, Estate Owners and Hotel Keepers. In 1929, it was transferred into the name of John Morrison. After his death, John Morrison's Trustees sold it for £2,000 in 1934 to John (Jock) MacCallum, a publican from Stornoway (and the subject of a Scottish fiddle tune, Jock MacCallum of Rodel), the grandfather of the present owner, Donnie Macdonald.

In the 1930s Rodel Hotel advertised regularly, identifying itself in glowing terms as a fishing hotel (see Fig. 4.5).

The Rodel Hotel brochure[39] in 1937 had advertised that the *"Meals are served to suit visitors' convenience"*. The ardent angler Professor Clem Mundle who fished extensively around Scotland and who wrote regularly in angling magazines praised it, probably referring to a visit in the 1960s: *"... The hotel was most relaxed and informal. If it had a clock, it was apparently kept as an ornament. Fishing times determined meal times, not vice versa. They seemed to have about ten sea-trout lochs per bedroom. Unfortunately they also had a drought ... ."* The drought had kept the sea-trout in the sea pools, so most rods on the freshwater lochs were unsuccessful and gave up. However, Prof. Mundle, unlike his fellow guests, then had good fishing success in salt water with a Forster's Favourite fly, a low-slung white wing, white hackle, silver body, and no tail that supposedly represented a small fish [41].

In 1965 the title in the hotel and lochs, also the land at Finsbay Lodge, was transferred to Rodel Crofting Lands, Ltd; then later to the Rodel Hotel Ltd.

The author remembers with nostalgia a fishing visit in 1970: the hotel had a leaking roof and plumbing problems and the public bar was spartan and smokey but lively and doing good trade. But the fishing, not too productive[40], was taken seriously; at that time, it was likely that all the hotel guests were anglers or their families.

In 1970 there was a Boardmaster at Rodel Hotel, as in many traditional Scottish fishing inns of an older generation. The Boardmaster was a "senior" guest, well experienced in the fishing waters, who allocated guests each evening to their place on the next day's fishing roster and gave kindly advice to newcomers. This relieved the fishing proprietor of such duties and, frankly, a well informed and conscientious Boardmaster gives much better advice than a non-angling proprietor or someone with a conflict of interest. The Boardmaster had the privilege of the pole position armchair by the fire in the lounge, the chair being adorned with a handsomely embroidered antimacassar. Woe betide any ignorant

---

39   The brochure for Rodel Hotel was produced by the well-known Perth firm of P.D. Malloch, tackle makers and sporting agents. The partner, Gilbert Malloch, was known to fish in Harris. He accompanied Robert C. Bridgett to the Lacisdale lochs and provided the photographs for Bridgett's chapter on Harris sea trout fishing [40]

40   My 2¼ lb sea-trout was regarded as quite a "trophy" that week! The charge for full-board accommodation plus fishing was 3 guineas (£3.15p) per person per day

newcomer who usurped this privileged seat! Most of the anglers, though, had almost certainly been regular guests over a long period. At this time, the Mill Pool was invariably the choice of the angler at the top of the roster; the next person on the list would generally choose Loch Steisevat. Nowadays the Obbe fishery is operated in a rotational beat system. This is more friendly to casual anglers seeking an occasional days fishing; the old "Boardmaster roster" system of allocation does disadvantage such people, as at least one prominent Scottish angling writer has complained [42]! Possibly the only angling hotel in Scotland now to operate a Boardmaster system is the old-established hotel at Scourie in Sutherland.

After a period of physical deterioration, the hotel had to be closed except for its public bar in the 1970s, this marking the end of some 75 years as one of Scotland's "serious" fishing establishments. However, the hotel has been given a new lease of life: it was completely renovated in 2001 with Highlands and Islands Enterprise support and it operates once again as a hotel. The hotel now functions more as tourist accommodation than as a serious fishing institution as it had done for nearly a century.

The fishings at Finsbay that had belonged to Rodel Hotel were partly disposed of separately (see Chapter 5), though the Rodel Hotel proprietor retains a part-share in the Obbe fishings.

CHAPTER FIVE
THE FISHING –
SOUTH HARRIS

The Lochs

In Harris (Fig. 5.1), most of the freshwater angling is in lochs rather than rivers, a notable exception being the Horsacleit system where pools, artificially created, on the river are a significant feature. Like much of the Western Isles[41], South Harris has a great number of freshwater lochs relative to the land area; it also has numerous tidal basins, potentially ideal for salt-water fishing for sea trout. In 1999 it was estimated that angling contributed about £5.6 million per annum to the economy of the Outer Hebrides, including about £5 million from visitors.

The leases granted by Viscount Fincastle to the Hebridean Sporting Association granted them fishing rights on no less than 38 named lochs which are listed in Table 1 and shown on Fig. 5.2.

Essentially these were almost the whole number of lochs on South Harris, except for the Laxdale system[42] which was reserved for Borve Lodge (at NG 034 949) and the Luskentyre system which was reserved for Luskentyre Lodge (at NG 071 991). The fishings in North Harris, mainly the legendary Amhuinnsuidhe[43] system and the Lacisdale chain of three lochs[44] are not being discussed here although some of their angling results are included below for comparison.

Fig. 5.1 Map of South Harris – 1929. The locations of Finsbay Lodge, Rodel Lodge/Hotel, and the Obbe are marked with arrows. Ordnance Survey Popular Edition, sheet 18. Surveyed 1848–1877, 3rd revision 1928–1929, published 1931. Reproduced by kind permission of the Ordnance Survey

---

[41] The Western Isles contain 15% of the surface area of freshwater in the UK

[42] L. Fincastle and L. Laxdale

[43] The castle at Amhuinnsuidhe in North Harris was originally named Fincastle, but this must not to be confused with Loch Fincastle in South Harris.

[44] The Lacisdale lochs have long been attached to the Harris Hotel, Tarbert. Remarkably, the hotel advertised rainbow trout fishing in 1907 & 1908, though the actual loch(s) were not identified

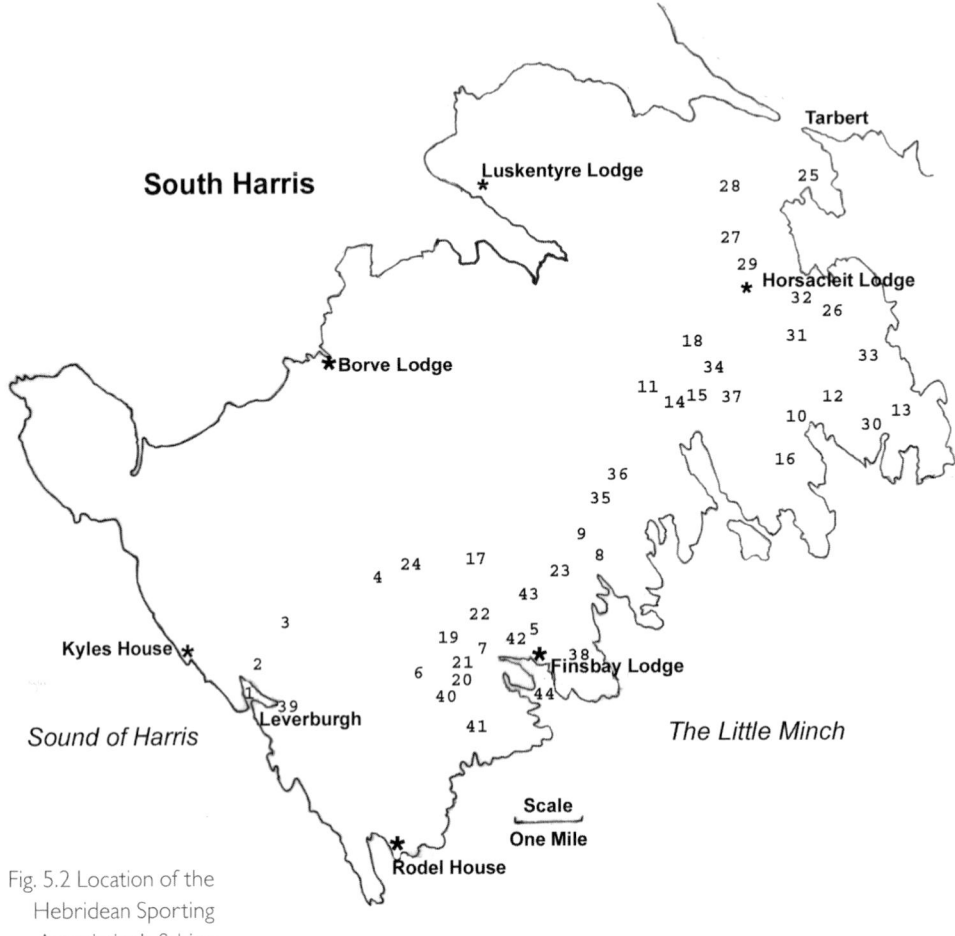

Fig. 5.2 Location of the Hebridean Sporting Association's fishing in South Harris and their two Lodges at Rodel and Finsbay. The key to the lochs is given in Table 1. The locations of Horsacleit, Luskentyre, Borve, and Kyles Lodges are also shown, though these Lodges, all originally the properties of the Earl of Dunmore, were never let to the Hebridean Sporting Association

The two leases granted to the Hebridean Sporting Association covered the Obbe fishings in the south-west part of Harris, attached to Rodel House, known then simply as the Rodel Fishings, and the Finsbay/Grosebay fishings on the east coast. In 1903 the Finsbay/Grosebay fishings included those that were subsequently described as the Horsacleit fishings. As time went on and the financial situation of the Hebridean Sporting Association became precarious, the fishings at Grosebay and Horsacleit were removed from the Association's revised leases from Viscount Fincastle. This, we believe, was probably the stimulus for the building of Horsacleit Lodge around 1909, to be let as a separate sporting tenancy, by the Earl of Dunmore (see Chapter 8).

Table 1: Lochs leased by the Hebridean Sporting Association. Lochs 1 to 38 were named in the Association's Prospectus in 1903. Lochs 39 to 43 were created later (spelling is as given in the Prospectus)

[No in square brackets shows No. of rods]	KEY	OS Grid reference	
Salmon and Sea Trout			
Obbe [2]	1	NG 015 868	Tidal, adjacent to Leverburgh harbour (no mention of Mill Pool)
Steisevat [4]	2	NG 015 875	At the township of Leverburgh
Na Moracha [4]	3	NG 023 885	Upstream from L. Steisevat, close to the "Peat Road" to Finsbay
Langavat [6]	4	NG 046 895	Upstream from L. na Moracha, close to the "Peat Road" to Finsbay
Sea Trout			
Huamavat [2]	5	NG 084 885	
Allityer [1]	6	NG 055 872	Head of Srath Leetein system (where L. Choire and na Criadh were built), to sea at Bayhead, Lingarabay
Na Ciste, River & chain of Lochs [2]	7	NG 070 878	Enters sea at tidal pond just N of Finsbay (at road bridge)
Manish [1] *	8	NG 101 898	Shown as A Clachain on modern maps (error). Lower L on Flodabay system
Vanish [2]	9	NG 097 905	Vanished from modern maps & shown as L. Manish. Headwater of Flodabay system
Groseby [1]	10	NG 150 930	Just W of Grosebay, close to sea
Strathgravat (Creavat) [1]	11	NG 115 938	(L. Creavat)
Harmasaig [1]	12	NG 160 935	NE of Grosebay, close to "Golden Road"
Plocrapool [4]	13	NG 175 935	Large loch
Glumra-More [1]	14	NG 123 935	Between Creavat and road
Glumra-Beg [1]	15	NG 125 935	Between Creavat and road
Mhic-Neacail [1]	16	NG 147 918	S of Grosebay on Stockinish peninsula
Rogavat [2]	17	NG 070 899	Headwaters of Holmasaig/Huamavat
Bearasta Mor [2]	18	NG 125 952	Close to main rd, W of turn-off of "old" Laxdale road
Brown Trout with some Sea Trout			
Meurach [1]	19	NG 062 875	Just N of "Peat road"
Aonais Mhic Fhionnlaidh and a Gleoidh [1]	20,21	NG 068 872	& 066 895 on each side of the "peat road"
a Dubha [1]	22	NG 074 884	

[No in square brackets shows No. of rods]	KEY	OS Grid reference		
Tarbert [1]	23	NG	094 891	Between Manish & Flodabay
Dubh-Sletteval [1]	24	NG	055 899	Headwaters of Na Ciste system
Diraclett [2]	25	NG	156 989	Roadside just S of Tarbert
A Mhonaidh [1]	26	NG	161 957	SE of Meavag, close to "Golden Road"
Mora [1]	27	NG	135 975	Upper (middle) L on Horsaclett system
Uamadale [1]	28	NG	136 987	N of Mora, headwater of Horsaclett system
Horsclett River [2]	29	NG	145 964	Enters sea near Meavag
Na-Cro [2]	30	NG	168 928	NW of Scadabay, close to "Golden Road", W of L. Plocrapool
Iolaire [1]	31	NG	150 952	SE of Horsaclett
Larach Leithe [1]	32	NG	155 962	S of Meavag, own inlet from sea just E of Horsaclett River
Brown Trout				
Cul-na-Beinne [1]	33	NG	168 945	S of Drinisheader
Strath Steachran [1]	34	NG	128 943	E of turn-off of old Laxdale rd from main road
Udromul [2]	35	NG	102 912	Large loch, W of Geocrab
Gamisgarva [2]	36	NG	107 918	Quite large loch, NW of Geocrab
Airidh-Tain Oig [1]	37	NG	135 936	S of junction of E coast road (C79) & main road (A859)
Nan-Caor [1]	38	NG	096 876	On Quidinish peninsula
Other Lochs not referred to in the Association's Prospectus				
Mill Pool	39	NG	021 867	Created between 1903 and 1909 – see text
Choire	40	NG	063 864	Probably created shortly after Loch na Criadhach
na Criadhach	41	NG	068 860	Probably created between 1903 and 1909
Dempster	42	NG	081 879	Almost certainly created by the Association in 1903
Malcolm	43	NG	082 890	Almost certainly created by the Association in 1903

The Prospectus stated: *At Horsaclett River and [its] Lochs and Loch-Na-Cro, salmon and sea trout cannot ascend due to obstructions. These are about to be removed at the expense of the Proprietor and it is expected that the fishing here will be very good. Others of the lochs can be greatly improved at a moderate expenditure*

* The position or naming of Lochs Manish, Vanish, and A Clachain on old Ordnance Survey maps has been inconsistent, and the Ordnance Survey have been unable to provide any explanation.

Figs. 5.3 & 5.4 Kyles Lodge, another of Lord Dunmore's sporting lodges in South Harris. The earlier picture is believed to be around 1905, and the later one showing the added verandah is a few years later. Pictures kindly supplied by Tony Scherr and Chris Lawson.

Fig. 5.5 Loch Dempster in about 1903. The track crossing the bridge was the track between Finsbay and Tarbert. The dam is about 140 yards long. From a postcard kindly supplied by Tony Scherr. (See Fig 5.6 for modern view)

Some of the fishing, that on Loch na Moracha and the rest of the Obbe system was shared with Kyles Lodge[45], another of the Earl of Dunmore's sporting lodges, at Huishnish point just west of the Obbe (NF 998 878) – Figs. 5.3 & 5.4.

The Hebridean Sporting Association's financial accounts show that they had spent £200 by June 1903, a further £193–9s-1d by the end of 1906 and only a further £18–17s-3d by the end of 1916 on "improvements to lochs" [sic]. The lochs improved (or created) were not specified, and we know that Viscount Fincastle had committed himself to make improvements to the Horsacleit system. It is difficult to be certain which of the improvements/creations in the early 1900s were funded by the Association and which were paid for by Lord Dunmore.

In February 1903, the Mill Pool dam probably did not exist; there was simply a tidal pond at the head of the Obbe basin shown in the Ordnance Survey map[46]. Likewise, Lochs Dempster and Malcolm, below and above Loch Huamavat respectively, did not

---

[45] The current owners of Kyles, the Lomas family, retain a part ownership of some of the present Obbe system

[46] 1901 revision of 1878 survey, published as 2nd edition 6–inch map in 1903

exist; we can be fairly sure that Lochs Dempster and Malcolm were created by the Hebridean Sporting Association early on in the Association's existence, and that these two lochs were named after John Dempster and John Malcolm who were founding Directors. Loch Dempster (Figs. 5.5 and 5.6) was constructed as a water supply for Finsbay Lodge as well as a fishing loch, so the cost of constructing its long dam may have been included in the cost of making the water supply rather than under the accounting heading of "improvement of lochs".

Loch na Criadh and Loch a Choire on the Srath Leetein system which drains into the sea at Bayhead just north of Lingerabay also were not shown on the 1903 (2nd edition) maps; nor were they mentioned in the Association's Prospectus detailing the waters being leased in 1903. However, the 1909 revision of the Ordnance Survey map, published in 1911, does show Loch na Criadh, but not Loch a Choire (see Fig. 5.7).

None of Watson Lyall's *Sportsman's and Tourist's Guides* ever mentioned either Loch na Criadh or Loch a Choire. However, as seen in Fig. 4.4 above , an advertisement in Watson Lyall's Shooting & Fishing Agency's catalogue[47] for *The Rodel Fishing Syndicate*[48] at Rodel Hotel in 1915 mentions both Lochs Na-Creagh and Na-Corrie [sic]. It therefore seems more likely that Lord Dunmore, rather than the Hebridean Sporting Association, was responsible for both: firstly L. na Criadh between 1903 and 1909, then L a Choire after 1909. However, Loch a Choire still was not shown on the 1929 map – this is possibly in error in updating the survey information. Loch Choire and its concrete dam are seen in Fig. 5.8.

The origin of the Mill Pool at Leverburgh is another mystery to be solved. It and its dam are shown in Figs. 5.9 and 5.10. It was not mentioned in the Association's Prospectus in 1903, nor was it shown on the 1903 map.

The first mention of the Mill Pool in Watson Lyall's Guide did not appear until the Summer 1910 edition[49]. However, the Mill Pool

---

[47] The catalogue is a separate publication from *The Sportsman's and Tourist's Guide*

[48] This syndicate succeeded the Hebridean Sporting Association as tenants of Rodel Hotel and fishing in 1915 – see pages 18, 54–56

[49] We do not know how efficiently the Guide was updated each year, so this only gives a "latest" date for construction of the dam at the Mill Pool

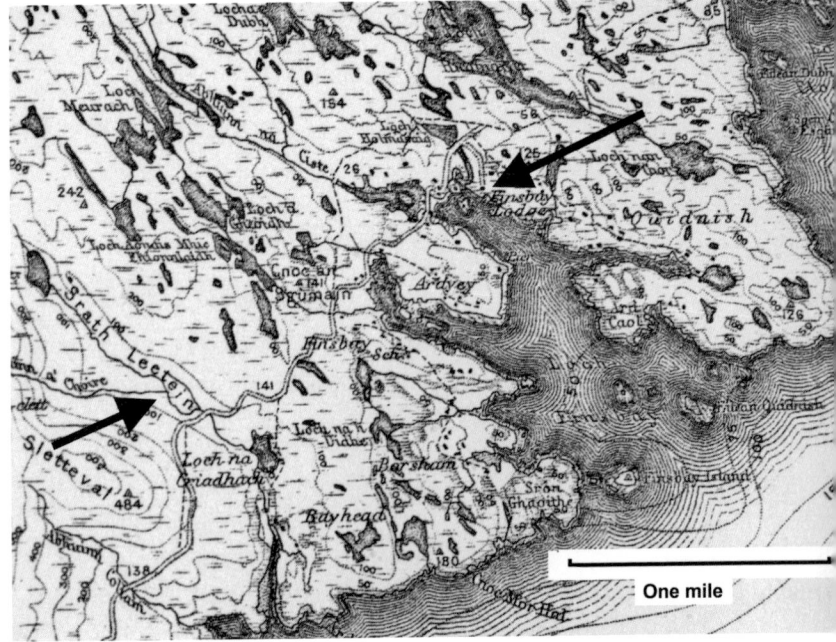

Fig. 5.6 Loch Dempster photographed in 2005

Fig. 5.7 Ordnance Survey map, 1909 revision, published 1911. No loch is seen where L. Choire subsequently is found (see arrow in Srath Leetein). The other arrow shows the location of Finsbay Lodge. Reproduced by kind permission of the Ordnance Survey.

One mile

Fig. 5.8 Loch a Choire, the middle loch on the Lingerabay (Srath Leetein) system. The concrete dam and sluice can be seen at the far right of the picture.

Fig. 5.9 The Mill Pool at Leverburgh. The Obbe at fairly high tide is in the foreground. The dam and, to its right, the outlet from the Mill Pool, can be seen.

is mentioned in the first edition of Calderwood's book which was published in 1909 [7]. So we can be fairly confident that the Mill Pool was created by damming between February 1903 and 1909, but it is not possible to say whether the Association or Lord Dunmore[50] was responsible. In the early 1900s Lord Dunmore (or Viscount Fincastle) made huge investments in fishery improvements with creation of artificial lochs, clearing obstructions, and establishing hatcheries, though this work has hitherto escaped record except for a single article in *The Scotsman* newspaper in 1914 – see Chapter 7.

From around 1911, Norman Robertson at the Estate Office, Obbe (i.e. Leverburgh) and J. Watson Lyall, London would receive enquiries for these fishings on behalf of the Hebridean Sporting Association, but earlier, according to the 1905 edition of Watson Lyall's *The Sportsman's and Tourist's Guide*, the Association's letting terms for Rodel House and Finsbay Lodge were to be obtained from Dowells, 34 St James's St, London or from George Stirling (the Association's Secretary) in Glasgow (see Fig. 3.12).

The Obbe system comprises the Obbe tidal basin with a narrow mouth to the sea (the Sound of Harris) close to Leverburgh harbour, the Mill Pool (mainly less than 8 feet deep) into which spring tides readily flow, Loch Steisevat which is deep, Loch na Moracha which is shallow, and the long and deep Loch Langavat[51] which is said to contain ferox trout[52]. The system, apart from the top loch, L. Langavat, is seen in the recent aerial picture (Fig. 5.11) and the panoramic view (Fig. 5.12). It provides a striking variety of fishing lochs, all within a short distance of each other, and both salmon and sea trout are caught.

The Finsbay systems are, on the other hand, almost exclusively sea trout (and brown trout) fishings, with very few salmon being caught. Three different systems drain into the sea loch, Loch Finsbay

---

50 Or Viscount Fincastle who succeeded his father to the Earldom in 1907 but who, legally, was the proprietor of South Harris from about 1890. The respective roles of these two men in the fishery developments in the late 19th and early 20th centuries have never been made clear in the literature and documentation – to our regret!

51 Not to be confused with L. Langavat in Lewis, one of the headwaters of the Grimersta system, and others of the same name derived from Norse "Long Loch"

52 In Scotland only lochs over 100 ha in area and containing Arctic Charr are likely to contain ferox trout [43, p.122]. L. Langavat in Harris meets both these criteria

– two can be seen in the aerial view (Fig. 3.5 above). Most of the Finsbay lochs are smaller and in much more rugged terrain than those in the Obbe system, and they are generally suited to fishing several lochs during an energetic day's walk – see Professor Irvine's account in Chapter 10. Further north from Finsbay, freshwater systems drain into the sea lochs Floddabay, Geocrab, Stockinish, and Grosebay. Even further north on the East coast of Harris is the Horsaclett system, of similar character to the Finsbay system but with the added benefit of a fishable river. Horsacleit and its lodge are discussed in Chapter 8.

While the Laxdale system which comprises Loch Fincastle at the head of the Luskentyre estuary and the small Loch Laxdale upstream was never part of the Hebridean Sporting Association's fishings, these lochs were an important part of Lord Dunmore's fishing improvements. Loch Fincastle was created in about 1898 by building a dam of substantial length at the head of tide across the mouth of the Laxdale river at a cost of £200[53] – see Fig. 5.13.

Though the construction of the dam at the Mill Pool is very different from that at L. Fincastle, the success of the latter is likely to have encouraged the creation of the Mill Pool. Loch Laxdale was described by Hamish Stuart as *"the smallest natural salmon loch in Europe"* [3]. Both these lochs have great charm, and they have been greatly successful for fishing, yielding about 6,000 salmon and 30,000 sea trout over the years, according to Tony Scherr, who was Estate Manager at Borve Lodge Estate for 38 years. He personally has caught over 1,300 fish off the system and has kept outstandingly detailed records of fishing results and conditions during his period of management. Additionally, Lord Dunmore opened up access to the lochs in the headwaters and spawning streams above Loch Laxdale. It can be safely assumed that the success of damming to create Loch Fincastle marked the start of a very busy period of development in which so many of the South Harris lochs were created, enlarged, or controlled – see Chapter 7.

We are fairly sure that the Association never operated a fish hatchery, though Lord Dunmore[54] had done so and, subsequently

---

53 This cost **may** have included other works on the Laxdale system
54 See information on his hatching ponds in Chapter 7 & Fig. 7.1. All these hatcheries were on the West coast systems, and it is unlikely that the waters leased to the Hebridean Sporting Association benefited from stocking

Fig. 5.10 The Dam at the Mill Pool. The building at the left of the picture is the An Clachan stores, where the Harris Millennium Tapestry can normally be viewed

Fig. 5.12 Panoramic view of Leverburgh showing A: The Sound of Harris, B: The Obbe, C: The Mill Pool, and D: Loch Steisevat

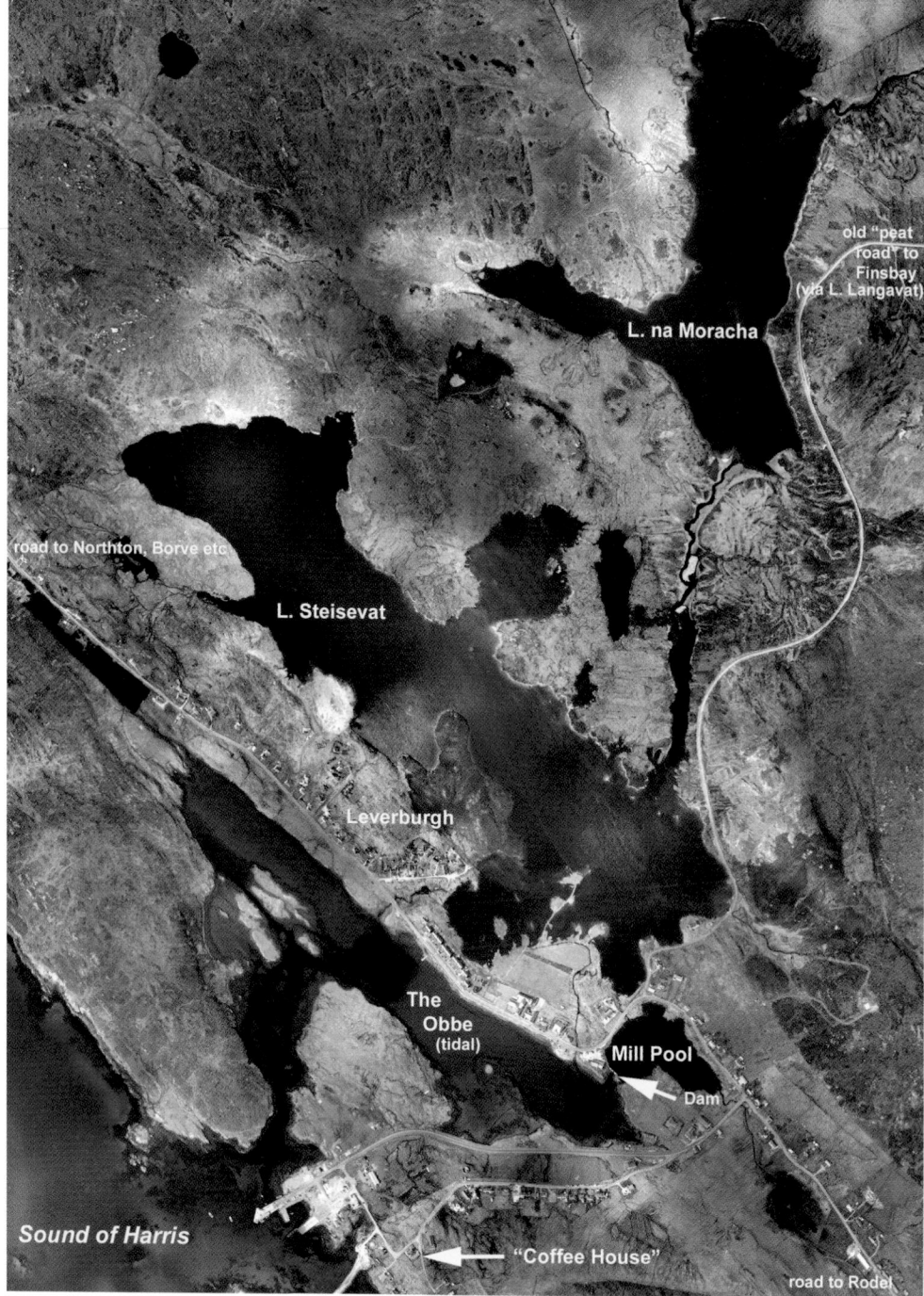

Fig. 5.11 Aerial view of the Obbe system. The township of Leverburgh is seen in the foreground. Except in low water conditions, it is possible to take a boat up from Loch Steisevat to Loch na Moracha. Loch Langavat, upstream from Loch na Moracha, is not seen in this picture. Reproduced under licence from Getmapping Plc

Lord Leverhulme and his factor, Norman Robertson, installed one at Borve Lodge: The 1925 sale particulars after Lord Leverhulme's death briefly refer to the Obbe fishings being stocked quite recently with spring salmon fry. In 1923, Norman Robertson had been in communication with the Kincardine Fisheries at Ardgay, Ross-shire[55] about acquiring spring-fish ova, but there is no record of how or whether this was progressed. Lord Leverhulme sanctioned the purchase of 2,000 yearling salmon to be released at Leverburgh [sic], at a price not to exceed £25 per 1,000 [44]. Norman Robertson indicated at that time to Lord Leverhulme that cement in the proposed hatchery (presumably the one being developed at Borve Lodge) would render the pond unusable for a year [45]. To the writer's knowledge, none of the Harris salmon systems has ever had a significant spring run of fish – as well as requiring the genetic make-up for spring running, spring salmon require large enough systems to maintain reproductive isolation during spawning, otherwise the dominant trait of later running will prevail [46], though the Obbe system would possibly qualify for the size aspect. Hebridean fisheries are not recognized for spring fish, though the Skealtar system in North Uist has had significant spring runs.

The fishings in the Obbe system (the Obbe, Mill Pool, Lochs Steisevat, na Moracha, and Langavat) are now owned by a consortium, the main owners being the Jourdan family, who make day and weekly lets available on a beat basis. Rodel Hotel and Kyles Lodge still retain a part-share in some of these lochs.

The fishings at Finsbay were sold in 1987 by Rodel Crofting Lands to Mr and Mrs Pat Mackreth for £55,000 who had plans to establish a hatchery, stock the fishery and regenerate it along the lines of the ranching operation on the Delphi fishery in Ireland which has been described by Rawlings [47, p.99–111]. Concerns about poaching and the whole viability of the operation caused the Mackreths to sell the fishings in 1991 to the Lees Group (Scotland) for £110,000 (this being said to include ... "comprising Finsbay Lodge &c ... "). The Lees Group planned to establish fish farming, but the company went into liquidation, and it sold these fishings in 1992 to Dr Jan Abel and Peter Brauchl from Austria who are the current owners. At that time the sale particulars stated that 12,000 smolts had been released into the Loch Huamavat system

---

[55] No relevant information exists at the present Ardgay hatchery

in 1989, plus a further 20,000 in 1990. In 1991, 15,000 pre-smolts had been released into the Flodabay system and 2,000 fry into Loch Huamavat; then in 1992 100,000 salmon parr had been introduced into the headwaters of the Abhainn Na Ciste system[56]. These fishings, now described as "The Hundred Lochs Fishery", are now available on a day or week ticket basis, but are not heavily fished. The owners have erected a substantial fishing hut close to the site of Finsbay Lodge – it can be seen in Fig. 3.3.

Some recent fishing results from both the Obbe system and The Hundred Lochs Fishery are shown below (Table 3, page 102), but comparisons with old results should be made with caution since the numbers of lochs fished are not identical. Also, we have no reliable indices of angling pressure, a serious but common obstacle for anybody trying to interpret fishing catches.

Historical Accounts

Hamish Stuart[57] had high praise for the creation of artificial lochs, including Loch Fincastle, and the other fishery developments in South Harris, giving particular credit to the Hebridean Sporting Association. His *"The Book of the Sea Trout"* (1917) [15] is regarded as a seminal, but sometimes controversial, work[58], and his description of the Harris lochs was as follows:

> " ... .. the writer is convinced from his experience of existing artificial sea-trout lochs that the sea-trout fishing of most watersheds can be improved by the construction of such lochs at suitable places in the watershed, where they will also serve other and almost equally useful and important purposes. In the first place, they increase the area of angling water in any watershed; in the second place, they almost invariably increase the number — one is not justified in the light of present experience in saying that they also increase the size — of the sea trout; in the third place, when constructed in a watershed of the purely

---

56 Despite these ambitious stocking attempts, it should be recognised that the Finsbay systems have always been productive for sea trout rather than salmon. The sale particulars in 1992 suggested that catches before 1985 had been 43 salmon and 126 sea trout per annum, but it is likely that these figures erroneously included all the fishings attached to Rodel Hotel, i.e. including the Obbe fishings.
57 He died in 1914 at sea, and his sea trout book was edited posthumously by his friend Rafael Sabatini
58 Republished in 1952

'river' type, especially when the river is one that can be fished by day with much hope of success only in times of spate, they ensure sport in conditions in which the river would yield few fish or none at all, except perhaps by night. In the fourth place, the lochs serve the useful purpose of storing water which, by simple mechanical means, can be utilized to keep the river up to a certain height or to create artificial spates which induce the fish to run.

The artificial lochs with which I can claim a fairly intimate acquaintance from personal inspection and actual angling are those of South Harris. These, however, were not the first to be constructed. The small artificial loch on the Iorsa River Arran, was constructed long before the first of the Harris lochs — the loch at the foot of the Laxdale River. The Iorsa Loch was in existence over forty years ago. ... ... the Iorsa Loch may fairly be regarded as the first artificial or semi-artificial loch frequented by salmon and sea trout. ...

The first of the Harris lochs to be constructed was, as stated, Fincastle Loch, which lies at the end of the Laxdale River, and though not strictly tidal, it is occasionally invaded by very high tides. This loch lies in a natural basin so far as three of its sides are concerned, but it was necessary to construct a barrier on the side nearest to the sea so as to complete the loch. The outflow was much the same as from Loch Stiesavat — a large, tortuous, natural loch, the first of the chain of lochs connected with that singular tidal basin the Obbe, South Harris — and the flow of water is generally quite sufficient to induce, or at least to permit, migrants to run. When this loch was being constructed I ventured to predict that it would probably prove a better sea-trout than salmon loch, the prediction being based on the habits of the two fish and on the fact that the sea trout is an estuary trout, always reluctant to travel far from tidal water unless the reproductive process compels it to do so. The salmon, on the other hand, becomes in this sense, and in this sense only, more of a fresh-water fish than the sea trout, and will push on to the upper water when it can, without lingering on the way like the sea trout. The prediction, I believe, has been amply fulfilled. The greater number of the salmon still push on to lie is that singular tarn, South Loch Laxdale — probably the smallest salmon and sea-trout loch in the world — and in the dark, still pools of the narrow river below the loch. In most of its length the Laxdale is a ditch of dark peat-stained water.

It is rather a startling experience to see salmon leaping in the manner usual to their kind in this narrow ditch-like river, which is often not more than six feet across, although here and there you find a fair-sized pool where the river widens. The fish, which do not approach in quality the salmon of the small rivers of the Southern Hebrides, occasionally take the fly well when there is flood-water and a good breeze. The Laxdale is probably unique amongst little rivers in which salmon take the fly.

The important point, so far as the subject under discussion is concerned, is that the artificial loch at Fincastle has proved a success in every way and has amply justified its construction. The other artificial lochs in Harris, at Finsbay, are due to the enterprise of the Hebridean Sporting Association, whose lodge at Finsbay is unique among Hebridean residences, for it boasts trimly kept grounds and one goes by garden paths to the nearer lochs. To approach an otherwise typical Hebridean tarn of dark peat-stained water and wild, rocky shores by a trimly kept

Fig. 5.13 Loch Fincastle at the head of tide in the Luskentyre estuary. This was created in 1898 by Lord Dunmore, and it success probably encouraged the subsequent development of artificial lochs in Harris. Note the dam. Loch Fincastle and Loch Laxdale above it were never part of the Hebridean Sporting Association's waters, but were attached to Borve Lodge. Borve Lodge Estate now has the rights on these 2 lochs

garden path, more suggestive of the fertile South than the most barren and rocky of all the outer isles, is a singular experience. These lochs, with the exception of one lake near Rodel Lodge — which lake might with greater fitness be described as a pond — have all been constructed on watersheds already frequented by sea trout and boasting two or more natural lochs; they are thus additions to an existing chain of lochs ... ..

To understand the principle upon which the lochs, which are now part of natural watersheds frequented by sea trout in great numbers, have been constructed, and to grasp the reason why all have realized expectations in almost every way — I shall presently note the only direction in which the expectations of the constructors have not been fully realized — it is necessary to give a general description of the watersheds of South Harris.

The Obbe watershed comprises a large tidal basin of almost circular shape. This is called the Obbe. Although the water is almost salt, the Obbe affords excellent fishing with the fly for salmon and sea trout. The salmon-fishing is at its best in July and early in August. The duration of the brief season depends largely upon the rainfall, or at least did so, for the Association can now command a good flow of water through a simple system of storage down the burn which connects the Obbe with Loch Stiesavat[59] through an upper pool, more or less tidal according to the height of the tides. The sea-trout fishing in the Obbe is fairly good in spring, but is at its best, not merely in point of the number but also of the size of the fish, during the period when the salmon-fishing is also at its best. The Mill Pool too is artificial, and the existing burn which connects it with Loch Stiesavat is therefore also not the original connection between the Obbe and the Stiesavat. The original burn flowed direct from the Stiesavat into the Obbe. But the Mill Pool and the existing burn are, nevertheless, perfectly natural in design; and if one did not know their history one would think that this part of the environment owed nothing to man, except some suggestion of his handiwork which the short burn shows in places where the banks have been 'shored up' with stones.

The environment, therefore, consists of a large tidal basin (which the salmon, of course, leave for the open sea, but in which the sea trout, being an estuary fish of very limited ocean range, remain), a large tidal pool and a short burn flowing from

---

[59] Stuart's original spelling has been retained here

the loch above, which in turn is connected by a canal or ditch-like burn with another large loch. One can go in a boat from the lower to the upper loch[60], and the boats, in consequence, all lie at the sea end of Stiesavat. At the head of the upper loch a burn of considerable dimensions forms a connection between another and still larger loch[61] lying some two miles up in the hills, If it were deemed necessary, artificial lochs could be constructed on the river between the upper loch and the highest loch of the chain with every certainty that they would become sea-trout lochs. In the meantime, however, there is no necessity for this, since the Obbe, the Mill Pool, Stiesavat and the upper loch together represent an area of angling water quite sufficient to keep fully occupied the limited number of 'rods' permitted by the rules of this admirably controlled 'fishery'.

The Finsbay environment is similar in its general aspects, but the extent of tidal water is much more limited. When one grasps the general character of this environment, it is easy to see why the lochs constructed on the natural watersheds frequented by sea trout have realized the expectations of their constructors. As already indicated, they have shown sound judgment in following Nature, and to the existing chains of lochs they have merely added lakes that are in all respects modelled on the same plan as the natural lochs. In some cases the artificial lochs afford even better fishing than the natural ones, and so form a permanent memorial to the foresight of the constructors in avoiding excessively ambitious projects.

These lochs, then, furnish the principle upon which all such lochs should be constructed, while in a negative way they show the limitations of our power in this matter and also provide a useful object-lesson in the advisability or otherwise of interfering in any way with a natural watershed frequented by sea trout. The Harris lochs thus indicate that in the case of certain watersheds any attempt to increase or limit (for limitation is possible, as I shall presently show) the existing area of angling water may be injudicious, even if one cannot dogmatize, through lack of data, upon the degree to which such increase or decrease may be the reverse of beneficial to the watershed as a home for sea trout and as furnishing sport for the angler. The principle upon which all artificial sea-trout lochs should be constructed is clearly this:

---

60   This refers to Loch na Moracha
61   This refers to Loch Langavat

one must follow natural models and must construct the loch at a point where there would be a natural loch if the means whereby such a loch is formed existed naturally, or, in other words, if the artificial barriers necessary to dam the water and to form a complete basin for the loch were natural barriers of the same height and length, though not, of course, of the same character and composition as the artificial barriers.

I here presume, of course, that the watershed is already frequented by sea trout and that the great difficulty of stocking the watershed with sea trout does not exist, and that one is not faced with the experimental and almost hopeless task of constructing a lake-and-burn watershed, which sea trout will prefer to existing natural watersheds already frequented. It is, indeed, more than doubtful whether a perfect watershed, in terms of the best natural models of the district, would draw sea trout away from the existing natural watersheds. The experience of those who attempted to convert certain natural lochs in Rum into sea-trout lochs seems to afford convincing proof of the accuracy of the proposition here advanced in theoretical form. But few experiments of this kind are likely to be made; they are too costly and the result is too uncertain. Moreover, there are so many watersheds already frequented by sea trout on which one or more artificial lochs can be constructed with every assurance of success that the construction of artificial sea—trout watersheds, *de novo* in every sense, need hardly be further considered.

The point of importance is that the construction of an artificial loch, or chain of lochs, is a simple matter and is assured of success in watersheds already frequented by sea trout. These lochs must vary in excellence, but on every burn or small river where there are suitable basins, a watershed in all respects superior to the original burn or river as a home for sea trout may be constructed by the making of one artificial loch or more. This fact is not recognized by proprietors. There are many small rivers on which the plan might be adopted with great advantage and with every assurance of the comparatively small expenditure being amply rewarded."

Hamish Stuart, however, drew attention to the relatively small size of the sea trout in the Finsbay system (see also discussion below at pages 95–99):

" ... .. The construction of artificial lochs has thus, so to speak, a negative as well as a positive aspect. It has already been indicated that the Finsbay artificial lochs have failed to justify expectations in one direction. Reference is made to the fact that the construction of the lochs has not, as anticipated, been attended by any increase in the size of the fish, though they appear to be, and probably are, more numerous. The Finsbay lochs have, however, always presented one peculiar feature. The sea trout, so far as is known, have always been small, while salmon have ever been so scarce that they may be said not to ascend into these lochs at all. A few salmon are taken each season, but the capture of a salmon is so rare — so much of an event — that the fish taken are probably 'wanderers', while it is doubtful whether the few that ascend into the lochs ever spawn in the watershed. They probably return to the sea. The sea trout are of small average size. If one captures twenty fish, then the largest will in all probability not be more than 1¼ or 1½ lb. in weight, while the majority will be herling size, from ½ to ¾ lb. A fair average is ¾ lb. Fish over 3 lb. are very rare, and even fish of from 2 to 2½ lb. are scarce. Large sea trout of from 4 to 7 lb are almost as unusual captures as salmon. The lochs may, then, be said to hold only small sea trout, there being a hundred of less than 1 lb. for every fish that exceeds this weight. Other Harris lochs, notably Groseabaigh, present the same feature. It is extremely difficult to account for the absence of large sea trout in the Finsbay lochs, for they present a striking exception to most Hebridean lochs. The difficulty of the problem is increased by the fact that the few large sea trout, and assuredly such salmon as are taken, are probably not natives of any of the Finsbay watersheds. They are so scarce that one is justified in inferring that they are 'wandered' fish belonging, in all probability, to the Obbe watershed[62].

There are three explanations of the absence of fish over 3 lb. and the scarcity of fish over 1½ lb. in weight. Upon attaining the maximum weight of the watershed, which may be fixed at 3 lb., the sea trout of the Finsbay lochs die, or their growth is arrested, or else they cease to ascend the Finsbay watersheds on attaining the said maximum weight, and migrate to the Obbe, the Laxdale or other Harris watersheds, in which sea trout of from 4 to 7 lb. are fairly numerous and fish of 10 lb. occur.

---

[62] This remains very speculative!

When one says that the fish either die or cease to grow one says, in effect, the same thing, because the cessation of growth is, in the case of common trout, the first step towards a rapid decline in health, weight and strength, and hence towards death. Strictly speaking, therefore, there are only two alternatives: the fish, after reaching the maximum weight, either cease to grow, and hence rapidly waste away and die, or they migrate to other waters. The analogy of the trout of certain waters is strongly in favour of the first alternative, whereas migration to another water is not only opposed to the habits of the sea trout but increases the difficulty of the problem, because it would be extremely difficult to state the reasons why the fish depart from their racial habits in the case of the Finsbay lochs. Some authorities, it is true, seem to hold that the salmon of certain waters in which large fish are scarce do migrate to other waters on attaining the maximum size of their native water, but no positive proof of such a departure from habit has been advanced in support of this speculative contention. As to the first alternative, strong and convincing proof of its probable accuracy is furnished by the well-established analogy of the trout of certain waters ... .."

Note that Stuart attributes the creation of artificial lochs (presumably including the Mill Pool) to the Hebridean Sporting Association, rather than to Viscount Fincastle or Lord Dunmore. However, there is no reason to suppose that Stuart, though a lawyer, had accurate knowledge of those responsible for the improvements. Of course, a significant stimulus for Lord Dunmore's (or Viscount Fincastle's) fishery improvements may have been the tenancy of the Association which must initially have appeared to have had long-term financial potential for the estate. At this time, deer-stalking was also an important source of revenue, so development of sporting assets was beneficial to the estate. It can also be noted that fishing developments did not intrude on other land uses, as deer forests had done, and would provide more opportunities for employment in the community than deer stalking had done.

The fullest historical account of the Harris fishings is that given by William Leadbetter Calderwood (1865–1950), who was H.M. Inspector of Salmon Fisheries for Scotland, in his *"The Salmon Rivers and Lochs of Scotland"* [7, 8], and it is worth quoting fully here:-

"The streams of Harris—the High Island—are, for the most part, sea-trout streams, and a very great many of the small lochs communicating with the chief streams yield good sea-trout fishing in early autumn. To other lochs sea-trout are unable to climb, but in South Harris—which is that part of the island south of the Tarbert—owing to the arrangement entered into by the proprietor, Lord Dunmore, and an association called The Hebridean Sporting Association, Limited, a good number of the obstacles have recently been modified, a new fishing lodge built at Inisbay[63], and roads and paths constructed by means of which access is more easily obtained to the various waters. Inisbay and Rodel are now the two bases of the Association from which fishing is carried on. At the former a deal of fly-fishing is practised in the narrow sea channels or kyles, and some large baskets have been made, especially in the year 1890, before the association took up residence. Rodel was formerly the residence of the proprietor, and from it the famous Obe fishings are reached at the south end of the island.

Obe: The principal features here are a fairly large fresh-water loch, called Loch Steisevat, close to a large salt-water channel, winding in from the Sound of Harris. From time to time artificial channels have been formed in different places so as to make the communication between the fresh and the salt water in the most advantageous manner, and these channels have commonly been sluiced for the purpose of controlling the water-flow. Now, the short run of water passes out at its south-eastern extremity, and in this way the most use is probably made of the tidal water.

The fresh water flows first into what is called The Mill Pool, a shallow basin not reached by salt water in the lowest neaps, but freely filled during spring tides. Ordinary half-neap tides raise its level about 18 inches. From this Mill Pool the tidal channel has a strong current up and down, and about half way to the sea there is a pool in which fish congregate.

The Mill Pool yields good sport with sea-trout as early as March and April, but the great bulk of the fish are finnock or herling, i.e. the juvenile grilse stage of the sea-trout. More adult fish of

---

[63] This typographical error for "Finsbay" was corrected for the 1921 edition, though the demise of the Hebridean Sporting Association by that time was not mentioned. This is a surprising lapse, as Calderwood was generally well-informed and authoritative

2, 3, 4, and even on occasion up to 8 lb., are, or have been, got. About 600 to 700 sea-trout, small and great, may be expected in a good spring.

The tidal channel lower down yields the chief fishing in summer and autumn, particularly in the pool already referred to. It is noticeable, however, that fish do not take well in the salt-water channel if much fresh water is descending from Loch Steisevat and the lochs above. If a flood or considerable rise is "on," fishing is transferred to Loch Steisevat into which the fish naturally travel.

A considerable sprinkling of salmon and grilse, mostly grilse, also enter fresh water at Obe. They are not usually susceptible to the lure of the angler in salt water, and do not hang about tidal channels as sea-trout do. Loch Steisevat is the chief place to expect the salmon to rise, and in its mile of water there is considerable space for plenty of sport. The salmon seldom exceed 9 or 10 lb. in weight. So far as I know, a fish of 14½ lb. (which in all probability was a big bull-trout, as known in the Tweed or Coquet, i.e. *Salmo trutta eriox*[64]) constitutes the record weight.

About 1000 to 1200 sea-trout and about 70 salmon are expected each season at Obe, but it may be noticed that sea-trout here have to be referred to before salmon, as in other Harris localities.

Laxdale: At low tide this stream winds over a sandy flat, called the Traigh Luskintyre, for about 1.75 miles. At high tide the great Traigh, or stretch of shore, is a lagoon shut off from the Sound of Taransay by a narrow barrier of sand and rock. I recollect crossing the narrow channel from the end of this barrier to Luskintyre House on one occasion in a boat which literally leaked like a basket[65]. I don't suppose the passage is more than some three or four hundred yards, but I had my feet on the seat, and we were all awash when we landed. "Row hard, row hard," shouted a man with me, "I cannot swim, I'll be drowned." He only ceased shouting when we touched bottom. The knee of one of the thwarts came away in my hands when we attempted to pull the boat up.

---

64 Calderwood deleted this for his 2nd edition
65 It is likely that this ferry boat was rowed by Norman Morrison, Keeper at Luskentyre and brother of Sam Morrison, the Keeper at Finsbay Lodge. See [48, p.144] and Fig. 13.14.

A pool[66] has been constructed just above the point where the Laxdale enters the head of the Traigh by the formation of a broad dyke from the left bank, a mass of rocks on the right hemming in the water largely in that direction. This and the sea-pool just below is said to fish well when the tide is out. It has to be remembered, however, that the Laxdale is a late river. On one occasion when I tried this pool on 5 July I was still too early. From the pool, fish are able to ascend freely to four lochs. There is also a Laxdale in Lewis.

Other sea-trout streams of similar nature occur along this eastern side, some fished by visitors to Tarbert Hotel, those further south by the Hebridean Association. July, August, and September are the best months."

Another valuable historical account on angling in South Harris was given in a chapter in the Rev. Joseph Adams'[67] book on *Fifty Years Angling* [49].

"South Harris has undoubted attractions for the angler. There is a good hotel at Rodel, under admirable management. Everything that courtesy and liberality can do is at the service of the visitor. Three miles' drive finds one at the lochs in Leverborough, and as we are the first rods of the season there are four lochs to select from. Steisevat is the highest loch from the sea, where we make our first attempt. There is another farther in amongst the mountains[68], but it is too early in the season to pay it a visit. As it is, Steisevat fails to fulfil our hopes on the first day, as the fish had not yet settled down, and after fishing the most promising parts of it we passed down to Mill Pool, as the middle loch is called. It is a comparatively small area of water, but we had not been five minutes afloat before the evidence of trout and salmon was unmistakable. One could not look in any direction—towards the high mountain that rises sheer from its bank, and casts its shadow on the water, or out towards the sea, where a mist is blotting out the hills—that the splash of a fish or a clear spring from the water did not attract attention. It is almost axiomatic that rising sea trout can be depended upon to take the artificial fly when it is presented to them. If there is an exception it is in the case of the big specimens. These we saw

---

[66]   This is L. Fincastle

[67]   Rev Joseph Adams published many articles under the pseudonym "Corrigeen"

[68]   This refers to L. Langavat. The fishings on L. na Moracha were specifically excluded from the Rodel Lot in the 1925 Leverhulme sale

repeatedly, and I estimated their weight to be from 4 lb. to 8 lb., and although I covered the spot where I saw them rise I could not persuade them to take. It may have been that, like the fish that had run up to Steisevat, they had not yet settled down after their adventurous sea journey. They have been taken later on in the season, fly fishing, up to 9 lb.

The smaller fish, running from ¾ lb. up to 2 lb. were of a different mind, and in the first drift I landed a couple of moderate dimensions. Then as we passed on towards the mouth of the brook that flows into the loch, I found myself on combative terms with a vigorous fighter. Before he showed himself by a leap from the water I might have judged him to rank amongst the leviathans of *Salmo trutta*, for he took very long runs, half stripped my reel, and bent my rod to the butt in the severity of the struggle. He only proved to be well on the way to a pound and three-quarters. This was the beginning of a chapter in which a similar fight was repeated of little less intensity, and did not close until the evening. Pounders figured in it freely, and plenty slightly below that size, but each of them a born fighter that gave most exciting play.

The Mill Pool flows into Obbe loch, from which it is separated by a small waterfall. Here the fishing is tidal, but the formation of the inlet is well adapted to angling. It only averages 2 ft. to 4 ft. at low water, and is therefore suitable for the fly. It always holds a liberal stock of salmon and sea trout, which are no doubt waiting for a spate to take them up to the higher lochs on the fishing. They have practically settled down in different parts of the water — the pools, in short — and there is always the chance of interesting them. A further advantage in connection with Obbe lies in the fact that with the first flow of the tide there is always a new influx of fish of both species. It is well to time one's visit to low water. The fish will be there and disposed to rise, and every moment there is a chance of getting hold of some of the new-comers. Several hours can be usefully employed before the tide rises too high for fishing. Even at high tide there is so much fresh water in the loch that angling can be pursued close to the shore, a place where sea trout, at least, frequent in quest of the sand eels and crustacean amongst the seaweed. I got my best fish within a few feet of high-water mark. Some of them showed they were recent arrivals by the parasites that copiously covered them.

This form of fishing is thoroughly enjoyable. There seemed a disposition on the part of many sea trout to rise short. One had a rise almost every cast, a nip of the feathers, or a tumble over the gut followed, with no further result, but there were times when the fly would be seized in no gingerly fashion, and a fish would dash off, cutting through high waves at express speed, and making the circle of the boat half a dozen times before giving in. It was no uncommon thing to get two fish on at the same time, and with a cast of three flies, both were taken. This is, as I have noticed before, undesirable, and I soon learned the wisdom of keeping to a single fly. The fact was that invariably one only succeeded in landing the smallest of the fish hooked. My best basket in a day was 14 sea trout, running in weight from ¾ lb. up to 1¾ lb."

Another account, brief but highly complimentary, was given also by John Stirling[69] of a visit in 1903 in his *Fifty Years with the Rod* [50]:

"In 1903 I was at Finsbay, South Harris, but not for long enough to give the place, with its very numerous lochs, a proper trial. I saw no salmon, there may however be a few in some of the lochs. The seatrout were numerous but, while I was there, herling predominated; it was probably their time for running. I got several two pounders and was broken by a fish which rose high; it was evidently about 4 lb. I had been using too fine gut, a foolish mistake as it was a gale most of the time I was there. The Hebridean Association were taking measures to improve the angling, but when the weather moderated the sport was good enough for anyone. There is such a variety of lochs, big and small, that one could spend a month or two at Finsbay without any risk of being tired of thrashing the same beats. Of the lochs which I tried I liked best Marnish [sic] and the loch below it; on these on 3 September I had ten seatrout; Langavat, where on the 4th I had four seatrout, heaviest 2 lb., and four brown of a half pound each; Dun Tack, where again I got four seatrout, best 2 lb. I had several days on Humavat, but it blew a gale each of these days. I thought its possibilities were good."

The enthusiasm of these authors from the early part of the 20th century is captivating; they were fortunate to experience a greater abundance of sea trout than would be possible nowadays.

---

[69] John Stirling had more extensive experience of the Lacisdale lochs in North Harris when he stayed in the Harris Hotel, Tarbert in 1902, 1913 & 1923.

The Fishing Results

Sadly the Association's fishing record books have never been found, and these may have been lost along with the Rodel Hotel's records. However, a summary for the years 1903 to 1907 was presented at the Company's AGM in 1908 – see Table 2. Salmon catches on the Rodel fishery, i.e. the Obbe system, were remarkably similar to the current levels of reported catches of around 40 salmon per annum. Salmon were rare, though occasionally caught, in the Finsbay and Grosebay systems.

As seen in Table 2 sea trout catches were high, at between 921 and 1251 each year from the Rodel fishery plus 951 to 1248 each year from the Finsbay and Grosebay fishings. While the biggest fish each year were noteworthy (14lb salmon; and 7 lb 12 oz and 4 lb sea trout for Rodel and Finsbay[70], respectively), the average sizes were 6 lb for salmon and 10 oz for sea trout – i.e. typical of modern figures for Hebridean salmon but distinctly small for sea trout. The average weights of sea trout at Finsbay and Grosebay were consistently smaller than at Rodel (9 & 12 oz respectively), a point stressed by Hamish Stuart in his account quoted above. In spite of these large catches of small sea trout, the catches of sea trout were well sustained through the period for which detailed records are available (1903–1907). Table 3 below summarises the historical results alongside some recent results from the Harris and some other Hebridean rod fisheries.

According to Jones [51, p.118], the annual catch at Finsbay and Obbe had been about 70 salmon and from 1,000 to 1,200 sea trout during the period 1887–1889, before the Hebridean Sporting Association's tenancy, when the proprietor of the Harris Hotel (then known as the Tarbert Hotel) leased these fishings.

Some information about the catches from the Hebridean Sporting Association's waters is also provided by contemporary issues of *The Scotsman* newspaper. Before the Second World War *The Scotsman* used to publish regular reports on a remarkably wide range of sports including angling, and the angling column often contained results from distant parts of Scotland including Harris[71] though it gave particular attention each week to Loch

---

70 In June 2006, sea trout of 4 lb and 6 lb were taken from L. Huamavat in the Finsbay system

71 The correspondent responsible for these reports is not known.

Table 2: Annual recorded catches by the Hebridean Sporting Association 1903–1907

YEAR		No of Salmon	Average Weight (lb oz)		Heaviest (lb oz)		No of Sea Trout	Average Weight (lb oz)		Heaviest (lb oz)	
			lb	oz	lb	oz		lb	oz	lb	oz
1903	Rodel	58	6	8	14	0	951	0	14	5	4
	Finsbay	5	4	14	6	0	1170	0	9	4	0
	Total	**63**	**6**	**6**			**2121**				
1904	Rodel	60	5	7	7	12	1219	0	11	6	8
	Finsbay	0					1205	0	7	3	0
	Total	**60**	**5**	**7**			**2424**				
1905	Rodel	31	6	8	7	12	1247	0	11	7	12
	Finsbay	1	5	0	5	0	1207	0	8	2	8
	Total	**32**	**6**	**7**			**2454**				
1906	Rodel	29	5	12	9	12	1152	0	12	5	12
	Finsbay	2	5	8	7	0	951	0	9	4	0
	Total	**31**	**5**	**12**			**2103**				
1907	Rodel	24	5	3	13	1	921	0	11	6	0
	Finsbay	3	4	13	5	14	1248	0	10	3	0
	Total	**27**	**5**	**3**			**2169**				
1903–1907	Rodel	202	5	15	14	0	5490	-		7	12
	Finsbay	11	4	16	7	0	5781	-		4	0
	Total	**213**	**5**	**14**			**11271**				
5-year average	Rodel	40	5	15			1098	0	12		
	Finsbay	2	6	0			1156	0	9		
	Total	**43**	**5**	**14**			**2254**	**0**	**10**		

Leven. Obviously, these reports are a poor substitute for a proper angling record book, as they are erratic in coverage and because they, understandably, do not record anglers with "blank" days.

Hence *The Scotsman* reports give just a snapshot of fishing results, and a probable underestimate of the number of anglers so that one can only guess at the total angling pressure. Nevertheless, these reports (see Appendix 4), even allowing for unsuccessful anglers, give the impression that no more than a dozen anglers were likely to be fishing each day in the peak of the fishing season – it is unlikely that the accommodation at Finsbay and Rodel (about 20 + 10 rooms respectively) was fully occupied by hard-fishing anglers: this perhaps suggests that the Association's founders had been over-ambitious in their expectations of numbers of anglers. (Optimism is a pleasant characteristic of anglers, but it is not necessarily conducive to good financial management or the provision of reliable records for historical use!)

The fishing results for the Hebridean Sporting Association were good, though not spectacular. It is hard to judge them objectively, in the absence of reliable information on fishing pressure and hence a measure of catch per unit effort, a common problem in the examination of angling records. We do not know what proportion of the shareholders took advantage of the sport available to them; it seems that some, or many, did not do so, but it is equally clear that many non-shareholders fished at both Rodel and Finsbay. Of the 60 different anglers' names appearing in 38 reports in *The Scotsman* between 1903 and 1914, only 19 (32%) were shareholders.

The catch records show an extraordinary number of small sea trout: it is totally unclear whether these include fish that were caught and released or fish killed – a complication that still exists in many modern records! It is probable that they include only the fish that were killed. However, the records also show that big sea trout were also being caught, though the available information does not allow us to determine the numbers of fish over, say, 1½ lbs.

Many of the small sea trout would have been finnock[72], i.e. sea trout that have not yet spent a winter feeding at sea. Without scale reading, it is impossible to be sure of the status of fish between ½ lb and 1 lb. Although it is generally assumed that fish of under 1 lb would be finnock, this is not necessarily true for sea trout in the systems at the east coast of Harris which are particularly slow-growing – see below.

---

[72] Finnock are also known as whitling, herling, school peel, and post-smolts

According to an advertising brochure for the Rodel Hotel in 1937 produced by Mallochs of Perth, the well known fishing tackle manufacturers and sporting agency, the sea trout catches at Rodel were 1,292 in 1935 and 1,077 in 1936, with an average weight of 14 oz[73] (excluding finnock *[sic]*); the corresponding figures for salmon were 23 and 4, with an average weight of 6 lb 11 oz. The heaviest fish were an 8 lb sea trout and a 15½ lb salmon. The Rodel Hotel brochure refers, without giving details or the date, to a catch of 96 sea trout being taken on one day by a Lord Cardross from the Finsbay fishings. The sale particulars when Lord Leverhulme's Trustees sold his Harris properties in 1925 describe the 1924 catch in the Obbe fishery (presumably referring to all of Lochs Langavat and Steisevat and the Mill Pool, but excluding L. na Moracha[74], as 35 salmon plus 1,172 sea trout, the latter averaging 13½ oz.

There are two striking differences between the fisheries at the Obbe and at Finsbay. First, salmon are rare in the Finsbay systems, but common in the Obbe system. Secondly, the sea trout caught from the Finsbay systems are distinctly smaller than those from the Obbe system. Why should this be?

Table 2 above shows that the average weight of sea trout caught between 1903 and 1907 at Finsbay was just 9 oz while the average at Rodel (the Obbe system) was 12 oz[75]. The biggest sea trout caught was 7 lb 12 oz at Rodel and 4 lb at Finsbay. There are three possible explanations for the fish in the Finsbay systems being smaller: (1) they may be growing more slowly in freshwater, due to poor feeding, hence are in effect "stunted" fish; (2) they may grow more slowly in salt-water, due to poorer or different food availability; and (3) they may be of a distinct "race" that is slow-growing and short-lived. It is now accepted that fish stocks in different systems do have sufficiently different genetic compositions as to be regarded as distinct "races".

---

[73] If the average weight was 14 oz, there must have been many fish weighing less than 14 oz, and it is hard to see why these were not recorded as finnock!

[74] Loch na Moracha was sold in a separate Lot (Lot 4) along with Kyles Lodge

[75] The average and maximum weights in Table 2 were based on catches of 5,490 & 5,781 fish at Rodel (Obbe system) & Finsbay, respectively, and therefore almost certainly represent significant differences

It is well known that sea trout[76] and brown trout belong to the same species, *Salmo trutta*. The former are migratory between freshwater and salt-water (anadromous), and the latter are resident in freshwater through their life cycle, though they do exhibit some short-range migratory behaviour within freshwater. It has increasingly been recognised that there is no sharp distinction between the migratory sea-trout and the freshwater-resident brown trout. There is a continuum, i.e. an infinite range, of intermediate patterns of behaviour. Biologically, trout demonstrate great plasticity, so that they adapt their behaviour to match optimally their own environmental conditions. Hence, some migratory trout spend their sea-feeding phases in estuaries and close on-shore in sea lochs; some venture further away, up to over 400 miles; and others seem to wander about. Both genetic and environmental factors are now regarded as relevant in determining the behaviour [52, p.5].

Some insight into the differences between the growth of sea trout in the two systems, Obbe and Finsbay, is possible, thanks to the pioneering work of George Herbert Nall[77], with the Fishery Board for Scotland in the 1920s and early 1930s [53, 54]. Nall collected fish scales from many systems in Scotland, and he tabulated the characteristics of each population of fish. Scale-reading[78] enables

---

[76] The life cycle, simplified, of sea trout is: eggs hatch into alevins that develop into parr which feed in freshwater. After a few years (typically 2 or 3 in Harris), the parr become silvery smolts and migrate to salt-water, the estuary or sea, in spring. Some return to freshwater after only a few months (no winters at sea) as finnock or post-smolts; others stay for one or more winters at sea, feeding and growing before returning to freshwater to spawn. Some that survive (as in long-lived populations) may make multiple visits to freshwater to spawn in subsequent years.

[77] G.H. Nall (1860/61–1940) was a retired schoolmaster, probably originally from London, who performed many series of scale-reading studies for the Fishery Board of Scotland though he never was actually employed by them. He worked on a voluntary basis for many years. His book, *The Life of the Sea Trout*, published in 1930 remains one of the seminal works on sea trout [53]

[78] Similar to the rings on tree trunks, fish scales deposit circuli (rings) as the fish and its scales grow. In periods of relatively poor growth (e.g. in freshwater or in winter) these circuli are relatively close together; it is therefore fairly easy to detect the time at which the fish enters a period of rich salt-water feeding. Spawning causes a mobilisation of calcium from the fish's skeleton and scales, and this is seen as a patch of erosion known as a spawning mark on the scale. It is thus possible to obtain a detailed life history of an individual fish, including an estimate of its length each year.

the biologist to determine the growth of an individual fish during each year of its life, the age at which each young sea trout migrates to sea as a smolt and the timing of its return to freshwater, and the timing of each occasion that fish has spawned.

Among the numerous sea trout populations studied in Scotland by Nall, scales were collected from angling catches on the Obbe system, the Laxdale system, and several fisheries on the East coast of Harris around Finsbay and Horsacleit. Despite Nall being one of the world's foremost experts at scale-reading and in sea trout biology, these studies do have some limitations which need to be recognised before the reader jumps to firm conclusions that may be scientifically unjustified. First and foremost and admitted by Nall, the numbers of fish examined from Harris were rather small – far fewer than the Fishery Board for Scotland would normally have regarded as necessary for reliable interpretation. Secondly, in the case of sea trout from "East Loch Tarbert", the fish had actually been captured from several different systems. Since we now believe that different river-loch systems, even close together, possess their own "races" of fish, it is unwise to pool together results for several systems. Thirdly, and more complicated, Nall's estimations of fish weight as calculated from the length of each fish relied on a "condition factor" formula which assumed that each fish is of the same shape, and that the shape approximates to that of a cylinder so that the weight is proportional to the length cubed. Fourthly, a problem with early biological data, no statistical information had been calculated to show the variance around the mean (average) values. Hence it is not possible to use statistical tests to ascertain whether suspected differences are statistically significant – i.e. whether they might simply have arisen by chance alone.

Notwithstanding these limitations, Nall's data do allow some fascinating comparisons to be made. In the Obbe system (referred to by Nall as "Steisevat"), 36% of the sea trout migrated as 2–year smolts, 54% as 3–year smolts, and 10% as 4–year smolts. In the Horsacleit/Finsbay systems (referred to by Nall as "East Loch Tarbert"), 44% had migrated as 2–year smolts, and 56% as 3–year smolts. So, in both these systems, 3–year smolts had marginally predominated. The average ages at which the fish had become smolts and migrated to sea were:

Obbe ("Steisevat"), draining into the West coast of Harris:
2.75 years

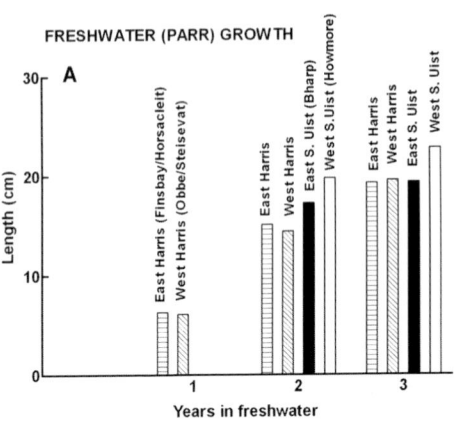

FRESHWATER (PARR) GROWTH

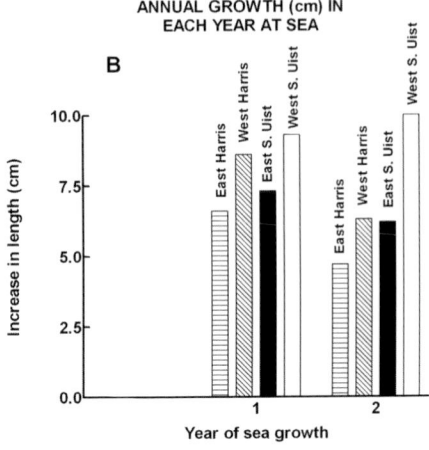

ANNUAL GROWTH (cm) IN
EACH YEAR AT SEA

Fig. 5.14 Growth of
sea trout in freshwater
and at sea. Note
that the fish in the
East coast systems
(Finsbay/Horsacleit)
grow at a similar rate
to those in the Obbe
system during the first
few years of life in
freshwater. However,
the East coast fish
grow less well at sea
than the Obbe fish.
Data recalculated from
Nall [53, 54]

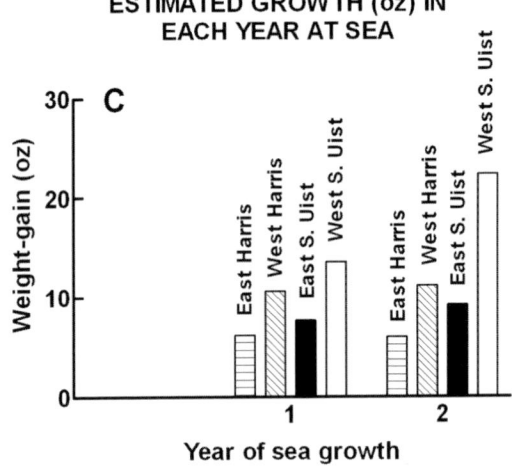

ESTIMATED GROWTH (oz) IN
EACH YEAR AT SEA

Laxdale/Borve: 2.62 years

Horsacleit/Finsbay ("East Loch Tarbert"), draining into the East coast of Harris: 2.56 years

So, in all these systems, the average ages at smoltification were extremely similar; therefore this age in freshwater cannot account for the difference in average weights subsequently seen in the fish caught.

Of particular interest is the fact that the young fish from both systems had grown at extremely similar rates in their freshwater life – see Fig. 5.14A.

Thus, the reason for so many small sea trout featuring in the Finsbay catches is very unlikely to be poor feeding of the young parr in freshwater. In contrast, when one looks at the growth in the first and second years of sea feeding (Fig. 5.14 B & C), one sees that the Horsacleit/Finsbay ("East Loch Tarbert") fish have grown less than the Obbe ("Steisevat") fish. While caution is needed because of the relatively few fish studied and the lack of a variance measurement, as discussed above, it seems highly likely that the smaller size of the Horsacleit/Finsbay ("East Loch Tarbert") fish is due to poorer sea-feeding. This may reflect either less food availability, a population of fish not migrating far enough to find more food, or simply a "racial" difference that imposes this behaviour or slow growth.

As an interesting comparison, data from Nall's scale-reading of South Uist sea trout are also shown in Fig. 5.14; those from L. Bharp which drains into the East coast, and those from the Howmore system which drains into the West coast. The South Uist sea trout grew faster both in freshwater and in the sea than the Harris ones, but there is also a striking difference between the Bharp system (East coast) and the Howmore system (West coast), reflecting different races and/or feeding behaviour.

Another difference noted by Nall was that 21% of the sea trout samples at Horsacleit/Finsbay had spawned (as judged from erosion on the scales) as finnock, compared to 1.7% of those at Steisevat/Obbe.

It is widely thought that finnock, i.e. sea trout that have not yet spent a winter at sea, do not spawn: Hence they are regarded as immature, and the term "adult sea trout" is reserved for fish that have spent at least one winter at sea. However, there is a body of good evidence that, in some systems, a sizeable fraction of the finnock population do spawn; in other systems, few or none spawn. Edward Fahy [55, p.87] [56] suggested that this fraction can vary from 1% to 60%. Biochemical markers of sexual maturity have also confirmed maturity in some finnock [57]. Most fisheries require or advise anglers to return these small fish so that they will return again in a future season and spawn, so contributing to the future fish population. Some anglers, such as H.P. Henzell, have expressed outrage at fishing hotels that permit their guests to take large bags of finnock, though he did concede that *"after all a finnock with a couple of rashers of bacon makes a most excellent breakfast"* [58]. The message is that taking a few finnock is acceptable, but the slaughter of dozens is unacceptable. Certainly any attempt to kill finnock in a "big-fish" system, such as those in South Uist, should be banned:

however, the position is not so simple in systems, such as Finsbay and some Irish systems, where a large fraction of the catch appeared to be finnock. Fahy [55, p.168] discussed some Irish populations of sea trout where 50% or 81% of the stock were finnock[79]. Based on the Inver system in Connemara, Fahy concluded: *"protecting a younger stage of sea trout produces a better quality of capture some time later. Whether the actual reduction in yield is adequately compensated by the quality of catch is a value judgement to be made by the individual fishery owner/manager"* [59].

Armed with this knowledge, it is easy to understand that the sea trout populations in the Finsbay systems may have a very sound biological reason to have adapted to behave so differently from the Obbe populations. It also follows that there is no sound reason, apart from regulatory convenience, for applying the same size-limit for anglers to return small fish in all fisheries.

At the present time of scarcity of sea trout in parts of the Scottish highlands and islands, a precautionary policy of catch and release is appropriate for conservation. However, the question of whether, in times of plentiful stocks, the return of finnock should be mandatory is less clear. Nall's figures suggest that the majority of fish over 10oz in South Harris would be 1–sea-winter adults, rather than finnock (0–sea-winter post-smolts). A size limit of 1lb would therefore require the return of some adult (over 1–sea-winter) sea trout as well as finnock. Even W.J.M. Menzies[80], a former distinguished Inspector of Salmon Fisheries for Scotland, who considered that anglers should ensure that every fish has the opportunity to spawn[81], conceded that *"to spare whitling [i.e. finnock] is, however, perhaps a counsel of perfection and almost unnecessary"* [60, p.223]. If a particularly large proportion of the fish population at any one time is finnock, then catching and killing a few finnock may be perfectly in order.

Proper analysis of the consequences of killing a certain number of finnock cannot be done without knowledge of the "stock-recruitment" relationship for that particular loch/river system. Killing of finnock may have a negligible effect on subsequent

---

[79] Sampling method unstated!

[80] Successor to W.L. Calderwood

[81] His logic is, unusually, flawed: the vast majority of salmon taken by nets or anglers are maiden fish that are never given the chance to spawn

returning adults; or it may reduce the number available to return as larger fish in subsequent years; or it might even enable better growth (through less competition for a limited food supply) among those returning in subsequent years. Which of these consequences will prevail cannot be predicted empirically.

Speculatively, an unusually high incidence of finnock spawning may be a reflection of the particular stock or "race" adapted for an environment such as that at Finsbay, with a large population of short-lived small sea trout, probably with a very restricted range of migration, and only a small number of larger individuals. At any rate, regulation on size limits should vary according to the particular local "race". The size of freshwater resident trout (non-migratory brown trout) is predominantly determined by supply of food: hence, the main strategy to improve the size of brown trout caught in acidic highland lochs with poor nutrients, where the average size can be pathetically small, is to reduce (cull) the number of fish [61].

Graeme Harris has suggested that *"the whitling [finnock] component may be of crucial importance to spawning success in terms of its contribution to total egg deposition ... ... [and they] may be very important in maximising the use of the available wettable area within a catchment for spawning ... as they are better able to penetrate the smaller tributaries and they spawn in gravel of a smaller size than that utilised by larger fish"* [62, page 448]. Thus, it is possible that the nature of the spawning areas in the Finsbay systems may be particularly conducive to finnock spawning; this may also have some bearing on the paucity of salmon in these systems.

It should be noted that environmental conditions, especially on-shore supply of food sources such as sand eels[82], small herrings, sprats etc, have changed since Nall's observations in the 1930s; so the growth rates and patterns discussed above are likely to have changed. Unfortunately there are no comparable modern data, and the practicalities and expense of obtaining large enough samples for valid statistical analysis make it unlikely that a new study will ever be undertaken. Poor marine conditions have been implicated in deterioration of Irish sea trout stocks [63]; Butler and

---

[82] Worrying losses of sand eel populations have been attributed to global warming; also to seal predation and industrial fishing

Table 3. Historical and recent fishing results for Rodel and Finsbay and several other Hebridean fisheries

Historical fishing results			Salmon	Sea trout
			No. per year	No. per year
Rodel	HSA tenure	1903–1907	40.4	1098
Finsbay	HSA tenure	1903–1907	2.2	1156
Rodel + Finsbay	HSA tenure	1903–1907	42.6	2254
Rodel + Finsbay	HSA tenure	1909	34	2653
Rodel + Finsbay	Rodel Hotel	1935	23	1292
Rodel + Finsbay	Rodel Hotel	1936	4	1077
Lacisdale	Harris Hotel	1916–1926	14.6	397.1
Borve Lodge Estate	Borve	1929–1939	29.0	247.0
Borve Lodge Estate	Borve	1963–1972	45.0	193.0
Borve Lodge Estate	Borve	1989–1998	47.0	115.0
Grimersta (Lewis)		1909–1913	1168	
Published fishing results for 2001 to 2007				
Obbe Fishings ("Rodel")		2001–2007	47.7	149.3
"100 Lochs Fishery" (Finsbay)		2001–2007	4.7	52.0
Lacisdale (North Harris)			Approx 20	
Borve Lodge Estate		2001–2007	39.7	46.7
Amhuinnsuidhe (North Harris)		2001–2007	155.6	384.0
Grimersta (Lewis)		2002–2007	419.5	69.3
North Uist Estate		2002–2007	20.0	116.7
South Uist Estate		2002–2007	54.2	650.0

It should be emphasised that these results take no account of fishing effort nor of the size of the fishery. Comparisons must therefore be made with caution. Further, changes such as transfers of ownership mean that the fishings now referred to as "Obbe Fishings" do not exactly correspond to those previously attached to Rodel; likewise, the fishings now referred to as "100 Lochs Fishery" do not exactly correspond to those previously attached to Finsbay . Further, the historical figures for Finsbay are likely to have been augmented by the taking of considerable numbers of finnock. The published fishing results for 2001–2007 have been taken from: http://fishhebrides.co.uk

Walker stressed marine feeding as a key factor in the abundance of sea trout [64], and a strong plea has been made that "... *marine phase studies will be essential if science-based management is to be informed and effective*" [65, p.485].

Finally, the complex behaviour of young sea trout has been described in a picturesque way by W.J.M. Menzies in 1936:

> "*The migrations of the whitling are therefore complicated in the extreme. A further confusion is caused by the fact that during the course of these indecisive to- and fro- movements they are not wedded to their native district or even to the immediate neighbourhood of it. They are full of the youthful spirit of freedom and adventure. They band together in companies and they travel hither and thither, making an exploratory visit here or pushing in there until the winter be spent and spring be again at hand.*
>
> *Sandy estuaries and long tidal reaches seem undoubtedly to entice whitling either for feeding or merely for shelter. Up and down these waterways they go, and from one to another they travel, as marking experiments on the east coast of Scotland have well shown. While so doing, however, the whitling apparently feed very little, and, though they do not fall off in condition as do those which settle down in the river, they make extremely little or no growth except in their particular area*".[60]

Little wonder that we do not fully understand the behaviour of sea trout in systems such as Finsbay.

The Fishing – Now and the Future

Sea trout stocks and their population dynamics have not benefited from the same international analysis that has been applied to salmon since the problems of over-exploitation of salmon in the Greenland and Faroese sea fisheries; sea trout conservation and their long-term financial value to the community have generally been neglected by political powers, although the general state of Scottish sea trout fishings is unanimously agreed to be poor[83]. It is heartening that a major international biological symposium devoted to sea trout was held in 2004 [52].

Several factors beyond the scope of full discussion here are

---

[83] The sea trout stocks of South Uist currently seem to be a pleasant exception; this may be related to the lack of marine fish farms in the vicinity

likely to be involved in the serious collapse in sea trout populations in Scotland which has been seen since the 1960s. Fish farming is a serious culprit[84], poaching is relevant in some areas, and seal predation may also be involved in some areas including the East coast of Harris.

A sudden and drastic collapse of sea trout populations has been seen in many Scottish and Irish locations, especially between 1986 and 1989 . Over the same period, English and Welsh fisheries (which do not have marine fish farms, as the Scottish and Irish fisheries do), have remained "healthy" [66]. Sound scientific evidence now shows that marine survival of sea trout is responsible for these collapses in stock in Scotland and Ireland, and it now confirms fish farms as culprits [64, 67, 68]. Biological evidence is now supporting what anglers have anecdotally blamed for years. Fallowing fish farms (i.e. leaving them temporarily disused) has shown beneficial effects, so the problem is not necessarily irreversible [68]. The detritus from on-shore fish farms leads to a proliferation of sea lice: these parasites attach themselves in great abundance to sea trout[85] before they migrate into freshwater with lethal consequences. However, the commercial successes of fish farming and the prospect of providing employment at the farms have been allowed to outweigh the ecological, fish conservation, and sporting consequences, a highly contentious issue for which political policies are widely blamed. There are some prospects that the short-sightedness of these policies is being recognised and that the relatively new Scottish Environmental Protection Agency (SEPA) may institute better management.

Although happily a conscience for conservation and preservation is generally present in Harris, it is true that narrow Hebridean streams offer easy opportunities for netting; off-shore netting is also easy and able to avoid detection except in carefully keepered or patrolled waters[86]. It has been said of Hebrideans that *"the urge to*

---

84 The value to employment has often been greatly over-estimated by politicians, and the environmental damage has only recently been exposed

85 One sea trout tagged as a smolt in the R. Shieldaig (Wester Ross) was found to bear as many as 977 sea lice after only 15 days at sea! [69]

86 It has already been noted (pages 18–19) that the feu charter granted to the Hebridean Sporting Association by Lord Dunmore requested the Association *"to protect the fishings in the sea coast or other waters on the Estate from injury by any unauthorised person ... "* [6]

poach is in the blood", and it would be fair to say that this has been a factor in the loss of the deer population in South Harris[87]. While the motto of Stornoway town, *God's Providence is Our Inheritance*, may originally have been based upon the benefits of rich herring stocks, the principle of exploiting natural resources is long rooted in the community and is hardly surprising, given the nature of the terrain and its poor prospects for agricultural cultivation[88]. Although times have moved on from the days of oppressive landowners and of limited access to food shops, old traditions die hard. While technically the law may not make a distinction, many proprietors show goodwill and now would see a difference between the odd fish being taken for the pot and a whole cohort of fish being annihilated by mass netting. The latter practice is bound to cause shortage in due course which is to nobody's advantage. The same remark is true for predation by seals[89].

The comparisons shown in Table 3 for the fishing results now and in the early 1900s give some confidence that salmon fishing is as good as ever, but that sea trout catches have fallen dismally as they have done elsewhere in the West Highlands of Scotland.

The fishings at the Obbe are currently undergoing a programme of regeneration by a separate Company, South Harris Fishery Ltd, and another private partnership is also working to re-establish the fishings around Finsbay in a venture known as the "One Hundred Lochs Fishings". So, we now have an active interest, once again, in conserving, developing, and using the freshwater fish resources of Harris and promoting the tourism associated with sporting angling. A relatively new Outer Hebrides Fishery Trust is taking an active involvement in the biological management of the environment and in trying to establish a balance between the conflicting interests of

---

[87] The inevitability of this was recognised in advance by the Scottish Office and the King's & Lord Treasurer's Remembrancer (i.e. the U.K. Government's Treasury representative in Scotland) in 1936 when they decided to sell Borve Lodge and associated sporting rights at a relatively low price before smallholders took up their crofts [70]

[88] It is also true that poaching provides adventure and excitement to its perpetrators. Patrick Campbell describes how the hydro-electric construction workers in the Highlands thrived on this activity [71, p.89].

[89] While the Scottish seal population is regarded as stable, the numbers of seals hauling up around the East coast of Harris in the vicinity of the sea trout systems is alarming. Legislation now prevents culling of seals except in restricted and licensed circumstances

Fig. 5.15. An t-Ob
(now Leverburgh)
photographed by
A.A. Chisholm on 17
November 1903. The
Mill Pool is visible at the
left of the picture, but
it is not possible to see
whether its dam has
been constructed or
whether it is still just a
tidal pond off the Obbe.
Picture kindly supplied
by Tony Scherr.

Fig. 5.16.
Loch Grosebay
photographed by A.A.
Chisholm on 31 May
1904. It is likely that the
building marked
by the arrow is the
fishing hut erected by
the Hebridean Sporting
Association. Picture
kindly supplied by
Tony Scherr.

commercial fish farmers and environmental and sporting interests. One successful phase of a mink eradication programme has been completed, and further work on this conservation measure is being undertaken by Scottish National Heritage. This project has already eradicated mink from the Uists. However, all these modern sporting developments are all on a tiny scale compared to the 1903 venture by the Hebridean Sporting Association together with their landlord, Lord Dunmore.

Fig. 5.15. An t-Ob (now Leverburgh) photographed by A.A. Chisholm on 17 November 1903. The Mill Pool is visible at the left of the picture, but it is not possible to see whether its dam has been constructed or whether it is still just a tidal pond off the Obbe. Picture kindly supplied by Tony Scherr.

Fig. 5.16. Loch Grosebay photographed by A.A. Chisholm on 31 May 1904. It is likely that the building marked by the arrow is the fishing hut erected by the Hebridean Sporting Association. Picture kindly supplied by Tony Scherr.

CHAPTER SIX
WATSON LYALL'S SPORTSMAN'S GUIDE – LOCHS OF HARRIS

Watson Lyall's *The Sportsman's and Tourist's Guide to the Rivers, Lochs, Moors and Deer Forests of Scotland* is an invaluable resource for information about Scottish fishings, shootings and deer forests in the period 1873 to 1915. This publication provides an encyclopaedic, though not necessarily infallible or entirely up to date, resource on Scotland's sporting facilities and the tenants and proprietors thereof. The extensive advertisements also give a fascinating insight into a past way of life.

James Watson Lyall was born in Blairgowrie in about 1832, the youngest son of John Lyall, a Congregationalist Minister. In 1852, he took over the Proprietorship of *The Stirling Journal and Advertiser*, with James Hogg as editor. In 1867, Watson Lyall withdrew, apparently to move to be editor of *The Perthshire Constitutional*, a local newspaper that ran from 1835 till 1951. One brother went on to become editor of *The Kelso Mail* and his other brother became a wholesale stationer in Edinburgh. Further biographical details are given below.

In 1873 James Watson Lyall published the first issue of *The Sportsman's and Tourist's Guide*; initially this appeared monthly but it soon settled down to be a twice-yearly publication, May and August, of over 500 pages until 1915, priced at one shilling (See Fig. 6.1).

As well as a wealth of information about individual rivers, lochs and moors, it generally included railway timetables for routes from England to Scotland (deliberately excluded from the 1915 issue because of national security during wartime), information about steamer services, lists of proprietors and tenants, and information about golf courses. As well as the advertisements, each issue contained a bespoke fold-out map produced by James Bartholomew

of Edinburgh showing deer forests. The publisher also offered an attractive tie-in hard binder with gold-blocked lettering. Many buyers had their copies hard-bound professionally as they were such valuable reference sources, though they now have become collectors' items. A rival publisher and sporting agency, Robert Hall, published a somewhat similar book, *The Highland Sportsman and Tourist, A Comprehensive Guide to the Highlands of Scotland* [72], annually from 1881 to 1886, but this lacked the detailed catch and bag records given in the Watson Lyall's *Guides*..

In 1873 Watson Lyall was still at *The Perthshire Constitutional* when the first issue of the *Guide* was published, but he also had an address in London at Union Bank Buildings, Ely Place, Holborn Circus. By 1894, he had moved to 118 Pall Mall, London, and the firm later moved in 1911 to 21 Pall Mall.

In 1879 he formed an estate agency in London, dealing with Scottish sporting properties. When launching this, he advertised in *The Oban Times* (22 February, 1879), naming 50 eminent "Noblemen and Proprietors" [sic] who supported him in this venture. The Earl of Dunmore was one of those listed. As well as continuing to publish *The Sportsman's and Tourist's Guide* (its full title varied a little over the years), Watson Lyall's firm also published a regular catalogue of Scottish sporting properties for sale or to let, and it is clear from newspaper advertisements that his firm was one of the major estate agencies of this specialised market. J. Watson Lyall & Co was registered as a limited company in 1901, trading from 118 Pall Mall, London, but subsequently dissolved: unfortunately, the records of dissolved Companies in England have not been kept, unlike the situation in Scotland where many such records have been lodged in the National Archives of Scotland.

After James Watson Lyall's death in 1902 *The Sportsman's and Tourist's Guide* continued to be published twice a year by his firm. The firm continued to exist with at least 2 partners, Mr William Murray and Mr Davies. Mr Murray was a member of *The Rodel Syndicate*, along with Lord Leverhulme and a Mr Collier, who leased Rodel Hotel and Fishings from about 1915 (after the Hebridean Sporting Association had been sued for arrears of rent) from the Earl of Dunmore (till 1919) and from Lord Leverhulme's Lewis & Harris Welfare and Development Co until 1923. William Murray, who died that year, had lived at Hitwick Manor, Ampthill, Bedfordshire.

Fig. 6.1 The cover of Watson Lyall's *Sportsman's and Tourist's Guide to the Rivers, Lochs, Moors & Deer Forests* for Summer 1898

In 1936 J. Watson Lyall & Co operated from 21 Pall Mall, and Captain P. Wallace had a very similar advertisement in *The Scotsman* but with differing telegraphic addresses. In 1938, both firms advertised, again with very similar wording, but by now both used the same telegraphic address, so it is likely that Captain Wallace had taken over Watson Lyall's business. In 1943, J. Watson Lyall & Co advertised from 20 Cosbyte Avenue, Herne Hill, Lambeth, London.

While he was in Stirling, James married Janet Bowie from Carlogie of Panbride in Forfarshire, the daughter of a farmer, in 1858. In 1871, he resided at Fairmount Villa, Perth which, I believe, subsequently became the house of the Episcopal Bishop of St Andrews, Dunkeld & Dunblane. They had 2 daughters Jane E. (b. 1859 or 1860) and Alice B. (b. 1867 or 1868). The wife, Jane(t) Bowie Watson Lyall (b. ~ 1833) died in 1897, aged 64, in the Croydon district, Surrey.

In the 1881 Census, James, Jane (wife), Alice B and Jane E. (daughters) lived with 2 servants at 6 Observatory Avenue, Kensington, London; he was described as "Newspaper Proprietor".

In the 1891 Census, James together with Jane B. (wife), Agnes Lyall (sister aged 60), Alice B.W. (daughter, now widowed, aged 23) and James Ross Sanderson (grandson, aged 2, born in Mysore), lived at Bridge Road, Barnes, Richmond, Kingston, Surrey; he was described as "Land Agent & Newspaper Proprietor".

In the 1901 Census, James (now a widower) was at 8 Southwick Place, Paddington, London (Hyde Park), together with Alice B. Sanderson (his widowed daughter, b ~ 1868). His profession was described as "Land Agent".

James died on 3 August 1902 at 50 Weymouth Street in London. He had colorectal cancer for at least 18 months and died 3 days after a colostomy operation. He had been resident with his daughter at Southwick Place.

Entries for Harris in *The Guide*. These are of considerable interest, and those from the Summer 1913 issue are reproduced in full below. Curiously, there never were any entries for the Horsacleit system except for L. Uamadale in its headwaters. There never was an entry for Loch a Choire; and Loch na Creagh [sic] was mentioned only in the 1910 to 1915 issues. [Where earlier issues or the 1915 issue have had different details, I have annotated the entries below accordingly in square brackets. The footnotes here are added by me.] The Hebridean Sporting Association referred in their Prospectus at the Association's launch to the Watson Lyall *Guide*, obviously in the knowledge that the Watson Lyall entries would present the Association's venture in a most enticing light to prospective shareholders. Like many sporting proprietors, the Association regularly advertised in Watson Lyall's Guide – some advertisements have been reproduced above in Chapters 2 and 3.

"LOCH-A-GHLINNE in North Harris, is a mile long by half a mile broad, and belongs to Lady Farquhar, whose permission to fish is necessary. It contains salmon and sea-trout, but is not often fished. A fair day's sport is a dozen of sea-trout and a couple of salmon. It is 20 miles distant from Tarbert Hotel. ROUTE :—By rail to *Mallaig* or *Kyle of Loch Alsh*, thence by steamer to Portree; thence by steamer alternate days.

LOCH ASHIEVAT—A little loch not far from Amhuinsuidh, in North Harris yielding middling good sport, but not open to the public. Proprietor, Sir Samuel Scott, Bt. The trout run 4 to a lb— 14lbs is a fair basket.

LOCH CHRAVADAIL is 20 miles from Tarbert, by a road not fit for driving. It is half a mile by about 400 yards, and contains small brown trout of which 7 lbs is a good day's take. It belongs to Sir Samuel Scott, Bt. There are no boats on it. April, May, and June are the best months. Fine rocky scenery. ROUTE :—Same as Loch-a-Ghlinne, which see.

LOCH CREAVAL is 5 miles from Finsbay Lodge, and is some 500 yards by 200. It contains sea-trout and brown trout, the latter 4 to a lb., the former much larger. Preserved. Proprietor, the Earl of Dunmore. [Before Summer 1910, lessee was stated to be the Hebridean Sporting Association]

LOCH CRUMBIVAT—Similar to Loch Ashievat.

LOCH FINCASTLE is an artificial loch at Luskintyre, in South Harris, into which the sea flows at high tides. It belongs to the Earl of Dunmore, and is let with shootings[90]. Very good for salmon and sea-trout. [Not mentioned in the Guide until the Summer 1910 issue, though we know that it had been constructed in about 1898. This shows that the Guide was not always up-to-date!]

---

[90]   Watson Lyall's entry under the Borve (Harris) shootings says: "The salmon and sea-trout fishing includes some of the best water on the west coast. There is no better sea-trout fishing in Scotland"

LOCH FINSBAY (tidal) is situated near Finsbay Lodge, and in July and August swarms with sea-trout and salmon ascending to the lochs above. The sea-trout take the fly freely, and sport is excellent. [Not mentioned in the Guide until the Summer 1910 issue, though we know that the Association fished it from 1903]

LOCHS GROSEBAY and HARMASAIG are about 5 miles from Finsbay Lodge, and are capital sea-trout lochs, and yield good sport. [Issues from Summer 1903 to Autumn 1909 refer to the Hebridean Sporting Association as lessees, but not subsequently]

LOCH HILLIDALE out of which the river Lisovay flows, is three-quarters of a mile long by 250 yards broad. Preserved. Salmon average 7 lbs., sea-trout, ¼ lb. to 3 lbs. A fair day's sport is 20 lbs. of salmon and 14 lbs. of sea-trout. Flies and best months same as Loch Lacisdale. Two miles from Fincastle[91]. ROUTE:—Same as Small Lochs, which see.

LOCH HUAMAVAT belongs to the Earl of Dunmore, and is a mile long by half a mile broad and is very good for salmon and sea-trout. One rod has killed 86 sea-trout in 3 hours. It is let on lease to the Hebridean Sporting Association Limited, and preserved. It is ¼ of a mile from Finsbay Lodge. [No change in entry between Summer 1903 and 1915 issues]

LOCH LANGAVAT in South Harris, is 2 miles from Finsbay Lodge. Contains salmon and sea-trout, and big loch-trout, and is about 3 miles long. It is the highest of a chain of lochs at the Obbe of Harris. It belongs to the Earl of Dunmore, and is let to the Hebridean Sporting Association, Limited. [Entry in 1915 show the new lessee as *The Rodel Syndicate*]

LOCHS LACISDALE —Three in number, in North Harris about 3 miles distant from the Tarbert Hotel by a fair road. The lochs are beautifully situated, and their sizes are as follows:—Top Loch, 1¼ mile in length by 380 yards broad; Middle Loch, 660 yards by 220; Lower Loch, 650 yards by 180. The season extends from July to October, during which time the salmon and sea trout fishing is consistently good, although very heavy baskets are seldom taken. The lochs are let to the tenant of the Harris Hotel, and visitors there have the sole right of fishing free of charge. ROUTE:—By rail to *Mallaig* or *Kyle* of *Loch Alsh;* thence by steamer to

---

91 Fincastle here refers to the former name for Amhuinnsuidhe in North Harris, not to Loch Fincastle which is at the head of the Luskentyre estuary in South Harris

Portree (where a night has to be spent); thence by steamer to *Tarbert* (latter part of journey can only be accomplished on Tuesdays, Thursdays, and Saturdays).

LOCH LAXDALE is about one mile from Luskintyre, and very good for salmon and sea-trout. Belongs to the Earl of Dunmore, and is let with shootings.

LOCH MORACHA[92] —In South Harris. a mile long by half a mile. The river Langavat falls into it, and Ath-dhu flows out of it. It is very good for salmon and sea-trout, and 20 lbs. of the latter and 3 salmon may be regarded as a good day's sport. It belongs to the Earl of Dunmore, and is next to Loch Langavat, in the chain of Obbe Lochs. It is 2½ miles from Rodel House, and is let to the Hebridean Sporting Association, Limited. [Entry in 1915 shows the new lessee as *The Rodel Syndicate*]

LOCH-NA-CISTE is in North Harris, and contains brown trout, which run about 5 to the lb., and good sport is to be had in May, June, or July. The Loch is 5 miles from Tarbert Hotel, by a good driving road. The tenant of the Harris Hotel can give his guests the right to fish this loch.

LOCH-NA-CREAGH is situated about 2 miles from Finsbay Lodge. It and the sea-pool below are very good for sea-trout. Let to the Hebridean Sporting Association, Limited. [First mentioned in issue of Summer 1910. Entry in 1915 show the new lessee as *The Rodel Syndicate*. There never was any entry for the nearby Loch Choire, further upstream]

LOCH-NA-MORCHA —A little loch in North Harris[93], belonging to Sir Samuel Scott, Bt. The loch adjoins Loch-na-Ciste, but contains heavier trout. Visitors at Harris Hotel may fish the loch. ROUTE:- Same as Loch-a-Ghlinne to Tarbert; thence 6 miles.

OBBE in South Harris is a place where the sea comes in at high tides. It abounds with salmon and sea-trout, so much so that as many as 13 salmon and 100 sea-trout have been killed in one tide by one rod. Above the Obbe is the Mill Pool into which the sea flows in spring tides. It affords steady and excellent sport with salmon and sea-trout. It is 2½ miles from Rodel House, and is let to the Hebridean Sporting Association, Limited. [The Mill Pool was first mentioned in the issue

---

[92] Better known as Loch na Moracha, but not to be confused with Loch na Morcha in North Harris

[93] Also known as Loch a' Mhorghain which was subject to unsuccessful improvement works in 1885 [7, p.314]

for Summer 1910; earlier issues had contained *"at low water the place is small, some 250 yards in circumference"*. The entry in 1915 shows the new lessee as *The Rodel Syndicate*]

LOCH SCOURST —In North Harris, half a mile by a quarter. It is 7 miles from Amhuinnsuidh Castle, and 9 from Tarbert Hotel. It holds salmon and sea-trout, and a good day's sport may be said to be four salmon averaging 7 lbs and 20 lbs. of sea-trout running ½ lb. to 6 lbs. Black and green flies best, and July, Aug., and Sept. the choice months. Can be fished only by leave of the proprietor Sir Samuel Scott. Bt. ROUTE:—Same as Loch-a -Ghlinne to Tarbert; thence hire, 9 miles.

LOCH STEISAVAT —Near Loch Moracha[94], and belongs to the Earl of Dunmore. It is 2 miles long by half a mile, and is 2½ miles from Rodel House. Let to the Hebridean Sporting Association, Limited. Three salmon and 20 sea-trout is a fair bag for this loch. The sea-trout run up to 8 lbs. [In 1873, the lessee was stated to be the Marquis of Ripon, but he was possibly primarily concerned with the shooting. Between Summer 1903 and Autumn 1909, the fair bag of sea trout was said to be 35, this being revised to 20 in Summer 1910. Entries from 1903 to 1914 show the Hebridean Sporting Association as lessee, then the entry in 1915 shows the new lessee as *The Rodel Syndicate*]

LOCH ULLEDALE in North Harris is a quarter of a mile by 300 yards, and belongs to Sir Samuel Scott, Bt. It is 6 miles from Amhuinnsuidh and 12 from Tarbert. Sport &c same as Loch Lacisdale. ROUTE:—Same as Lacisdale to Tarbert; thence hire, 12 miles.

LOCH VOSHIMID — In North Harris, half a mile by a quarter—the property of Sir Samuel Scott, Bt., and cannot be fished save by his leave. The river Stolidle falls into it, and the river Reasort flows out of it. It contains salmon and sea-trout, and four salmon and 25 lbs. of sea-trout are a good day's take, Season and flies same as other Harris lochs. ROUTE: Same as Loch Lacisdale to Tarbert; thence 12 miles— the last 4 miles of which is only a bridle-path.

SMALL LOCHS —There are three small lochs in North Harris, about 12 miles from Tarbert. The River Leosit falls into them, and the Amhuinnsuidh flows out of them. They belong to Sir Samuel Scott Bt. Salmon and sea-trout are got in these lochs, and 5 lbs. of the latter, and say 5 salmon (which average 7 lbs.), are a good day's sport. Season

---

94   Between Loch na Moracha and the Mill Pool

and flies same as Loch Morcha. ROUTE:—Same as Loch-a-Ghlinne to Tarbert; thence hire, 12 miles.

SMALLER LOCHS —There are a great number of smaller Lochs, and the following, among others on the Earl of Dunmore's property, are rented by the Hebridean Sporting Association, Ltd., viz. :—Loch Allityer, Loch Clachan, Loch Dempster, Loch Dhu Sletteval, Loch Flodabay, Loch Holmasaig, Loch Manish, Lochs Meurach (Upper and Lower)." [Issues between 1904 and Autumn 1909 also included Lochs Bearsta Mor, Mhic Neall, na Cro, and Uamadale which were let to the Hebridean Sporting Association. These smaller lochs are included in Table 1.]

There has been no comparable publication containing this level of detail about sporting properties, the proprietors and tenants since Watson Lyall's *Guide* ceased publication. Nowadays, sportsmen may rely on the Internet for details of currently available sporting facilities[95], but these sources seldom give historical information. The *Guide* had also provided an integrated reference source.

---

[95] The Fish Hebrides web-site is an excellent example – see http://fishhebrides.co.uk

CHAPTER SEVEN
LORD DUNMORE'S FISHING IMPROVEMENTS IN HARRIS

The 5th Earl of Dunmore, George Murray (1762–1836) bought Harris from Alexander Hume Macleod in 1834, and it remained in the Dunmore family's ownership until the sale to Lord Leverhulme in 1919. The family's history goes back to the first Marquis of Atholl. The wife, Lady Catherine Herbert Dunmore, of the 6th Earl is well known for her pivotal role in promoting the production of Harris tweed [73]. Indeed, if it had not been for her support, it is unlikely that this industry, which has been of great importance to Harris and Lewis, would have gained momentum let alone its international reputation and economic value. The 7th Earl of Dunmore, Charles Adolphus Murray (1841–1907), is thought to have had many interests in sporting activities, though we have never seen any of his fishing records. In 1923, Rodel Lodge was said to have had *"rows and rows of antlered stags' skulls, inscribed with the year in which they were killed and the name of the person ... the dates going back to the early years of the previous century"* [74]. Presumably many of these had been stalked by the Dunmores. These trophies are no longer in Rodel Hotel. He travelled around his estate, staying at Amhuinnsuidhe Castle, Ardvourlie by Loch Seaforth, Borve Lodge, and Rodel House engaging in sport, but Rodel, at least in the 1870s, was his main residence. He sold Amhuinnsuidhe and the North Harris estate to Sir Edward Scott in 1868. The South Harris estate was transferred to the 7th Earl's son, Viscount Fincastle, Alexander Edward Murray VC (1871–1962), who was famed for his military service and subsequently became the 8th Earl of Dunmore; it was Viscount Fincastle who legally was the lessor to the Hebridean Sporting Association.

In 1885 attempts had been made to open up the Ballan a' Ciste system in North Harris to sea trout and salmon by Sir Samuel Scott,

Figs 7.1 & 7.2 Hatching ponds adjacent to Loch Laxdale. These are just visible, now being overgrown. Photographs kindly supplied by Tony and Heather Scherr

involving building of dams and sluices and blasting to try to reduce the gradient. Though these were initially reported by Archibald Young, Inspector of Salmon Fisheries, to be a great success [75], his successor, W.L. Calderwood later, (1909) described them as *"a complete failure"* [7, p.313–314].

The 7th Earl recognised the potential benefits of improving the fishing. In 1876 he attempted unsuccessfully to sell South Harris and referred to *"… several other inland lochs could be made accessible to salmon at very small expense … ."* [76]. Apart from the references by Hamish Stuart [3, p.128] to the creation of Loch Fincastle at the estuary of the Laxdale River near Luskentyre, the sole known written account of the Dunmores' substantial work to develop the salmon and sea trout fishings in South Harris is provided by the following anonymous (except for the initials N.A.J.) article in *The Scotsman* newspaper on 1 April 1914. Curiously, there is no reference to the Hebridean Sporting Association who must have been the main lessee of the fishings. While the creation of fish hatcheries on the estate was very progressive, this practice was already in place in many other parts of Scotland. Around 1840, John Shaw at Drumlanrig, Dumfriesshire had started work on artificial rearing of salmon, and in 1853 experimental hatching ponds had been established at Stormontfield, beside the River Tay [7, p.60–61]. However it was soon recognised that more benefit was likely to accrue from the removal of obstacles to fish migration [77, p.54].

> **"HOW TO IMPROVE TROUT[96] FISHING ON MOORLAND LOCHS: THE EXAMPLE OF SOUTH HARRIS.** An instance of what may be accomplished by judicious and well-directed efforts to improve trout and salmon fishing on moorland lochs is furnished by the results achieved on Lord Dunmore's estate of South Harris. Since 1897 the estate officials, led by Mr Thomas Wilson, the then factor, who is himself an authority on trout-breeding, have worked strenuously at great expense to improve the fishings, with the result that the rent derived from the sport has been trebled. It will interest landlords throughout Scotland to know that, notwithstanding the initial expense connected with the work, the undertaking has been a highly profitable one. Harris is naturally hilly, and abounds in pools and burns, which provide excellent natural nurseries for fish. So as to take

---

96   This clearly is meant to refer to sea trout

advantage of this fact, four hatcheries have been established in different parts of the estate[97], and as a result from 80,000 to 120,000 fry have been hatched out each season for the last ten years.

These have been placed on small burns in order to give them a chance of development under the most favourable circumstances. A keeper takes charge of each hatchery[98], and the duty of this individual is to catch trout going up the river in October and November. These are spawned by the hand, and the ova are placed in hatcheries, which are placed in charge of an experienced man, who extracts dead ova each day.

About the month of March the fry come out, and five or six weeks later are in such condition that they can be distributed in the burns. It may be remarked that the men in charge take a lively interest in the work, and their enthusiasm is no small factor in the success which has been achieved.

It was, however, recognised that the benefits of these hatching operations could not be fully reaped unless lochs and rivers were constructed in such fashion as to provide a suitable habitat for the fully-sized and developed fish. Attention was primarily turned to Loch Laxadale, of which Mr Hamish Stuart speaks in his book as being the smallest salmon loch in Scotland. This was always a fairly good fishing place, for the fish used to run up the river Laxadale (Gaelic – Lachdasdal) into the loch and spawn in the small rivers above it. At the mouth of the river there was a pool, and Lord Dunmore and his advisers conceived the idea, of forming here the loch now known as Loch Fincastle. This idea was successfully carried out by the construction of an embankment 120 yards long, 25 feet broad, and 14 feet high, at a cost of about £120. There is thus left between Loch Fincastle, at the mouth of the river Laxadale and the loch of the same name, a whole mile of extremely suitable spawning ground, and there is also above the upper loch a stretch of ground suitable for spawning purposes.

---

[97] These were located at Luskentyre (NG 072 991), Laxdale (NG 109 964), Carron (NG 088 959), and Borve (NG 038 949). Figs. 7.1 & 7.2 shows the ditches used as hatching ponds at Laxdale. In addition to hatching ponds, there was a stone & slate hatchery adjacent to Luskentyre Lodge, according to the Inland Revenue (Scotland) Valuation field books – see Fig. 7.3

[98] It is likely that Sam Morrison, who became Keeper at Finsbay Lodge in 1903, had been in charge of the hatchery at Laxdale

Above Loch Laxadale there are four large lochs, but the fishing on these was practically valueless on account of the fact that few sea-trout and no salmon got up because of the extremely bad fall. To improve this state of matters a ladder was constructed of huge boulders, skilfully arranged, up which sea-trout ran quite easily. The extent of the improvements carried out here can be gauged from the fact that the fishing of Laxadale river, which before 1897 was one loch and one pool, now consists of six lochs and two pools, yielding a yearly average of 40 salmon and from 350 to 400 sea-trout. This annual yield clearly shows that, as a result of these improvements, the fishings have been enormously increased in value.

The success which attended Lord Dunmore's efforts at Laxadale encouraged him to persevere in the work of loch construction. Loch Carron[99] was formed on another river at the head of Luskintyre Sands, and four lochs were made on the Horsaclett and Grosebay rivers. These lochs were formed by constructing embankments, and here again the fishing has been vastly improved. On Horsaclett river there were two steep falls, up which fish could not go, and to counteract this difficulty a very ingenious ladder was built of large stones, to permit the ascent of sea-trout and salmon from the pools next the sea. The river itself was diverted from its course for upwards of a mile so as to avoid an upper fall, which was effectively blocked off. Salmon are thus able to get up to the large lochs on the hills. His Lordship's efforts in this part have already improved the fishings, and it is anticipated that in a year or two the expenditure of from £400 to £500 which has already been made will have been justified.

The three rivers flowing into the sea loch of Stockinish were so small that the fishing on them was practically valueless; and to improve matters, the three have been gathered into one large stream by the exercise of an ingenious system of blocking. There are now seven lochs connected with this stream, each of them yielding excellent fishing.

An original method of avoiding a steep fall was adopted in one case. The course of a river was changed in such fashion that the water was made to flow down a natural hollow in a volcanic dyke for several hundred yards. By cutting an opening in the volcanic dyke the river was got to flow quite easily down a slight incline into the loch below. At the point where the course of the

---

99   Normally spelled "Carran"

stream was altered, an embankment was built, which served the intended purpose admirably. The original estimate for this work was £200, but it was carried out for £80.

The result of these efforts is that, instead of the ten or twelve lochs which yielded trout in South Harris prior to 1897, there are now upwards of eighty which provide excellent fishing. As every angler knows, weather is an element in trout fishing, and in July, August and September sportsmen are busy in South Harris. During these months, droughts are liable to occur, and if such be the case no fishing can in ordinary circumstances be had. To provide against such droughts, sluices have been constructed, by means of which water is stored up in May and June. When, at a later period, the fish come to the mouth of the river with a view to ascend, the flood-gates are opened, an artificial flood is created, and the trout thus find a means of getting up. This operation of letting the flood loose is performed by the head-keeper about half an hour before high tide, so that the fresh water reaches the sea just when the fish are waiting to get up the river[100]. If trout appear sluggish after getting to the loch, the gates are again opened, and this proceeding has an appreciable effect in stirring up the fish. The head-keeper on the

Fig. 7.3 Remains of the former fish hatchery at Luskentyre. Photograph kindly supplied by Tony and Heather Scherr

---

[100] The trick of creating an artificial spate was not novel. This technique had been used on the Grimersta system in Lewis in 1888 when A.M. Naylor made his record-breaking catch of 54 salmon in one day; Rev Hely-Hutchinson ("Sixty-one") described using it on the Blackwater system at Soval in Lewis in 1875 and stated that he had previously seen it used at Costello in Galway, Ireland [78]

South Harris estate — Mr Roderick MacLeay[101] — has a natural aptitude for the work, and his efforts have been ably seconded by the present factor, Mr Robertson[102].

Since 1897 from £6000 to £8000 have been spent by Lord Dunmore on the improvement of the fishings of South Harris. A most pleasing feature of the situation is that the work has given employment to quite an army of people, and thus the material welfare of the tenantry has been considerably enhanced. Farmhouses vacated when land has been allotted for small holdings have been converted into miniature but extremely convenient lodges, and thus we have agriculture and sport thriving side by side on the same estate, to the mutual advantage of a generous landlord and a contented tenantry. The fact should not be lost sight of that the influx of anglers to this estate each season is the means of providing a great deal of local seasonal employment. The tradesmen of Harris reap great benefit from the increased currency of coin, and an impetus is given to the sale of the well-known Harris tweed. It need hardly be mentioned that the combination of happy circumstances detailed above tends to strengthen the goodwill which has always existed between the Dunmore family and their tenants

N.A.J."

This article gives a costed evaluation of these schemes, and it also confirms Thomas Wilson's involvement with the fishery improvement work. At present-day prices this work would amount to some £0.5 million.

---

[101] Roderick Macleay (~1848–1938), a native of Lochbroom, Ross-shire, was Gamekeeper at Borve from about 1878. His eldest daughter, Alexandrina, married Kenneth Campbell, Farmer at Rodel in 1901 – he was presumably the person who, together with John Morrison, bought Rodel (Lot 3) in the Leverhulme sale in 1925. Alasdair Alpin MacGregor refers warmly to Mr Macleay at Scarista Beg with a picture [48, p.132–134]

[102] Norman Robertson (1882–1961) succeeded Thomas Wilson as Factor in 1911. He previously had been Lady Gordon Cathcart's assistant factor at Askernish in South Uist. See also p.205 below.

Chapter eight
HORSACLEIT

Also known as Horsaclett (Norse: Horse cliff). Some of the history of this Lodge and small sporting estate has recently been provided in David Jones' illustrated history of sporting estates of the Outer Hebrides [51]. As one travels on the A859 road about 2 miles south of Tarbert one sees a remarkably attractive white wooden lodge on the shores of a small loch. This is Horsacleit Lodge (see Figs 8.1 & 8.2) at Ordnance Survey grid reference NG 141 964. It has been recorded by Historic Scotland as a Category B Listed Building since 1994, but these particulars do not include any details of its history. Although no records are available of the construction of Horsacleit Lodge or its House Loch, the lodge first appeared in the Valuation Roll for 1910/11: its fishings and shootings also appeared as separate entries in the Rolls for 1910/11 and 1911/12 respectively. It has been suggested that the lodge might have been built from a kit imported from Norway (note that Finsbay Lodge was said to be in Norwegian style), but it has not been possible to confirm this. It is interesting to note that the St Magnus Hotel in Hillswick, Shetland has been widely reported to have been constructed from a kit that was shipped from Norway to Glasgow for a Great Exhibition of 1896[103] and subsequently shipped to Shetland and reassembled: however, contemporary accounts do not support this, recording the hotel opening in 1900 and giving credit to a local architect and contractor, John M. Aitken [79, 80]. This hotel, built for the North of Scotland Steam Navigation Company, was said to be built "on the Norwegian style, the architectural design being Swiss" [80].

As explained above, the Horsacleit fishings were included in the original lease in 1903 by Viscount Fincastle to the Hebridean Sporting Association. He then undertook to improve the access for

---

[103] In fact, the first Great International Exhibition in Glasgow was in 1888 and the second in 1901

ascending salmon and sea trout up the Horsacleit river which enters the sea at Meavaig [2]. It appears (see Chapter 2) that the financial situation of the Association made them reduce the extent of their fishing tenancies in 1905/6 and they ceased leasing the Horsacleit and Grosebay fishings. We presume that the 8th Earl of Dunmore created Horsacleit around 1909 as a separate sporting tenancy to capitalise on the improvements already made for the Association. The entry in the Valuation Rolls makes it certain that Horsacleit Lodge existed before Lord Leverhulme's ownership of the South Harris estate.

Horsacleit Loch (also known as the House Loch) was not shown on the Ordnance Survey map surveyed in 1909 (published 1911), but it did appear on the next map which was surveyed in 1928. It is likely – see below – that the Loch had been created by Lord

Dunmore, probably at the time of building Horsacleit Lodge. Some people have believed that Professor Henderson constructed the loch, but it almost certainly was created before his tenancy.

The first tenant recorded in Watson Lyall's *The Sportsman's and Tourist's Guide* was Mr H.D. Mann Thomson in 1911, though the Horsacleit fishing records go back to 1909 when the angler was recorded as the "Luskentyre Tenant".

In Watson Lyall's shooting and fishing agency catalogue[104] for May 1915, there is an advertisement for an un-named lodge, the description of which matches almost exactly the description of Horsacleit Lodge as provided later in the Leverhulme sale particulars in 1925 in the details of the number of rooms and outside room (dining room, sitting room, 6 bedrooms, plus outside ghillie's room and boiler house). The only discrepancy between the two descriptions is a statement in the 1915 advertisement that there is a yacht anchorage about half a mile from the lodge.

As part of the sale of South Harris by Lord Dunmore in 1919 for £36,000, Lord Leverhulme acquired Horsacleit. Technically, Lord Leverhulme promptly transferred the whole South Harris property to his Lewis & Harris Welfare and Development Company which was almost wholly owned by him personally. In 1919 Horsacleit was let to an unknown tenant for £200 from 1 July to October [81]. Horsacleit was subsequently leased to Professor George Gerald

---

[104] A separate publication from the *Sportsman's Guide*

Fig. 8.2 Horsacleit Lodge in the 1950s, during Norman Jamieson's tenure. Note the fishing rods and landing nets neatly stored under the verandah. Reproduced by kind permission of Gillian Bertram, granddaughter of Norman Jamieson.

Henderson for the period 1922 to 1925 at an annual rent of £150. His name first occurred in the Horsacleit game records in 1921. After Lord Leverhulme's death in 1925, Professor Henderson bought Horsacleit for £2,100. He regularly visited in the summers until his death in 1942. Professor Henderson was a regular angler in Harris, both at Finsbay Lodge and at the Harris Hotel, and he had looked forward to spending his retirement at Horsacleit. *"Mrs Henderson's sudden death coincided with his resignation from his chair in 1937, and it was a weary broken-hearted man who retired to the Isle of Harris to seek consolation in scenes hallowed by precious memories"* [82]. Further biographical information about Professor Henderson is given in Chapter 10 (The Three Fishing Professors).

It appears that there were interior alterations to reduce the number of rooms after 1925.

The 1925 sale particulars by Lord Leverhulme's Trustees refer to the 1924 catch at Horsacleit as 29 salmon plus 338 sea trout. For comparison, these particulars also mention that 30–40 salmon and 200–300 sea trout are expected per annum at Lochs Fincastle and Laxdale on the Borve Estate, so at that time the two estates were recording very similar catches[105]. Later, in 1957 during the Bertram's ownership (see below), the year's bag was 12 salmon (average 5 lbs) and 345 sea trout (average 15 oz) [83, p.17]. The game book then recorded that salmon spawn had been placed in the system at Grosebay and at Collam [83] so, like the other systems, there were stocking attempts at Horsacleit.

Horsacleit Lodge, fishings and shootings were then sold successively to a John Hart for £1,272 in 1943, then to John Anderson Service for £3,800 in 1947, and then in 1955 to Mr (Edward) Norman Jamieson for £2,000. It appears, though, from property Deeds that Norman Jamieson had rented the estate for some years before buying it.

Norman Jamieson OBE (1902 – 1956), the surgeon at The Lewis Hospital in Stornoway, was an influential and greatly respected person who played a huge role in the development of medical services in the Outer Hebrides – he was also a keen and accomplished sportsman: Horsacleit provided an ideal opportunity for him to shoot and fish while enjoying relaxation and entertaining a wide circle of friends (Figs. 8.3 to 8.7).

---

105 Though we have no estimates of fishing effort at the 2 fishing systems

Though he was not a native of the Isles (he was born in Edinburgh), he very effectively fitted in well to Hebridean life – not always easy for an "incomer" and, by all accounts, was well trusted both by the local community and by the medical authorities.

The world-renowned neurological surgeon, Professor Norman Dott[106] (1897–1973) in Edinburgh who had fished at Horsacleit (Fig. 8.8), summed this up well in an obituary of Norman Jamieson:

> "... To succeed to this post at that time one had to be able to tackle every kind of surgical emergency, a very wide scope of surgical practice, to do one's own radiology and clinical pathology – all with a minimum of technical facilities. Moreover, the people of the islands are a proud and somewhat exclusive community[107], and to succeed among them required unusual gifts of adaptability, personal and social sympathy, and tact. Mr Jamieson met these formidable challenges with ever-widening success ... he was a big man though of small stature. We shall not look upon his like again as heroic pioneer and gently successful immigrant of the islands for men with his attributes are rare ... .. he was a keen sportsman, an excellent shot, and a skilful angler; and he loved to share these pleasures with his friends. It was a revelation to travel with him on the island. High and low, young and old greeted him with affection and reverence wherever he appeared ... ". [85]

Another medical obituary concurred with:

> "... It was a pleasure to see him return to work refreshed and invigorated after a holiday in Harris, the island he loved so much and knew so well. He will long be remembered with respect, gratitude, and reverence in every island home". [86]

Norman Jamieson's medical skills encompassed a remarkable range of surgery, also radiology, and he had an additional qualification in dentistry: what an asset to an island community! Several streets in Stornoway are named after him and at least one

---

[106] Professor Dott also was a keen angler who had fished at Horsacleit with great success – see Fig. 8.8

[107] It would be unkind and unfair to judge this remark as patronising. Interestingly, Sir Samuel Scott, owner of North Harris, gave this advice to Lord Leverhulme in 1919 on Lord Leverhulme's acquisition of Harris: "I believe I have some influence at present among the N. Harris people. They are a curious race, extremely nice in many ways but very suspicious. It is simply a question of gaining their confidence. I shall do all I can to help you."[84]

Fig. 8.3 to 8.7 Norman Jamieson. Surgeon at Stornoway, keen sportsman, and owner of Horsacleit. Reproduced by kind permission of Gillian Bertram.

prominent citizen of Stornoway has the middle name of Jamieson given in honour of the surgeon! His portrait hangs in the Lewis Hospital (Fig. 8.9).

After his death, Horsacleit passed to his widow, then to their daughter and her family who owned James Bertram & Sons, a well known engineering firm in Edinburgh specialising in paper-manufacturing machinery. The estate (house plus fishings) was transferred in 1965 for £10,000 to the Bertram's Sinclairtown Property Co. In 1972, the estate was bought by the Lucas family who currently own it, though it is now used as a holiday retreat rather than as a serious sporting estate. Interestingly, the Lucas family also own the very long established Warnham Park estate in Surrey, a renowned Red Deer park and stud. There are records of the Earl of Dunmore having introduced bloodstock from Warnham Park to Harris to improve the deer population in 1898. While part of South Harris at Borve and Luskentyre was a distinguished deer

Fig. 8.8 Professor Norman Dott, the renowned neurological surgeon, with a fine bag of fish at Horsacleit Lodge. Prof Dott is standing behind his dog. Reproduced by kind permission of Christopher Rush and John Shaw FRCS.

Fig. 8.9 Portrait of Norman Jamieson being unveiled by Mrs Jamieson in Stornoway Hospital. Apparently, the artist painted the hands of daughter (Elizabeth) Anne Bertram (née Jamieson), rather than those of Norman Jamieson. Reproduced by kind permission of Gillian Bertram

forest in the late 1800s and early 1900s, human intervention has extinguished most of the deer population.

Sadly, the Horsacleit fishings are now minimal compared to their original anticipated potential and their results in the 1950s. From remarks above, it will be clear that the Horsacleit river system was originally not a "natural" system for sea trout and salmon. In 1903, Viscount Fincastle undertook to remove obstacles from the river course, and there was great optimism that a good fishing system would result. In the short term this was very well achieved with the catches in 1924 being similar to those at Borve Lodge[108]; however, in the longer term, nature has overtaken the man-made system. The physical improvements made in the early 1900s, and we do not know how much of these were due to Viscount Fincastle (subsequently 8th Earl of Dunmore), to Professor Henderson, or latterly to Norman Jamieson, involved altering the river's course so as to reduce the gradient for ascending fish. It is believed that Mr Jamieson created the Canoe Pool which was very successful for angling, and it is rumoured that Professor Henderson may have created the Grassy Pool.

Unfortunately, the alterations and minor dams created were simply not capable of withstanding major spate conditions – one has to witness personally the difference between normal low summer water and serious spate water to appreciate the civil engineering issues underlying a seemingly simple water improvement scheme. In the past, floods from the Horsacleit system have threatened the public road. Furthermore, seasonal spates deposit silt in pools, conditions not conducive to good fishing.

Repeatedly, dams and river banks have had to be mended and reinforced. Recent European water directives place major responsibilities on proprietors to maintain and upgrade dams and similar structures to modern engineering standards even in remote places; in some cases, including Horsacleit, the burden of doing this is simply impracticable. Also, small systems such as at Horsacleit, with narrow streams, are very vulnerable to human predation. Unless a proprietor is going to use the system as a seriously managed fishery business with employed keepers/watchers, these factors will soon deplete a fishery, especially in times of threatened sea trout stocks.

---

[108] The 1925 Sale Particulars state that 29 salmon and 338 sea trout were caught at Horsacleit in 1924. Jones quotes results for 1929 to 1945 which give annual averages of 8 salmon and 140 sea trout, with maximum weights of 15½lbs and 3½lbs respectively [51, p. 128]

CHAPTER NINE
SHIPPING TO SOUTH HARRIS – FINSBAY AND RODEL

In modern days of reasonably good roads and roll-on/roll-off ferries, it is easy to underestimate the challenges of travelling to and around Harris at the time when the Hebridean Sporting Association was functional. In the early 1900s, travellers to Harris had the choice of two routes: by David MacBrayne's steamer on its Portree-Dunvegan Royal Mail route from the Isle of Skye, or Martin Orme's *SS Dunara Castle* from Glasgow.

MacBrayne's mail steamer went from Portree to Tarbert, Rodel, Lochmaddy, Dunvegan, Uig (Skye), Lochmaddy, Rodel, Tarbert, and back to Portree; each of these ports was served daily, three times in a week on the northbound route and three times in the week on the southbound journey. A traveller could leave Portree at 6 am on Tuesdays, Thursdays and Saturdays and arrive at Tarbert at 10.45 am and at Rodel at 12.45 pm. It was this route, on *SS Lapwing*, that Professor Irvine took in 1914 – see Chapter 10. Fig. 9.1 shows the ship-to-shore flit boat at Rodel Harbour.

One could travel directly to Finsbay Lodge via Martin Orme & Co's *SS Dunara Castle*[109] which sailed each week[110] from Glasgow to the Western Isles, calling at Finsbay Loch. Leaving Glasgow every Thursday at 2 pm, she would call at Greenock, Colonsay, Iona, Bunessan, Tiree, Carbost, Struan, Colbost, Dunvegan, Stein, Uig (Skye), Tarbert, Finsbay (on request[111]), Obbe (i.e. Leverburgh), Kallin, Carnan, Skipport, Lochboisdale, Barra, Tiree, Bunessan, Iona, Colonsay and so back to Glasgow. Calls at Finsbay started long before the Hebridean Sporting Association took up residence,

---

[109] She was named after a ruined castle on the Island of Mull
[110] Every 10 days in winter
[111] The bill stated "And any other places of call or recall that may be agreed upon"

Fig. 9.1 Flit boat delivering passengers between Rodel and MacBrayne's steamer. Probably most of the passengers were destined for Rodel House. Ca 1934

and they continued until the 1950s when a road service enabled transport of cargo from Tarbert to Finsbay. The good access by sea to Finsbay must have been one of the key factors to influence the Association in their choice of site for their Lodge. John McCallum's steamer, *SS Hebrides*, followed a similar route, but without regular calls to Harris in the early 1900s.

Martin Orme's company merged with its rival, John McCallum, to become McCallum Orme & Co in 1929; this was subsequently absorbed by David MacBrayne Ltd, the forerunner of Caledonian MacBrayne, which is now CalMac Ltd. The *Dunara*, as she was affectionately known, served the Isles unfailingly and with legendary punctuality for the long period from 1875 to 1948 winning the hearts and esteem of all who sailed in her or were supplied by her. She was scrapped in 1949 shortly after David MacBrayne Ltd had taken over the McCallum Orme fleet with, importantly, the associated goodwill, and had reorganised the cargo sailings. With a crew of some 25, she was primarily designed to convey cargo, but she had a passenger certificate and was popular among passengers too. She also sailed several times in each season to St Kilda and, famously, assisted in the evacuation of that island in 1930. She continued her service during both World Wars, undaunted even by the hazards of

U boats in The Minch. Fig. 9.2 shows the *Dunara Castle*[112], sketched by Professor Donald Meek who, as well as being a Gaelic scholar, is an authority on the history of Hebridean shipping.

At Finsbay Loch, passengers and cargo were off-loaded to the shore via a flit-boat, a wooden hulled rowing boat owned initially by Jack Brothers then by McCallum Orme, as there was no deep water pier at Finsbay or Quidinish.

Though many people might regard a shipping call every week or 10 days as adequate for a remote spot, this was felt by the Hebridean Sporting Association to be inadequate for the full benefit of visitors to Finsbay Lodge – another instance of the Association wanting the very best for their Hebridean venture and being willing to pay for it, also having helpful contacts in appropriate places. Therefore, Thomas Wilson, in his capacity as Clerk to the Harris Parish Council, approached the Congested Districts Board[113] at the Scottish Office in 1907 with a request for a subsidy to allow David

Fig. 9.2 *SS Dunara Castle* sketched by Prof Donald Meek. This ship gave outstanding service in the Western Isles from 1875 to 1948. Reproduced by kind permission of Prof Meek

---

[112] She was built with 2 funnels, but was converted to a single funnel in 1894

[113] The Congested Districts Board was appointed in 1897 to administer the sums available for the improvement of congested districts in the Highlands & Islands; it was succeeded by the Board of Agriculture in 1911 which also took over the land settlement functions of the Crofters' Commission which had been formed in 1886

MacBrayne's steamers on the Portree-Dunvegan route, rivals to the *Dunara*, to make a call at Loch Finsbay three times a week en route to and from Tarbert. There were protracted discussions with the Congested Districts Board at the Scottish Office about this proposal; the records of these provide interesting insight into the curious workings of the Congested Districts Board [87]. Sir Reginald MacLeod[114], Permanent Under-Secretary for Scotland, commented that *"I cannot but think the Convener is right in objecting to subsidies. The people should see that the steamer cannot be sent in just for the fun of the thing and that they must show it is wanted ... "* He further made the point that the extra steamer call would not result in increased traffic, but merely divert it from one port to a different one, though Wilson tried to refute this. Initially, the Board failed to realise that there already were calls at Loch Finsbay by the rival company's ship, the *Dunara Castle*. However, they did have the sense to realise that Thomas Wilson had vested interests other than as Parish Clerk, and they concluded (almost certainly correctly) that the request was made almost entirely for the benefit of the Hebridean Sporting Association[115]. Thomas Wilson had written that the extra shipping calls would greatly benefit the lobster and herring fishermen; however, the Fishery Board did not support him in this claim. The request for a subsidy was rejected, but this did not deter the Association from trying to increase the steamer calls at Finsbay. John Malcolm and William Fergusson from the Association met with David Hope MacBrayne in Glasgow in July 1907, agreeing to make a payment to MacBraynes of £5 per month for July, August and September for the extra call and to provide the ship-to-shore arrangements.

Just as nowadays, there was much commercially sensitive information involved in tendering for shipping services, including the Royal Mail contract, to the Highlands and Islands and in applying for subsidies. In replying in 1907 to the Congested

---

114 Sir Reginald MacLeod (1847–1935) became 27th Chief of the Clan MacLeod; it was he who sold St Kilda in 1931

115 Mr Patten MacDougal noted to the Congested Districts Board: *"I confess I don't like this. The Dunara Castle has provided a service with the enterprise that characterises her owners, and now we are to kill it or at least endanger it and mainly, I take it, for the benefit of the Sporting Association and in the interests of Messrs MacBrayne whose monopoly is not used to the public good. Are we to do this without communicating with the Dunara Castle people? It seems very hard ... ."* [87]

Districts Board's requests for information about MacBrayne's costs and about what cargoes were being carried to and from Harris, David MacBrayne firmly refused to divulge his cargoes and their respective destinations on grounds *"... It is contrary to the interests of our Company to give information which might enable competitors to learn what are and what are not the places to which a considerable volume of traffic goes ... "*. [87] He did, though, offer to provide the Congested Districts Board with a certificate from his company's auditor. Any alteration to MacBrayne's shipping routes or scheduled timings needed also the approval of the Postmaster General, as changes might impact on mail deliveries.

Having gained a shipping call at Stockinish, Thomas Wilson persisted again in 1908 in his requests for a public subsidy for MacBrayne to call at Finsbay saying that the Harris Parish Council *"takes the opportunity of impressing the urgent necessity which exists for the mail steamer calling at Finsbay also, for want of which the development of the district and prosecution of the Fisheries is seriously impaired ... "* [88]. The Board again referred to the Fishery Board which was unequivocal in denying the need for the benefit of the sea fishing. Finally, the Congested Districts Board again turned down the request *"... we were formerly impressed by the fact*

Fig. 9.3 The pier at Tarbert, Harris in about 1903. Postcard photograph by Archie Chisholm in his *Cairt Phostail* series. The ship approaching the pier is either Martin Orme's *S.S. Dunara Castle* (1875–1948) or her quasi-sister ship, John McCallum's *S.S. Hebrides* (1898–1955).

East Loch Tarbert, looking to Scalpay, Harris. (Copyright.)

or belief that the call at Finsbay was desired in the interests of the Hebridean Sporting Association of which Mr Wilson was the chief, if not sole, promoter[116] ... "

A similar, but less lengthy, set of discussions had already taken place in June 1903 when Thomas Wilson, again ostensibly acting in his capacity as Parish Clerk, requested that the General Post Office extend the telegraph to Finsbay; the Post Office in turn asked if the Scottish Office, via their Congested Districts Board, might subsidise this provision [89]. Neither the GPO or the Board were willing to provide a subsidy and, to their credit, this time the Board saw that the request might have been motivated for the benefit of the Hebridean Sporting Association[117]. This is another instance of Thomas Wilson working tirelessly to gain benefits for the islands or the Association – but, of course, it should be remembered that he had a significant financial shareholding in the Hebridean Sporting Association.

Shipping services to the Western Isles have always attracted controversy and even parliamentary debate. Technically these are "lifeline services", essential for the existence of populations. Hence they have been eligible for subsidies of various sorts over the years; it is now becoming clear that in earlier times they were supported by benevolent individuals who identified with the need. Inevitably, such services are in the public eye and, as Robins and Meek have recently commented, "MacBrayne bashing" is a common practice [90]. However, such criticisms are by no means new: Lord Leverhulme was less than enthusiastic about David MacBrayne's service: *"I think we shall always find Messrs MacBrayne unreasonable in their charges. I have got the impression that it is not a very well organised firm. I know there is seething discontent in the Island of Lewis with regard to the way they serve*

---

116 In view of the Wilsons' shareholding in the Hebridean Sporting Association, this comment may be very pertinent

117 Mr R.R. MacGregor, Secretary to the Congested Districts Board, noted *"... this may require careful scrutiny and enquiries as to the population to be benefited. With Mr Wilson in his many capacities it is not easy to be sure of one's ground. He has recently been occupied in floating a company, the Hebridean Sporting Association Limited, ... it is just possible that he is thinking as much of this as of other things in his wish for a telegraph ... ."* [89]. While this is true, the underlying motive may have been to benefit the local community through the success of the Association.

the island. I am not surprised that you have found them difficult to make satisfactory arrangements with, and therefore your proposal to charter from time to time when the cargoes have accumulated sufficiently to justify a charter is excellent ... .” [91] and later *“I think it will be best for all of us if we none of us accept favours from steam boat companies. We do not know when we might have to run an opposition service from Tarbert or Leverburgh ... ”* [92]

According to Nigel Nicolson [93, p.106], Lord Leverhulme bought £10,000 worth of shares in MacBraynes in order to try to influence their policy, and he wrote irate letters to numerous government departments complaining that MacBrayne's service to the community was a disgrace to the government who, he judged, was making false economies by failing to subsidise the service adequately.

CHAPTER TEN
THE THREE FISHING PROFESSORS, AND PROFESSOR IRVINE'S ACCOUNT OF A WEEK AT FINSBAY LODGE

It is unlikely that the residents of Harris ever realised that among their angling visitors were three of the world's most distinguished professors of chemistry, all Fellows of the Royal Society! Professors Henderson, Purdie, and Irvine were considered a major "dynasty" in Scottish academia and in world chemistry. Luckily for us, one of them recorded his adventures at Finsbay Lodge in the form of letters to his wife, and transcripts of these are reproduced below. Of the three, Professor Henderson was the most senior academically, since the other two had been his pupils and clearly had been greatly influenced academically by him, though Professor Purdie was actually the eldest – as explained below, Prof Purdie did not enter academic life until his 30s. Each of the three had a common background in that each had spent formative time early in their careers working in Leipzig under the famous Professor Johannes Wislicenus (1835–1902).

A keen angler with a particularly long association with Harris was George Gerald Henderson FRS (1862–1942) a Glaswegian from a merchant family who had been a scholar of both Greek and chemistry – see Fig. 10.1.

He became Professor at Glasgow's Royal Technical College and subsequently occupied the Regius Chair of Chemistry at Glasgow University from 1919 till 1937. It was said that *"his personality, his lecturing skills and his appearance (tall, slim, athletic, and well tailored) commanded respect, and that he was a man of habit who never altered his appearance or his customs"* [82].

He was a regular visitor at Finsbay Lodge and at the Harris Hotel,

Tarbert. He became a shareholder in the Hebridean Sporting Association (taking over the late John Dempster's entry in the Company's share folio) in 1919, the last year before the Association's liquidation. He was the last person to acquire a shareholding in the Hebridean Sporting Association; this was rather curious as, by then, the Association was in financial difficulties and no longer had their lease of the fishings.

Professor Henderson was so attached to Harris, though, that he then rented and later bought Horsacleit for himself and his guests – see Chapter 8. He died there in 1942, leaving an estate of £13,337.

Several Harris people with memories of Finsbay Lodge, at least in its latter days, had mentioned the names Mr & Mrs Purdie, even suggesting that they had "run" the Lodge. It is now clear that this refers to another distinguished chemist, Professor Thomas Purdie FRS (1843–1916), a native of Biggar, and his wife, Mary Anne (neé Rotherham). Professor Purdie was professor of chemistry at St. Andrews University from 1884 to 1909. Surprisingly though, the records of shareholders [2], which are complete for each year of the Hebridean Sporting Association's existence, show that Prof. Purdie was never a shareholder. Ill health, particularly asthma, dogged Thomas Purdie, but his long summer vacations fishing in the highlands and in Harris refreshed him. It appears that he and his wife were regular visitors for long stays at Finsbay Lodge – his long summer retreat to the Hebrides away from the greenery of St Andrews was beneficial for his health.

The log-book at Finsbay School records Prof. and Mrs Purdie, staying at Finsbay Lodge, visiting the school several times in 1908 and 1914 and that they invited the children to teas and treats at the Lodge; also a gentleman from Paisley, mentioned but unfortunately not named in the School log, who was staying at the Lodge presented the school prizes in 1909. Another person recalls that the school sports days were held at the Lodge[118], so it seems happily clear that Finsbay Lodge was well received as a benefactor to the local community. Prof Purdie was a Governor of St Leonard's School in St Andrews (where he helped design the science building which was opened in 1908 by Sir Ernest Shackleton), so he clearly was keenly involved with school education as well as University teaching and research.

Professor Thomas Purdie was another avid angler who had been a chemistry student of Professor Henderson. He, however, came into his academic career at an unusually late age. He was the son of the bank agent in Biggar and had initially considered a career in business. This proved not to his taste so he,

Fig. 10.2 Professor Thomas Purdie FRS. Reproduced by kind permission of The Royal Society

together with a step-cousin, Thomas Farquhar Paul, boldly went to the Argentine to start a large wheat-farming ranch there at Estancia Los Garrobitos in 1865. Though he loved this outdoor life, and he subsequently regaled his university students with tales of adventures on horseback in the Pampas, his ranch was raided by South American natives, Gauchos, who were unhappy about immigrants taking over the land and so, after seven years, he decided to return to Scotland. Conversations with his wealthy uncle, also named Thomas Purdie, in St Andrews and with T.H. Huxley led him to explore an academic career which he took up and which turned out to be a great success. As well as contributing greatly to the world's knowledge in organic chemistry, he became a great benefactor of St Andrews University where he founded

---

[118] See Fig. 13.2 in Chapter 13. We strongly suspect that the two ladies in elegant hats are Mrs Mary Anne Purdie and her niece, Miss Agnes Rotherham. The school register records a visit by Mrs Purdie and Miss Rotherham on 31 August 1914 – this was a month after Professor Irvine's stay at Finsbay Lodge – Chapter 10

(and substantially funded[119]) the now famous School of Chemistry. Its building is now named "The Purdie Building", and one of the professorships of chemistry in the university is designated "The Purdie Chair". Fig. 10.2 shows Prof Purdie in his laboratory.

Contemporary accounts indicate that he was a greatly popular lecturer who accompanied his lectures with lively – sometimes over-lively! – experimental demonstrations.

Mrs Mary Anne Purdie (née Rotherham), the professor's wife, was a sister of Alexander Rotherham of Coventry who had owned a silk dyeing company and was chairman of the Premier Cycle Company which was possibly the largest bicycle manufacturing firm in the world[120]. One of their sisters, Charlotte, had married Canon Frederick Evans, nephew of the writer George Eliot (Mary Anne Evans) and long-standing Rector of Bedworth in Warwickshire. Their father had been a very prominent watchmaker[121], an industry for which Coventry was then famous.

Just as Mrs Purdie was highly regarded in Harris, she contributed greatly to the social activities among the academic community of St Andrews. Lady Irvine wrote: " ... *Mrs Purdie was so stimulating, so gay and amusing, that she drew forth from the dullest witted person sparks that came from her own personality more than from theirs ... "* [94, p.32]. This atmosphere was clearly formative for the Irvines who would, in due time, be giving warm hospitality in the home of the Principal and Vice-Chancellor to many important international visitors to the University of St Andrews.

Prof. Sir James Irvine, see below, commented in his obituary of Prof. Purdie for the Chemical Society *"During the long vacation, he [Purdie] travelled extensively and, nearer home, the humble crofters of the Outer Hebrides will remember him for more than his skill as a fly fisher ... ."* [95], and Purdie's obituarist for The Royal Society

---

119 His uncle, also named Thomas Purdie, and the Carnegie Trust were major contributors
120 The Coventry Premier Company, which also had a factory in Germany, was taken over by Singer around 1922 who then concentrated on car production. William Hillman had been an early partner in the Premier Cycle Co, but went on to found Hillman motors. At this time, the transition from cycle to cyclecar to motor car production was occurring, with Coventry a particularly prominent centre
121 At that time, watch-making was a major industry in Coventry. John Rotherham Jr, Mary Anne's father, employed some 400–500 staff plus about 200 outworkers producing 100 watches per day

wrote "*... Purdie took his relaxation in golf on the far-famed links [of St Andrews], in foreign travel, and in trout-fishing in various remote parts of Scotland, latterly at Finsbay on the Island of Harris where both he and Mrs Purdie will long be remembered for their kindly relations with the crofters*" [96]. It is pleasing that Finsbay should be mentioned so warmly in these journals that are mainly concerned with esoteric academic matters! Unfortunately, neither the Purdies nor the Hendersons had families, so any diaries they may have kept of their Hebridean activities have not been traceable.

Though Professor Purdie never wrote any books on fishing, one of his students, Robert Currie Bridgett was renowned as the author

Fig. 10.3 Professor Sir James Irvine FRS. Reproduced by kind permission of Mrs Julia Melvin and Dr George Gandy, grand-daughter and grandson of Sir James Irvine.

of 6 fishing books[122] and as the fishing correspondent of the *Glasgow Herald*. R.C. Bridgett (1878–1960) went on to become Rector of Lanark Grammar School, and it is remarkable that in 1938 he built a small trout hatchery accommodating 200 ova in his classroom so as to introduce his pupils to the rudiments of fish biology!

Completing the trio of distinguished professors was another greatly successful student of Professor Henderson, Professor Sir James Irvine FRS (1877–1952), also a native of Glasgow. See Fig. 10.3.

As a young student in 1895 at the Royal Technical College[123], Glasgow he had been advised by Professor Henderson to continue his studies by going to the University of St Andrews and to follow an academic career rather than train for a technical post. He became a lecture assistant to Professor Purdie, describing his relationship with Professor Purdie as *"almost that of father and son"* [97]. After Professor Purdie's retirement on ill health grounds, Irvine succeeded Purdie as professor of chemistry at St Andrews University; he then went on to become Principal and Vice-Chancellor of that university, a post that he held for the period of 1921 to 1952, an extraordinarily long period of senior stewardship and substantial international influence[124]. Indeed, there is also a named "Irvine Building" in St Andrews University.

On 8 August 1913, Professor Purdie wrote from Finsbay Lodge[125] to his friend Professor Irvine saying:

> " ... Your fishing can scarcely have been less successful than ours here. The sea trout are congregated in the sea pools when however they do not look for flies, and the can't get up to the lochs. I have never seen the latter so low, & have never seen the fishing so long delayed. No rain to speak of has fallen since our arrival. We have now got 10 "rods" in the Lodge, & we don't know what to offer them. They have mostly to amuse themselves with small "brownies". But I hope things may be much better when Macdonald comes on 6 September. I got his wire & he is booked for the date mentioned. Surely the spate cannot be much longer delayed ... . My asthma gives little trouble, but

---

122 One of these was *"Sea Trout Fishing"* which included a chapter on fishing the Harris Hotel's Lacisdale lochs in 1926 [40, p.247–275]
123 Now Strathclyde University
124 Professor Irvine was knighted in 1925 and promoted KBE in 1948
125 Copy of correspondence kindly supplied by Mrs Julia Melvin, Sir James Irvine's grand-daughter

the giddiness continues ... .. A Glasgow Consulting Physician, Dr Middleton, a friend of the Hendersons, now among the visitors, has overhauled me ... ... I got Mr Macdonald's wire all right & have booked a room & rod for him for 6 September. Tell him that waders are not of any use here, our fishing being all in lochs ... .."

Following in Professor Purdie's footsteps in the new laboratories in St Andrews, Professor Irvine performed world-class research on sugar chemistry and made a major practical contribution to the nation's supply of essential dulcitol[126] and novocaine[127] and various other chemicals needed in the First World War. Many ordinary citizens of St Andrews became involved in the manufacture of these vital compounds on a grand scale. Fishing provided one of his much needed relaxations from this relentless scholarly and administrative work, and we now believe that his visit to Finsbay Lodge in 1914 to fish with his friends Professors Henderson and Purdie was formative for his subsequent enthusiasm for fishing. We are fortunate that he provided a detailed account of his stay at Finsbay to his wife, Lady Mabel Irvine (known by him affectionately as "Mabs"), who then included the following passage in her biography of Sir James (reproduced by kind permission of the University of St Andrews who holds the copyright) [94]. His letters to her, which follow, reveal his private – almost intimate – record of his holiday at Finsbay Lodge.

[From: *The Avenue of Years: A Memoir of Sir James Irvine, Principal and Vice-Chancellor of the University of St. Andrews 1921–1952 by his Wife*. **pp. 77–78. Blackwood, Edinburgh, 1970]** **[94]**

"In July 1914 Jim went to the island of Harris on a fishing holiday with Professor and Mrs Purdie. They were members of an anglers' club which had its headquarters in Finsbay. Here, too, were Professor G. G. Henderson, Jim's early teacher in Glasgow, and his wife. Jim delighted in this life at Finsbay; it was after his own heart; open-air freedom and pleasant company, long days on the moor or on the lochs, home in the evening sunburned and pleasantly tired, to have his catch weighed and entered in the club book. Then a hot bath and change for dinner, followed

---

[126] Dulcitol is a sugar that was needed in diagnostic bacteriology to identify *S. typhii* (the bacterium causing typhoid)

[127] Novocaine is a local anaesthetic, much needed in the field hospitals

by good talk and a smoke by the log fire. During the summer months Dr Purdie, bronzed and well, his old enemy asthma forgotten, strode over the heather to the lochs and fished all day. The worn, pale face and difficult breathing and walking, that we were sadly accustomed to in St Andrews, vanished during his long vacation.

This holiday of Jim's in that tragic summer is vivid in my mind because of his tales and descriptions on his return home. I cannot believe that I have not been in the Island of Harris, nor ever seen the crofts in the heather, the kilted bare-foot children, the busy womenfolk who spun and dyed the yarn, and wove the tweed in the colours of the world around them, sea, sky, clouds, heather, peat and bog-myrtle. I knew the ghillies, too, their names and their personalities. I knew the story of the two Englishmen visiting the lodge for the weekend who wanted to fish on Sunday. No ghillie would go with them in the boat, nor carry their catch when they returned. The cook would not allow it into her kitchen, so it could not be cooked, and when in despair the fishermen tied their sea-trout up in rushes and baskets, the postman on Monday morning refused to carry it to the post office. "Na, na," he said, "they were caught on the Sabbath, Ah'll no' handle them."

Mrs Purdie and Mrs Henderson, knitting in the sun at the door of the lodge, smiled with satisfaction, the member-anglers preparing their rods for the day's work, chuckled behind their cigarette smoke and the fish had to be cast [thrown] into the sea. Perhaps in our falling away from grace it is different now even on the Island of Harris, but it is fine to think of simple folk loyally standing by their convictions.

War was imminent as July drew to its close. At home there was tension, but the island was a land apart, as islands always are, and still the weather, the day's catch, the beat for tomorrow, filled their thoughts. The 4th of August dawned and the fiery cross went round like wind moaning over the moors. The ghillies laid down their oars and their fishing tackle, said goodbye to their wives and children, and before the sun was low in the sky they had disappeared over the heather, and the crofts were silent; for all were Navy and Army Reservists. St Andrews brimmed over with rumours. Everyone was excited and strained, yet buoyed up with strange exultation, an emotion which was the preparation for suffering and sacrifice to come.

On that first evening of war, police called at every house to order all windows to be blacked out and no light to show after dark."

Recently, Sir James' grand-daughter has delved into the family papers and has been able to provide extracts of his letters written to his wife, Lady Mabel Irvine (MVI), during this fishing holiday which give a unique insight into daily life at Finsbay Lodge, also telling dramatically how fishing there came to an abrupt halt at the commencement of the First World War. I am much indebted to Mrs Julia Melvin and Dr George Gandy for kindly permitting these to be included here. In making these transcripts Mrs Melvin has replicated the Irvines' punctuation just as it was written. She commented that Sir James himself was generally most punctilious in the use of punctuation, but that in writing to his wife, however, its absence is merely an attempt to be vivid, and to have, as he saw it, a personal conversation with his wife. He saw his letters home, when he was away on anything more than professional business, as a log for recording his experiences. They use the nicknames: Mabs, Mubbles (MVI), and Jim, Dimbie (JCI) variously. Sir James (JCI) was a romantic, and had the literary power to evoke the least experience, which in his imagination would be highlighted with a sense of drama. It is easy to see how the scenery and Hebridean life would provide the ideal backdrop for an evocative story.

His grand-daughter recently described him thus:

"He was a man who always drove himself to the point of exhaustion; at this juncture of his life he was the young (36 years old – unusually young at that time) and very ambitious Professor of Chemistry in the University of St Andrews. He was also Dean of the Faculty of Science. He had a gift for administration as well as for chemical research which secured many long-term benefits for his University. The fumes of the chemistry laboratory[128] coupled with his tendency to burn the midnight oil, would give him blinding headaches. Fishing in these remote highland lochs gave him the inner release from tension that he needed, and restored his health. He was very athletic, and a fine sportsman in several sports, but

---

[128] It appears that these chemical fumes were quite overpowering, not conceivable under modern Health & Safety legislation, and that Prof Purdie's asthmatic condition mentioned above also was badly exacerbated by them – hence the great benefits of his visits to remote highland fishing places

at this period of his life, fishing in the Highlands above all was to become the best form of escape he knew. As he grew older, and his public responsibilities grew heavier, he sought other forms of outdoor relaxation, and highland fishing became less a feature in his life, although he taught his son, Nigel, to fish in Scotland and later enjoyed fishing with Nigel both in the Highlands and in the West of England, where his wife liked to holiday.

In 1914, Jim [as he was known by his friends and family] was invited to Finsbay by Professor and Mrs Purdie. Several letters between Jim and Mabs (JCI and MVI) describe the journey there and all that he found when he got there. His family opinion is that this experience was a turning point in his life as a sporting fisherman".

29 July 1914. Station Hotel, Inverness.

[Jim has had to wait in the train for his connection for another train, which will take him to the boat for Skye. It is very delayed.]

> "Such a confusion of sportsmen, fashionable ladies, guns, rods, dogs, luggage and Boy Scouts you never saw in your life. I have the party in the carriage who are going to Kyle for the day ... .".

[The next arm of the journey was picturesque:]

> "....through wild mountain passes, alongside of lonely lochs and finally a wild run downhill to the sea on the West. The country is simply superb Mabs and some day we must do this trip together. You would enjoy it.
>
> How you would relish the next part is less certain. I did grin when I saw the boat which was to take us 'over the sea to Skye'. About the size of a tug, with old fashioned donkey engines and a dear old fashioned skipper who was as stately and genial as if in charge of the "Lusitania".

[note the irony here; in July 1914 Britain is on the brink of war. Within 12 months, the glamorous *Lusitania* had been sunk 8 miles off the coast of Ireland by a German torpedo]

> "As soon as we got on board I went and had a good dinner – very plain but substantial. It was well I did so for the trip across was no picnic and no mistake. A stiff N.W. wind was blowing although the sky was serene and blue, and the sun strong. We pitched and splashed our way across and it really was fine to see those gorgeous mountains in Skye. Still I wasn't sorry when we

got under the lea of the islands and got in smoother water. If anything is certain in this world it is that we shall have a heavy time in the Minch tomorrow morning.

Portree is a weird place – a quaint little town lying in a land-locked harbour in the midst of the hills. The Hotel is very good indeed, more homey and more comfy than the Station Hotel at Inverness."

29 July 1914. Portree.

"6 A.M.

What do you think I am doing now? Sitting on a coil of rope in the bows of the S.S. *"Lapwing"* which is fast aground in Portree Harbour. Really, a trip to Harris is as good as a play!

What a wild rush everyone had this morning to catch the boat and how impatiently the noble *Lapwing* sounded her siren to hurry us up. On went the luggage – "any more for the shore", "clear away that gangway", the sound of the engine room telegraph, the churning of the screw and then a sudden lurch to starboard. She was aground.

... Fortunately it is a most glorious morning and I write this in full view of the Cuchullin Mountains which are beyond description. The wind too has died down overnight and the sea is quite smooth in the bay and seems quieter outside as well."

[The next bit of this letter is written that afternoon from Rodel.]

"Here I am at Rodel waiting till Sam Morrison[129] brings over the fishing boat to the jetty at which we landed from the ferry. What a place! The sky above, rock under foot and the sea all around. If this is "the back o' beryont" then Finsbay must be "the back of the back o' beryont". The promise of the morning was fulfilled and the sail across the Minch simply perfection. The sea was like glass."

That night JCI finally has arrived and is able to write to his wife from Finsbay. He is using the headed writing paper of the Finsbay Angling Club (South Harris) – see Fig. 10.4.

Four letters in all were written by Professor Irvine to his wife from this address during his week's stay there. They provide a vivid description of the place, of Finsbay Lodge, of the *dramatis personae*, and of the sport.

---

[129] Sam is the Keeper at Finsbay Lodge

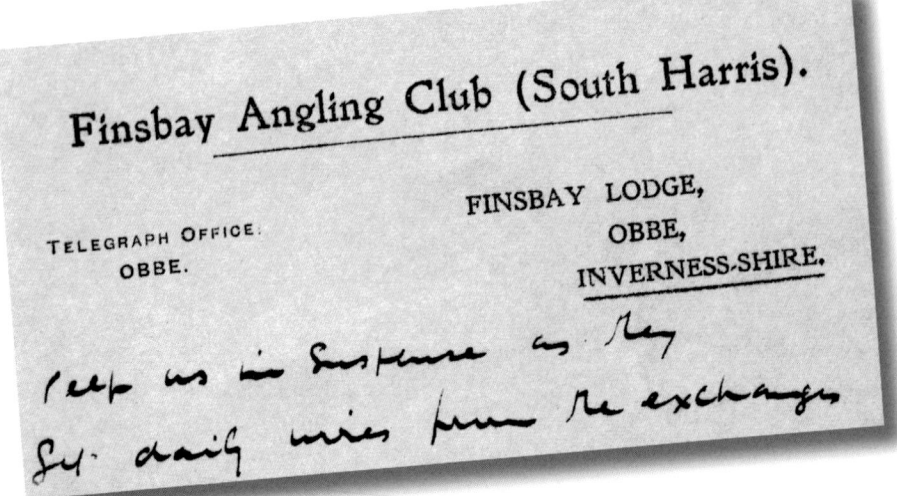

" ... the trip across the Minch was, in fact, perfection itself and so was the last stage in the fishing boat. We fairly tore along from Rodel and got our first sight of the Lodge from the head of the Bay. It is a splendid place and looks most imposing from the sea. Sam's sharp eyes caught sight of Mrs Purdie & Nessie[130] on the veranda and he told me they were waving handkerchiefs & so I did the same. When we got nearer I found he spoke truly.

Dr Purdie was still out fishing so we had tea, and meanwhile I told all the news I had. It was strange to bring the first news of the European war to the island. They were all greatly excited about it. Then Dr Purdie came in for tea and at once hauled me off to his loch. I wouldn't take a rod but was quite happy to lie in the bows and watch his elegant casting which, within the hour landed two fine sea-trout. Meanwhile Mrs Purdie sent off a wire to you via the postman who was just leaving. You should get it to-morrow morning.

Then home at 7 to unpack & dress for dinner. Afterwards a talk by the fire and, so, to my letter.

... I can do it better justice if I write about Finsbay by degrees but I must say it is the most desolately beautiful spot[131] I have ever seen.

---

130 "Nessie" is Miss Agnes Rotherham, Mrs Purdie's niece
131 The "desolate" description is the same as that by Lord Leverhulme's niece, Emily Macdonald, but she did not qualify her description with "beautiful"!

... Henderson, by the way, is also here and was upbraiding me for not bringing you with me!! He sends his regards."

Mrs Purdie sent a telegram (received in St Andrews on 31 July) to Mrs Irvine:

"Dr Irvine arrived safely – good journey – out fishing.
Purdie"

31 July 1914. At Finsbay Angling Club (South Harris) – as before

" ... Well, I've had my first day's fishing and both my rod and my new waterproof have been "blooded". We set off this morning at 9.30, Dimbie and his ghillie climbed the most awful hills, through peat bogs and over stones, until we came to a chain of three small lochs rather like Loch-a-Tairt[132]. Within an hour, I had my first fish a trout of over a pound. The second loch gave a blank and the third yielded 2 brown trout and 1 splendid sea-trout of 1 ¼ lbs. It fought like a fury but we got him in. By this time it was raining cats and dogs but the ghillie would not come home – he thought I would get some more if we stayed. At length we toddled home about 6 (I forgot to say that we took sandwiches & a Thermos with us and lunched on the moors).

Out of 8 rods[133] I had the second heaviest basket for the day and am in great delight (so is Purdie).

Tonight it is a howling gale & raining hard so a spate is in prospect and the sport may improve. I ought to say that I caught 12 fish in all but there is a rule that no fish is kept unless of a certain length & weight. Each boat has a measuring rod so as to test this. In my case most of the fish caught had to go back into the water[134].

The life here is very pleasant and the Lodge is a quaint place, built of wood and like a Canadian house. My own room is like an explorer's den – - wooden walls with shelves, a narrow camp bed and everything clean and simple. It is a curious mixture of Spartan simplicity and dress clothes which goes to make up the life here ... "

---

[132] L. an Tairt is a small hill loch north of Glen Urquhart, Inverness-shire, where the Irvines used to have family holidays

[133] More evidence that the full compliment of 20 rooms was not filled by anglers in the peak of the fishing season

[134] Unfortunately, he does not say what the size limit is nor whether the small fish are included in the fishing records

[JCI is boyishly proud of his first fish and wishes his wife had been there to see it]

2 August 1914. Sunday morning. Finsbay Angling Club (South Harris) as before

" ... I am writing in the smoking-room, a huge timbered room like the saloon of a house-boat, and my view is straight down Loch Finns Bay and out to the Minch. It is raining hard, the mist is down on the hills and not a breath disturbs the grey stillness of the bleak Hebridean Island of South Harris. It is a wonderful view outside. Inside there is a roaring peat fire and round it a little group talking of past fish and fish to come, of possible spates and flies and tackle and all the machinery of Isaac Walton's art. At each writing table there are others like myself who have sweethearts to write to or business to do – it is easy to say which kind of task they are engaged on. On the walls, hang fishing maps of the island showing the lochs and the "beats", lists of available ghillies, the record of the catches for the past week and all sorts of information of that kind. One wall is entirely covered with the rods which are ready to go out to-morrow.

So much for my immediate surroundings, Mabs, now for the daily routine which I shall give in detail so that you may be better able to picture my doings. To begin with, however, you know the general appearance of the Lodge which stands at the head of the Bay quite close to the edge of the sea. Behind us, the sea pools run up into a small stream which joins on to the first loch of the chain. There are in all about a dozen small lochs each about the size of Loch-an-Tairt but bounded by little islands. They are very beautiful but gloomy and desolate. The main hall of the Lodge is quite imposing and so is the staircase – everything is of wood and severely plain but strong and good.

... the day's sport begins the night before: when Henderson arranges the "beats"[135]. That is to say the total fishing ground is divided into ten sections so that each man may have a reasonable chance of getting a basket. Meanwhile there is a "list of rods". When you arrive, your name is put at the bottom of the list and you go up one place each day. After dinner the "beats" are arranged and then each man selects which he will take each day. You should see the solemn care devoted to this momentous decision. The barometer is consulted, the direction

---

[135] This corresponds to the "Boardmaster" regime mentioned on p. 62

of the wind, and the fishing records of previous years before a beat is selected. This is a bit awkward for Dr Purdie as some of the lochs lie well up the hills and he is not able to walk to them but Henderson is very good in juggling the arrangements so that Purdie gets a beat near to the Lodge.

The morning bell goes at 7 o'clock: there is a scramble for baths, and breakfast is at 8 sharp. It is a running meal, each person helps himself and I need hardly say the menu never varies: – porridge, trout, eggs – well cooked and devoured with zest. Meanwhile the ghillies are running in and out of the place getting rods and baskets ready, the Thermos flasks (and other flasks) are filled up, and off we go about 9.

The little parties of two wend their way up the steep rocky path and scatter over the moors to their respective lochs and there they remain all day long. You scramble through peat bogs, over streams, and up rocky crags – the ghillie leaping on ahead with all the gear and the endurance of a deer. Suddenly a lonely loch opens out, a boat is at the bank and in you go and begin. It is very different from Loch Meiklie [where he must have fished during the Irvines' 1913 Highland holiday at Balnain.] for the fish are plentiful and so the interest never flags. Each moment you may get one on the line and you work away landing plenty of fish although only allowed to keep the big ones – the ghillie sees to that and measures all doubtful cases.

When you've been twice round the loch you pack up and go off to another one for the afternoon, lunch being taken on the moor. Lunch is well done and is quickly devoured.

About five o'clock you find yourself high up in the hills and the return journey begins, the ghillie picking the track so that as far as possible advantage is taken of the lochs and you boat down.

Then there is a great inspection and weighing of the catches and at 7 we go into dinner, each man looking a different being in his sober black.

The Purdies have a private sitting room, and I divide my time between them and the company in the smoking room. By 10 o'clock we are off to bed and glad to get there.

..so let me tell you about yesterday's doings.

It was a hopeless day for fishing – blue sky, blazing sun, and no wind. Dr Purdie and I took beats close to each other and so met at lunch where we were joined by Mrs Purdie and Nessie. I had one fish and he had nothing as the result of the morning's work ... It was gorgeous up there at lunch-time

..After lunch we went back to our boats and tried again but it was useless and so we reeled up and trudged home. Just as we got back, the fishing-boat came in from Rodel with 11 people for the Lodge and herein lies a great joke. Rooms had been engaged for a Mrs Samuelson and maid and also for her son.

Imagine a fashionable dame with maid and jewel-case stepping out of a fishing boat on to slippery tangle-covered rocks. It was a case of what might be called lack of perspective. She thought she was coming to a kind of hotel I suppose and she simply had the whole place furious, ordering special meals (which couldn't be supplied) and generally behaving as if she had bought the island. You can imagine the situation – also her appearance at dinner in a fashionable filmy gown with the Samuelson ancestral diamonds. Bets are now freely offered as to the length of their stay here.

... You asked about my fittings, dearie. Well, they are all right except that my clothes are too good. The men are, during the day, simply in rags, but the only real mistake I seem to have made is in my waterproof. Everybody wears cheap oil skins (the 16/- kind) and my silk-lined garment is out of place in a boat. ... .That's the only flaw however and, for beginners at this game, we did well. It is a mercy you marked everything darling, for your clothes are whipped away without warning to be aired and dried.

With the exception, mentioned above, the company is most delightful. In addition to Mrs Purdie and Nessie, there are only two ladies (not including Mrs S. and maid). The men are largely academic – a Rugby housemaster[136], & a master at Charterhouse who knew Jack [MVI's 3rd brother] at Oxford, two medical men, and two business men. The latter keep us in suspense as they get daily wires from the exchanges and so there is a great war scare here. It is impossible for us to realize how bad the European situation is, but it looks as if the big war has come at last ... It is a terrible thought but it may have the effect of teaching Britain that there are graver issues in the world's affairs than votes for

136 This is likely to be John Collins who was a shareholder in the Hebridean Sporting Association

women and Home Rule in Ireland. We were rapidly becoming a petty little nation.

> ... Mrs Purdie sends her love. She often talks of you.
> Perhaps Mabs you would send me
> Some good sweets for Mrs Purdie
> Some cheap sweets for the little school children[137]
> More milk chocolate for my return journey
> A clothes brush
> I am an awful old nuisance am I not?"

[At the foot of the letter is a little pencil drawing of a man wearing sou'wester and oil skins standing up in a boat fishing, while the oars are manned by a cloth-capped ghillie. See Fig. 10.5]

Fig. 10.5 Professor Irvine's drawing at the end of one of his letters to his wife. Reproduced by kind permission of Mrs Julia Melvin

<u>Sunday evening</u>. A wire has come in telling of the war between Germany and Russia.

4 August 1914. Finsbay Angling Club (South Harris) as before

[He hopes his wife is not worried by the war scare. She is alone in St Andrews]

> " ... .We are more liable here to a panic in this out-of-way spot as our news comes in the form of skimpy telegrams which are inclined to be sensational. When out fishing today there was a little incident which you could put into words so well. Imagine

---

[137] Finsbay Lodge had a close relationship with the Finsbay School, probably fostered particularly by Mrs Purdie – see pages 188–191

a little lonely loch, dreary and grey, with the rugged hills all around and the mists swirling over the rocky precipices – I am quietly fishing in company with my gillie [sic], John[138] who, as a seargent [sic] in the Reserves, lives in the hourly expectation of being called out. For the moment, we have given up talking of war and casting for a big sea-trout who is coming again and again at the line, when out of the mist, leaping from rock to rock, comes an old white headed man who shouts to us in Gaelic. "My telegram" cries John, and he bends to the oars and we dash across the loch. A quick question and answer in the unknown tongue. "Have you any news" I ask the messenger – a shake of the head and "I hav' no Engleesh" is his reply. He has telegrams for the gillies [sic] who are in the Naval Reserve and he dashes off from one loch to another so as to find them. Half an hour later three men in oil-skins with sacks over their shoulders march down the rocky path. They have, in a moment's notice left homes, wives, children and their scanty livelihood to obey the call. A shouted farewell in Gaelic and they disappear – we got on casting with the feeling that it is unworthy for men to play themselves at such a time – meanwhile three brave men trudge through the rain to Stornoway. That gives a poor idea Mabs of a picture I shall never forget.

No wonder we reeled in early so as to get back to the Lodge for news. There was little to hear save that a wire from Glasgow advised us to order in extra supplies for the Lodge. This reminds me Mabs that perhaps you should order in some flour, oatmeal, and possibly also some coal. It is most unlikely that there will be any shortage of these or other foods but prices may dash up to extravagant rates for a bit and it is well to be prepared.

Unless there are peaceful developments I shall postpone my visit to Glasgow[139] and come straight back to you – either at the close of the fortnight or earlier if you wish it, or if things get more serious.

Needless to say, Dr Purdie is much upset – you know how even the mildest politics affect him.

..But for the war and rumours of war, I am having a splendid time spending about 10 hours a day out of doors. I can hold my

138 John, the ghillie, is likely to have been either John MacKay or John MacKinnon
139 His parents lived at Springburn, Glasgow

own now as a fisherman & got the third highest catch today
– one sea-trout and four brown trout[140]."

[There is no evidence in the family papers that JCI ever returned
to Finsbay Lodge to fish. Subsequent letters about fishing are sent
from rather more accessible parts of the Highlands]

Next in sequence are three letters from G.G. Henderson to
Irvine several years later.

13 December 1920. Chemistry Department, University of Glasgow.

"My dear Irvine[141]

I congratulate you most heartily on your appointment to the
Principalship and I congratulate St. Andrews equally warmly.
You will succeed, I know, and my wish is that you will find your
future path as free from troubles and obstructions as is humanly
possible. I am more than proud to feel that I had at least some
share in directing your steps at the beginning of your career."

26 December 1920. 7 Marlborough Drive, Kelvinside, Glasgow

"My dear Irvine

Just a line in answer to your welcome letter to say firstly that we
shall be more than glad if you can see your way to continue to
act as examiner. If there is no precedent, let us create one. Of
course if you find yourself too much occupied, there is no help
for it, but if you can hold on I promise to make the work as light
as possible.

As regards Finsbay, the Hebridean Assoc. offered to sell house,
furniture, and everything else to Lord Leverhulme, and I
understand from Malcolm that their offer has been accepted,
and that the Assoc. will now proceed to dissolve. I shall make
quite sure of this, but if you don't hear from me again please
take it that the sale has been completed[142].

---

[140] He was obviously enthralled by the fishing, though such a catch is
hardly headline news – perhaps a very typical sentiment about fishing
in the wilds of Harris, both then and now

[141] The formality of correspondence, even between friends, was
characteristic of much of the first half of the 20th century. Its demise
perhaps reflects a change in attitudes to respect and to attention to
detail

[142] As explained in Chapter 3, the sale was completed in January 1921; the
final winding-up of the Association was dated 24 November 1922

Meantime we send you all possible good wish.

Yours always

G.G. Henderson."

1 January 1925. 7 Marlborough Drive, etc.

"My dear Irvine

Heartiest congratulations on the new honour. [knighthood] Of course it was no surprise to find your name included in today's list, but it is most gratifying to all your friends that your work is receiving recognition. Long may you flourish!

Yours always

G.G. Henderson"

[The next passage describes something of what these fishing expeditions meant to JCI, who not only was thrusting ahead with his plans for the university, but had retained some Chemistry research students and authority over his Chemical Research Institute in the university. He writes of the family holiday ahead, and says *"... I shall help you in every way I possibly can. I'm able to do it now and I wasn't able a week ago at this time when I left you, for then I was ready to explode at anything or nothing, and indeed not fit to think. This week has worked wonders and I feel like a boy again ... ."*]

Professor and Mrs Purdie continued to take holidays at Finsbay Lodge, even despite the War, including in the last summer of his life, 1916. On 27 August 1916, Prof. Purdie wrote to Prof Irvine from Finsbay Lodge saying:

" ... . The fishing here has continued as bad as bad can be. The only rain we have had all the time of our stay is one spate, at a time when there were few fish in the sea pools. Now there are many, often jumping like mad, but they can't get into the lochs. For 15 consecutive days we have had E & NE breezes which blow across all the lochs & are anathema to the Harris angler. Today the wind is round to N & that is better. We had rather a fine display of Northern Lights on Thursday night extending from Roneval & the range of the loch up to the zenith. What a weird phenomenon it looks in this solitary country ... ... Hendersons leave on Tuesday for Rodel & on Wednesday go on direct to Glasgow arriving there on Thursday morning. We remain till Monday 4th Sept & on that day, always granted wind & weather favour the project, sail in the herring boat for Tarbert. Should that day fail & Tuesday be suitable we shall still make Tarbert by boat; if not, then to Rodel to catch the steamer there for Kyle on Wednesday 6th Sept ... . I leave accounts of our life here until we meet. Finsbay is as delightful as ever, & grows more & more upon us. The sunlit bay, the rocks tinged with the setting sun as they now are, while I write at the big oriel window in the smoke room [see Fig. 3.16 above, page 49], the "green island" where lambs just parted from their mother are passing some weeks of solitary discipline, the Dunvegan cliffs on the far side of the Minch are as enchanting as ever they were, & familiarity breeds no contempt. I refer to the Minch as lonely, for neither sail nor funnel is to be seen there nowadays, or at least seldom, unless an occasional patrol boat passes north or south. I was told by Malcolm that shippers have secret orders from Government not to sail this way, so as to avoid constant patrolling ... ... .I have walked twice to Manish & three times to Clachain. My wife too is greatly the better in mind & body of this place. She walked to Lingerbay the other day, beyond Na Creagh to call on the Sandy Morrisons[143]. She & N. Rotherham & Mrs Henderson have worked long hours at sphagnum[144]. The sun is off the bay; the cormorant sitting on a rock nearby has also gone ... ... ".

---

[143] Alexander Morrison, who owned the shop at Bayhead, Lingerbay, used to supply the milk to Finsbay Lodge. His daughter, Marion, walked over the hill to Quidinish to deliver it.

[144] Dried sphagnum moss was in great demand in the War for emergency field dressings, as it is 20 times more absorbent than cotton wool. Many civilians made big contributions to the War effort by collecting this moss

Fig. 11.1 Lord Leverhulme. The gentleman on the left, pointing, is Norman Robertson, the factor for South Harris. Reproduced by kind permission of The Leverhulme Family Archive

CHAPTER ELEVEN
LORD LEVERHULME IN HARRIS

L ord Leverhulme was the penultimate owner of Finsbay Lodge, and it was he who determined its fate, namely not to repair or maintain the Lodge which was in some state of disrepair at the time of his acquisition of it. Further, the only source of written information about the last years of Finsbay Lodge is to be found among his personal business correspondence in the Unilever Archives. Therefore some discussion about his activities is given here, though this is not the place to analyse in detail Lord Leverhulme's personality nor his great efforts to develop commercial enterprises in Harris. Good accounts about Lord Leverhulme, his work on Harris and Lewis, his fascination for designing new schemes, and his obsessive attitude to hard work have been written by several authors including: The 2nd Lord Leverhulme [98], Roger Hutchinson [99], Nigel Nicolson [93], W.P. Jolly [100] and Harley Williams [101]. The story of his efforts in Lewis and Harris and the counter-efforts by some crofters (probably a minority in Harris, but rather more in Lewis) and the involvement of the Scottish Office is well worth reading by anyone interested in social history or the history of the Western Isles. See Figs. 11.1 & 11.2.

For the benefit of those who may be unaware of Lord Leverhulme's association with Harris and Lewis, it is appropriate to give the following summary.

William Hesketh Lever (1851–1925) and his wife Elizabeth Ellen (neé Hulme) had visited Lewis in 1884, and it is said that they had one of the happiest holidays of their lives together and that it was in Lewis on this trip that he had first had the idea of specialising his business activities into the soap-making industry[145]. He clearly,

---

[145] His father had been a wholesale grocer

though, was struck by the primitive nature of the dwellings[146] and the obvious lack of opportunities for the community to prosper. Indeed, when his family house at Rivington near his native town of Bolton in Lancashire was burned down by a suffragette while he and Lady Lever were out dining with the King in 1913 he replied to a letter of sympathy with the emotive remark that "… .*no doubt she will be given a long sentence and be out in three days. She should be whipped and sent to the Isle of Lewis in NW Scotland where boats rarely call and where she could have suffrage and vote everyday of the week to her heart's content*"[102]. He later likened the poverty and hardship that he saw in Lewis to that which had existed 100 years earlier in Bolton and had now been converted into prosperity.

Lady Lever died in 1913. In 1918 Lord Leverhulme, aged 67, bought Lewis for £143,000, and he immediately made it publicly clear that he intended to bring commercial developments, especially fishing industry, to Lewis. He had rejected the idea of retirement – this was typical of the energy and personality that continually drove him. He unquestionably was a workaholic[147]. He had already made his mark on a world-wide scale by his soap industry and its overseas companies, also by the creation of the model village of Port Sunlight on the Wirral peninsula just south of Liverpool where his soap works were located. Planning new developments on a grand scale was always one of his joys, almost a hobby. His son commented that he was never happier than when seated at a drawing-board with ruler and T-square [98, p.86]. Wherever he went, his houses were always being modified and developed in grand (but successful) ways. Leverhulme had engaged expert landscapers to assist him to create memorable gardens at each of his 13 houses in the U.K[148]. While he engaged the very best professional planners and architects, as his great personal wealth enabled him to do, he enjoyed participating personally in drawing up schemes and improvements: It has been said that, if his father

---

[146] Many outsiders were so blunt as to describe them as hovels: certainly, the idea of living in the same building as one's cattle would have been most uncomfortable to visitors including Lord Leverhulme

[147] Ironically, he was a strong promoter of a shorter working day for workers (except himself), and Port Sunlight had been one of the earliest employers to institute an 8–hr working day [98, p.84]

[148] Thomas Mawson of Windermere was a close friend. Several of Leverhulme's gardens were illustrated in Mawson's classic work on landscaping [103]

had not encouraged him to enter the family grocery business, he would have wanted to become an architect. So, developing new industries and domestic improvements in Lewis became his latest activity – perhaps a hobby. In 1919 he bought South Harris from the Earl of Dunmore for £36,000[149] and, shortly afterwards, North Harris from Sir Samuel Scott for £20,000. The South Harris Estate included both Finsbay fishings and Rodel Lodge. In 1919 he gave an address in Edinburgh which summarised his opinion that " ... *Lewis and Harris have too long been the Cinderella in the Government pantomime*" [98, p.211]

While Lord Leverhulme was commercially very astute most of the time[150], he was also somewhat whimsical and he spent funds on

---

[149] In 1876, Lord Dunmore had advertised South Harris for a sale, quoting a valuation of £155,000 [76]

[150] He had some financial aberrations: for instance, he failed to realise that Lord Dunmore would cease to pay Norman Robertson's salary after selling South Harris [104]! (Lord Dunmore had been paying Norman Robertson £150 p.a.) Lord Leverhulme rectified this but, in 1922, he reduced Mr Robertson's salary on the grounds that "*the cost of living is so much reduced*" [105]

Fig. 11.2 Lord Leverhulme. Though he is sitting in the boat, it is unlikely that he has any intention of fishing! Reproduced by kind permission of The Leverhulme Family Archive

some peculiar things – for instance, he sent seeds of red flowering gum trees from Australia to his head gardener, Mr J. Stewart, in Harris as he thought that these trees would be attractive at Borve Lodge!

Understanding his way of thinking and whether the activities of his Lewis and Harris Welfare and Development Association were beneficial in the long term to the Western Isles will always be controversial and a source of debate. The same is still true of land reform issues and the relationships between tenants and proprietors. It was undoubtedly unfortunate that Leverhulme's land ownership in the Western Isles coincided with the end of the First World War, a bleak time for employment and for the national economy.

His plans were proceeding well until a major obstacle disrupted them. While many of the local crofters, unsurprisingly somewhat in awe of him, were keen to see his developments progress, others were determined to prevent him from obstructing the breaking-up of farms to provide crofts. There was a serious impasse: the Secretary for Scotland[151] had promised land for crofts to returning servicemen[152] and was minded to purchase these farms for land settlement purposes under the new legislation of the Land Settlement Act (Scotland) 1919. On the other hand, Leverhulme abhorred the crofting system as he regarded it as an impossible way to provide a decent income[153], though it must be stressed that he regularly pronounced his respect for crofters as people. He always saw them, rather than himself, as the beneficiaries of his plans, though he would always expect them to put effort into the new industries that he planned rather than be passive beneficiaries. During his ownership, the notorious "land raids" of Lewis occurred to try to force the Scottish Office to take over farms and convert them into crofts for land settlement. Such raids, though, and so-called "crofters' wars" were not new – resentment of bad (sometimes evil) landlords' behaviour to their tenants had been common in the mid-1800s and had already resulted in the Crofters' Holdings

---

[151] The title of this office became Secretary of State for Scotland in 1926

[152] Lewis and Harris contributed very large numbers of men to the 1914–18 War, and sustained great losses

[153] He had, of course, witnessed at first hand the benefits of the industrial revolution in Lancashire and the benefits of providing a good housing environment for the working community at Port Sunlight

Act 1886. This Act, aimed to provide protection for crofters, was passed in response to the Napier Commission's report[154]. Further, the Land Settlement (Scotland) Act 1919 had just been through Parliament, and Lord Leverhulme must have been freshly aware of its implications.

It is remarkable and most unfortunate that Lord Leverhulme had not foreseen the issues raised by the demands of crofters for land settlement as these had already been causing much anxiety since the mid-1800s and that he greatly underestimated the strength of the crofters' desire, above everything else, to have land. This was probably his biggest mistake in a great career. The Scottish Office was in a difficult, even untenable, position: it, and all the political parties, had committed themselves to make land available for resettlement by crofters even though it could not have, even by compulsory purchase orders, provided anything like enough land to meet fully the crofters' (especially the returning servicemen) demands[155]. On the other hand it did not want Lord Leverhulme's development plans to be axed because it saw them as a lifeline opportunity for development. It did not, though, have unreserved confidence that the plans would come to full fruition, and some political officers were said to have privately felt that Leverhulme was past his best. Leneman has recorded that Lady Cathcart had been considering offering her South Uist estate for sale to Lord Leverhulme, but she had been advised by her solicitor that *"For your Ladyship's own private information solely I may say that I have been told that his Lordship's brain power is not what it used to be ... I have an apprehension that all these Lewis schemes might tumble ... "* [106, p.67]. Lever Brothers, like every other organisation, had been affected by post-war recession. The herring fishing industry had lost much of its export market. The Company also had financial problems, albeit very temporary ones, due to a financial blunder over its purchase of the Niger Company in 1921 without realising the extent of that company's debts. In

---

[154] The Royal Commission of Inquiry into the Condition of Crofters and Cottars in the Highlands (1883–84) had been chaired by Lord Napier.

[155] Land settlement was politically a very "live" issue at this time throughout the UK, not just the Highlands and Islands. There was agreement that is was desirable to inject large amounts of money into the procurement for crofters, irrespective of the potential financial return. The plans were an investment only in terms of goodwill rather than with expectation of financial benefits.

the Western Isles, haste and obstinacy prevailed on both sides. An impasse developed, and the situation caused Leverhulme to leave Lewis, donating it to the people though only the town of Stornoway was actually taken up[156] in this way.

Colin MacDonald[157], himself a highlander from a Ross-shire crofting family, who wrote from first-hand understanding of the Scottish Office viewpoint and from several personal meetings with Lord Leverhulme, summed up the story briefly but clearly in his *Highland Journey or Sùil air Ais*. Among all the written accounts and prejudiced pontification on the situation, his account is unique in providing first-hand insight and honest recollections of both sides. It was clear that he did not relish his task of being the Scottish Office's "man on the scene". His account ended with the following conversation just after Leverhulme had met the land-raiding crofters which gives unusual insight into Leverhulme's misjudgement of the importance of land to the crofters, a rare admission from the great man:

> "When I joined Lord Leverhulme later in a near-by shooting lodge he was in great form, and it was with keen regret that I began the task of disillusioning him. At first he was incredulous. He could not understand what he called such "double dealing." I tried to explain and let both sides down gently. When he realised the truth he became very downcast. But after a few minutes he brightened up and said: "Anyhow, that was a great meeting! They are an intelligent people, and I never give up hope so long as I have an intelligent opposition to deal with. Besides, there is not the same enjoyment in things that are easily won. I am enjoying this fight and I shall win them over yet!"

> "I am very sorry," said I, "to have to resort again to the cold-water jug, but if you could see the position as I see it you would be less optimistic—unless you are prepared to compromise on the question of the land, which I venture to think you could do without material hurt to your schemes."

> "I shall *not* compromise," he retorted with emphasis, "and as for optimism, I have always been an optimist. I am like the Irishman who fell from the roof of a New York skyscraper. His

---

156 By the Stornoway Trust
157 Colin MacDonald (1882–1957) was a senior member of the Board (later Department) of Agriculture and was the Gaelic-speaking member of the Scottish Land Court

friend working at a window lower down yelled as Pat shot past: 'Hello, Pat! Are yez all roight?' 'Yes, bejabbers,' shouted Pat, 'so far!'" [107, p.149]

Leneman [106, p.117–131] has analysed the Scottish Office correspondence, including Thomas Wilson's reports to the Board of Agriculture (she quoted from [108]), and she sums up the situation fairly:

> *"No one could accuse Leverhulme of self-interest. He had radical plans to improve the living standards of the Lewis people by transforming the economy of the island, and he injected large amounts of his own capital in order to do so. His genuine concern for the people was unquestioned. The difficulty was that he had fixed ideas about what was and what was not good for them, and crofting was anathema to him..........*
>
> *Wilson sent a long report back to the Chairman on 26 September 1918. He found Leverhulme totally opposed to the tenure of Small Landholders Acts and convinced that his various plans (developing the fisheries and establishing a canning industry, establishing weaving sheds and developing a tweed industry, and so on) would solve everything. Wilson wrote:*

With his aspirations I expressed the most cordial sympathy and approval. I am satisfied his Lordship has taken up the Lewis problem with the intention of solving it, and he has the energy and resolve to carry his plans to completion. He has great admiration for the Lewis people, who have done such great and noble service for the Country in the War, and I think feels he should do what he can for them. His whole life, however, has been industrial, and I question if his experience of three months among the Lewis people has taught him their sentiments or desires. He does not realise that they will never feel satisfied until the farms in Lewis are divided into Holdings and given to them. The Lewisman is not by sentiment, tradition or inclination at all inclined to become a Factory-hand, and the present race cannot be satisfied by industrial methods alone... the older people will not change their present mode of life no matter what his Lordship may do. What the Lewis man wants is a small piece of land for a house site, two cows grazing and potato and corn growing. That is his ideal and it cannot be eradicated—save by allowing the present generation to die out and train up the young generation coming......... That Lord Leverhulme is convinced the solution of the Lewis problem

GROUP OF FISH WORKERS AT LEVERBURGH

Fig. 11.3 A brief period of glory with excellent herring catches at Leverburgh. This postcard picture must have been taken in 1924

lies in the development of industrialism seems to me clear, and that he is honestly bent on taking such measures as will in his opinion solve that problem I have no doubt. But the mass of the people of Lewis are quite convinced and determined that the land must be given them, and I do not think any solution will be final which does not give them the land.

Wilson also suggested that it would do no harm to suspend further consideration of the schemes briefly to give Leverhulme time to assess them. However, Leverhulme was to prove immovable." [106]

Following his departure from Lewis which caused considerable sadness both to him and to part of the local population, Lord Leverhulme concentrated his efforts on Harris; here he had begun to establish a major fishing industry based around An t-Ob (re-named Leverburgh in 1920). Crofters in Harris were notably less militant over the land settlement issues than the Lewis men had been, possibly because there were hardly any large farms in Harris suitable for land settlement purposes. There was, however, some opposition to his schemes and a good deal of scepticism as to whether they would be successful – a completely understandable reaction since they were so revolutionary, also because the population of the Outer Hebrides had previously witnessed some extremely bad experiences, as well as some good ones, at the hands of landlords.

While his developments at Leverburgh were still not complete, enough work had been done for herring drifters from Fleetwood to operate from there in 1924. The results, closely watched by Leverhulme[158], were exceptionally good, considerably greater than the catches landed at Stornoway (Fig. 11.3).

While this augured well for his schemes, which were going to be extended to white fish in 1925, nobody could have predicted the future demise of the herring industry which had enjoyed such buoyancy in Scotland. Hence it cannot fairly be said that Lord Leverhulme's death had snatched Leverburgh's future wealth from the people. As more recent events have shown, the Scottish sea-fishing industry has a precarious history. Iain Anderson, a visitor from Giffnock with considerable affection for the Hebrides, described the scene in 1937: *"Leverburgh is the most pitiful sight in the whole Hebrides, but still in its dismal ruin a glorious memorial to one who sought to do a great thing for the Outer Isles – Lord Leverhulme"* [109, p.177]

Finally, while huge construction work at Leverburgh and its pier was continuing, Lord Leverhulme unexpectedly died of pneumonia in May 1925 at his London home. He had just returned, full of vitality, from a 6 month tour of his estates in the Congo where he had plantations for palm oil production. His activities in Lewis and Harris had been personal ones, distinct from the commercial activities of Lever Bros (though very entangled with them through complex company subsidiaries); the board of Lever Bros had no hesitation, on his death, in winding-up these Hebridean ventures.

People are still divided in their opinions as to whether Lord Leverhulme's motives in the Western Isles were for his own benefit or for the people's good. Having read most of his biographies

---

158 He personally watched the initial landings by 12 Fleetwood drifters; later he insisted on receiving daily telegrams about the catches

and some of his personal correspondence, I have no hesitation in concluding that his intentions were wholly philanthropic and that his critics have studied only part of the complex story of a very unusual man whose personality was difficult to understand. He had no interests in making money for himself from the Lewis and Harris activities. Unfortunately, he despised the term "philanthropy" as, to him, it implied giving money with no expectation of a return of effort by the recipient. Leverhulme already had accumulated immense personal wealth[159] and had spent huge sums in Lewis and Harris[160], so a financial gain to him was not relevant. There are many examples of how he declined personal income in Lewis and Harris in favour of the monies being given to local charities: for several years he declined to let the potentially lucrative fishings of the Grimersta and other rivers. He chose to keep them for providing hospitality to his personal guests; on occasions when he granted an outsider permission to fish (he turned down many requests), he would make a charge but donate the proceeds to charities in Lewis or Harris. In 1921, he charged £4–4s for a day's fishing on the Grimersta, and a smaller sum for other systems[161] [111]. Welfare in communities was of great importance to him both in the Hebrides and at Port Sunlight.

It is clear from his correspondence with Norman Robertson, his highly respected Factor in South Harris, that Lord Leverhulme had been reluctant to buy Finsbay Lodge and that he initially did not see any merit in refurbishing it. However, it must be said that Finsbay Lodge, being one of the largest buildings in the Western Isles, was not an economically attractive proposition, quite apart from its physically deteriorated condition. Lord Leverhulme did not respond to Norman Robertson's suggestion that a new, but smaller lodge, should be built there to provide accommodation for fishing tenants. However, as explained in Chapter 3, he eventually did look at the possibilities of repairing Finsbay Lodge and an alternative idea of moving it to Leverburgh to accommodate people

---

159 His personal wealth in 1921 was stated to be £9,486,954 [93, p.167]
160 His expenditure in Lewis & Harris was estimated to be £1,400,000 [93, p.237]
161 In 1915, the Lewis estate was charging £120 per month for Grimersta fishing, exclusive of accommodation. Rents at Morsgail, Uig, Gress, and Soval were £80, £75, £30, and £30 respectively, inclusive of use of a lodge [110]

associated with his works there. This latter idea is an example of Lord Leverhulme's highly imaginative approach to his projects.

Lord Leverhulme's ownership of Finsbay Lodge has gone almost entirely unnoticed. Indeed, his biographer, the late Nigel Nicolson who had conducted extensive research including studying the Unilever Archives and the sale particulars for Leverhulme's properties in 1925, told the author in 2003 that he had never heard of Finsbay Lodge.

One might wonder what role Lord Leverhulme played in the sporting fishings of Harris. The answer appears to be remarkably little. Leverhulme was personally not keen on sports though in his younger days till about 1897 he enjoyed shooting [98, p.101], and he certainly appreciated the pleasure that he could give to his guests by providing shooting and fishing. His son recalled that Lord Leverhulme had rented a moor in 1898 specifically to entertain his relatives and friends though, by this time, he did not carry a gun. However, by the time he had come to the Western Isles he had developed a rather cynical attitude to shooting:

> "Up goes 10/-, bang goes 2d, down comes half-a-crown ... I am not at all enamoured with the game-keeping side of life here in Lewis. It does not appeal to me at all to keep a number of strong healthy men[162] looking after pheasants, rabbits, deer, salmon[163]etc, when the country is wanting men to make roads, cultivate the soil for food and carry on the life of the nation. I feel myself entirely out of sympathy with it ... " [93, p.66]

Nevertheless, Lord Leverhulme enjoyed entertaining guests, and he was keen to ensure that they had access to good sport, though it appears that some of those from his Port Sunlight staff came and participated more out of a sense of duty (a refusal might have been very detrimental for them!) than out of pleasure. If Leverhulme had been an avid sportsman himself, one suspects that Finsbay Lodge (or another building on the same site) might have enjoyed a renaissance after the departure of the Hebridean Sporting Association.

Sadly, there are now not many tangible signs of his Landlord-

---

[162] At this time, 1918, the estates directly employed 11 gamekeepers, 25 game-watchers, and 28 foresters [men involved with the deer forests, not with trees]

[163] This rather indignant outburst was not consistent with his subsequent establishment of a salmon hatchery at Borve Lodge!

ship in Harris, apart from the name Leverburgh (formerly An t-Ob until 1920, the manner of the re-naming being discussed in Nigel Nicolson's *Lord of the Isles*, page 210) and several streets and buildings named after him. The construction of several roads, including the "peat road" from Leverburgh to Finsbay (which passes L. Na Moracha and L. Langavat) and the east-coast road to Tarbert, the road to Kyles Scalpay, and the road to Hushinish, was substantially funded by him[164], though few drivers on these roads will be aware of this fact! Nigel Nicolson commented that *"today, though it requires steady nerves and sound tyres to make the passage by car from Leverburgh through Finsbay up the east coast to Tarbert, the roads that he made in Harris, almost as an afterthought and to meet a sudden emergency, have become Leverhulme's chief legacy to the island"* [93, p.223]. The magnificent round-walled garden at Borve Lodge, now a private residence, is still kept in immaculate condition unlike other of his gardens elsewhere in the U.K.

Undoubtedly, Leverhulme, while a generous benefactor who pumped huge amounts of his personal wealth into developments for the islanders, attempted to do far too much and far too fast. He totally failed to appreciate the personal characteristics of the islanders, their natural slowness of pace, and their demand for land which had been precipitated both by harsh and cruel land-owning tyrants and by their needs to survive in a difficult environment for agriculture, as well as their fierce loyalty to their native background. In such a situation it was inevitable that Landlord-Tenant relationships would be complex. As in other small island communities, it was (and still is) inevitable that there was a paradoxical mixture of mutual resentment and mutual interdependence, a sort of constant love-hate tense relationship. Lord Leverhulme never could understand the extent of this, a situation to which he had hardly been exposed in his developments at Port Sunlight with the mainland Lever Bros. workforce.

Leverhulme's desire to make the crofters take up more productive (in his eyes) employment than crofting further sensitized the local community's schism between Landlord and Tenant/Crofter, a consequence originally of harsh and greedy landlords and their

---

[164] He pressed the government to proceed with making these roads, especially to provide employment during the winter crisis of 1923, by guaranteeing to pay half the cost

highland clearances. On the other hand, it forced the Scottish Office to take a strong interest in the Western Isles and the issues of land ownership, and its support and beneficence has been significant over a long time – e.g. in the provision and maintenance of a strong integrated transport system and attempting to support crofting, rather than extinguishing it as Leverhulme would have preferred. There can be no doubt that Leverhulme, like many business innovators, had a complex personality – an utopian mixture of workaholic, innovation, benevolence, loneliness, and an expectation of development and perfection that could never be fulfilled. His reception in the Western Isles, though, was always bound to be dependent upon the environmental and genetic background of the island community, factors way beyond his control. Any fair analysis, though, should agree that he left a trail of generous philanthropy wherever he went; the disagreements that arose over land settlement issues were unfortunate, but inevitable. While other people might have handled the land settlement issues more sensitively, there was no one else with the personal wealth, ambition for planning, and energy to hasten new developments for Harris and Lewis. However, the Harris and Lewis of the late 20th century was already very different and well progressed from the region familiar to Lord Leverhulme. It will be interesting to look back in a hundred years time how the recent political and community initiatives in land reform have developed.

CHAPTER TWELVE
THOMAS WILSON AND ARCHIE CHISHOLM – PIONEERS OF LAND REFORM

Both these gentlemen were shareholders in the Hebridean Sporting Association, the only people in Harris and the Uists, apart from Mr Wilson's second wife, to be shareholders. However, their significance to the story and to the Hebridean community is far greater.

Archibald (Archie) Alexander Chisholm (1859–1933), a native of Kiltarity near Strathglass, Inverness-shire, was a notable figure in the Western Isles for several quite separate reasons. See Figs. 12.1 & 12.2. Professionally, he was the Procurator Fiscal for the Western Isles, based in Lochmaddy, North Uist from 1881 till 1913, and he had practised as a solicitor there for at least some time under the name Chisholm & Co[165]. He was also a most accomplished photographer, responsible for many fine picture postcards of the Western Isles including the best known picture of Finsbay Lodge (Fig. 3.8 above). The Hebridean Sporting Association's accounts show that the Lodge had a considerable stock of postcards (worth £8–3s-0d in 1916), presumably emanating from Chisholm's camera. The fact that he had been responsible for the Gaelic postcard series Cairt Phostail had nearly faded into oblivion until Bob Charnley, an avid collector of Hebridean postcards who had a great interest and talent for discovering their origin, launched an investigation into these postcards. Bob Charnley was a retired police detective and he tracked down a cousin of Archie Chisholm, a Miss Josephine Chisholm, who confirmed – seemingly unequivocally – that

---

[165] At this time it was quite common for the Procurator Fiscal also to run a legal practice, on the grounds that in remote areas there would be insufficient work to employ a full-time Procurator Fiscal. This was in due course outlawed because of the potential for conflicts of interest

Archie Chisholm had been the photographer of the entire Cairt Phostail series. This has recently been confirmed to me by Alastair Chisholm, who has a good collection of his grandfather's photographs. Mr Archie Chisholm was a member of the Hebridean Sporting Association, though we do not know whether he fished or not! If he was not an angler, then his shareholding may have been a matter of support for a worthwhile local venture; alternatively, but much less likely, it might have been a gift from the founding directors. He was a close friend and professional associate of Thomas Wilson. In 1913 he became Sheriff Clerk of Inverness-shire, where he had been deputy Sheriff Clerk before he had gone to Lochmaddy. One of his daughters, Margaret, became deputy Sheriff Clerk in Lochmaddy in the 1940s.

Archie Chisholm's father-in-law, Alexander McHardy (1839–1911), had been a Chief Constable for the remarkable period of 45 years, first in Sutherland, then in Inverness-shire. In the latter capacity, he had been involved in trying to maintain peace and order during the Glendale riots on the Isle of Skye and, later, would have become involved in any police action in the land agitation cases in North Uist. Incidentally, Mr McHardy had been a keen angler and golfer, being responsible for the foundation of the renowned Dornoch Golf Links [112].

Archie Chisholm had a great interest in Highland history. As soon as he moved to Inverness in 1913, he joined the Inverness Field Club and Scientific Society, becoming a Council member from 1914–18 and from 1924–1926 and President in 1923–1924. He presented extracts from ancient documents on topics such as mortcloths and coffin-coverings [113], "A few Vestiges of Old Days" especially on northern place-names and Norse influence [114], and on the indentures of an apprentice chirurgeon-barber and periwig maker in Inverness in 1710 [115]. At a meeting in 1927, he gave a paper on "In Western Fringes of Our Shire" which included his comments on land reform issues thus: "*Passing to his experiences in the Islands, the story of the Land Agitations, the ineptitude with which politicians and notably the Board of Agriculture had dealt with the problem was amusingly related"* [116][166]. He also became a founder of the Inverness Rotary Club, one of the oldest in Scotland.

Thomas Wilson (1856–1936) was born in Wick, the son of Peter Wilson, a fishery officer who was regarded as an expert on herring. Initially he pursued a career in Edinburgh as a law agent in partnership with his brother David Hay Wilson. Unfortunately, Thomas became bankrupt, and David was expelled from the Society of Solicitors to the Supreme Court due to an incident in Court. Thomas then went in 1882 to Lochmaddy as solicitor, initially working with Chisholm & Co. In due course he held a great many public appointments throughout the Long Island, including as Parish Clerk for Harris, until he left in 1911 to become Factor and law agent for the Congested Districts Board (which became the Department of Agriculture's) lands on Skye – he was well prepared for this post as he had a great interest in land settlement schemes. While he was in Lochmaddy, he was Factor for the Earl of Dunmore and Viscount Fincastle[167]; it is almost certain that he would have drawn up the leases for the Hebridean Sporting Association's tenancies in Harris. Indeed, without his personal co-operation, it is unlikely that the Association could ever have been founded or floated as a Company[168]. It is likely that he saw the Association's ventures in Harris as excellent employment opportunities for

---

166 The subsequent sentence in these Minutes that *"This led to a* [word obliterated] *of the evil effect of deer forests and emigration of the population, whose fine qualities deserved better treatment"* was scored through, presumably before the Minutes were approved. Perhaps his views were too forthright for other members.

167 He was succeeded in 1911 by Norman Robertson, and it appears that the factorship then became a full-time occupation

168 In commenting on Mr Wilson's request to the G.P.O. for an extension of the telegraph to Finsbay in 1903, Mr MacGregor, Secretary of the Congested Districts Board, had commented that *" ... he has recently been involved in floating a company, The Hebridean Sporting Association Limited ... "* [89]. It is perfectly possible, especially in view of his and his wife's shareholding, that Thomas Wilson was the instigator of the whole venture

people in Harris as ghillies and domestic staff at Finsbay Lodge and Rodel Lodge. He was a frequent correspondent to official bodies such as the Congested Districts Board and the General Post Office, requesting improved facilities at Finsbay. His fluency in both Gaelic and English made him a particularly valuable advocate for the local community in discussions with external bodies. Hamish Stuart names him as being involved in the creation of Loch Fincastle, and *The Scotsman* article discussed in Chapter 7 gives him substantial credit for the fishing developments in Harris implying that Wilson was knowledgeable about trout breeding. His personal thoughts and motives about the Hebridean Sporting Association will, I suspect, never be known.

Thomas Wilson appears to have lived in both Lochmaddy and Harris. At the time of his first marriage in 1892 to Mary Reid, his address was Lochmaddy. At the time of his second marriage which was to Christina Paterson from Berneray, 1901, his address was stated to be Luskentyre[169], Harris as it was at the time when he joined the Hebridean Sporting Association in 1903 as a shareholder. However at the 1901 Census date he was resident in the Lochmaddy Hotel. Later, he and Mrs Christina Wilson were at the Coffee House in An t-Ob, till they left around 1909 – after the haunting incident, and probably just after the fire there. In 1909–10, he was a tenant at 1 Northton, Harris. Subsequently they lived at Taigh na Hearradh (Harris House) in Lochmaddy. His early years in the Western Isles had been punctuated by very unhappy events: his own bankruptcy in 1882–85 and the suicide of his first wife (Mary Reid) by drinking liquid ammonia in 1885 at his brother Peter's Manse in Greenlaw, Berwickshire where he was United Presbyterian minister. Her death was just six months after the birth of their daughter, Alice Margaret Wilson, in Lochmaddy: it appears from Thomas Wilson's Will that Alice subsequently went to Vancouver.

Both Wilson and Chisholm featured prominently in a legal dispute and eviction proceedings with Sir John Campbell-Orde (1827–1897)[170], the proprietor of North Uist. Part of this colourful

---

169 He probably lived at Luskentyre farm. Alasdair Alpin MacGregor tells an amusing story about three Thomases who tenanted Luskentyre farm successively [48, p.145]. We do not know if Thomas Wilson was one of these, but it seems likely.

170 He was the 3rd baronet and had changed his name in 1880 from Sir John William Powlett Orde

story is told in Bob Charnley's (1992) first volume of postcard pictures *The Western Isles: A Postcard Tour – Barra to North Uist*, though Charnley was never able to establish the cause of the acrimonious rift between these two legal men and Sir John Campbell-Orde. Thomas Wilson gave evidence to the Royal Commission on the Highlands and Islands (chaired by Sheriff Brand[171]) in 1892, speaking out vigorously against Sir John Campbell-Orde. The Royal Commission published, at Wilson's request, full copies of no less than 21 mainly vituperative letters between Wilson and Chisholm and Campbell-Orde's solicitors. Additionally, the pro-land reform newspaper *The Scottish Highlander*[172] also published a considerable number of letters from both Chisholm and Wilson, and these strongly hint that the rift started in the early 1880s when Campbell-Orde asked the legal firm of Chisholm & Co to act for him in a contested action to evict crofters[173]. Chisholm and Wilson had strong empathy with the crofters, and I believe that they refused to act as legal agents on behalf of Campbell-Orde. This must have infuriated the landowner.

All accounts of evictions by Campbell-Orde lend weight to the view that he had adopted an anti-crofter stance and continually was behaving in a harassing way towards them – it was behaviour of this nature by various proprietors in the Highlands and Islands that had already led to the Napier Commission and then provoked the passing of the Crofters' Holdings Act (Scotland) 1886 to protect crofters from abuse. It appears that Campbell-Orde paid little heed to the new legislation, and there is some evidence that Chisholm photographed some crofting evictions on North Uist. At one stage Campbell-Orde denied Thomas Wilson access to any accommodation on North Uist, so that Wilson was obliged at one time to live on a barge moored in Lochmaddy harbour. He also refused to grant a lease to Archie Chisholm. Accounts in *The Scottish Highlander* reported evocative scenes such as that when

---

171 Sheriff Brand, sheriff of Ayr, was Chairman of the Crofters' Commission

172 *The Scottish Highlander* had been founded and was edited by John Murdoch (1818–1903), a founder of the Gaelic Society of Inverness [117]

173 The majority of members of the Napier Commission (1883–4) had expressed disapproval of Procurators Fiscal being allowed to engage in private legal practice, and they had been emphatic that the Procurator Fiscal should not work for landed proprietors.

Campbell-Orde blocked off access to Lochmaddy pier, and Wilson leaped over the wall to establish a public right of way! Matters both for crofters and for Wilson and Chisholm became substantially more harmonious after the death of Sir John Campbell-Orde when he was succeeded by his son, Sir Arthur John Campbell-Orde (1865–1933). Archie Chisholm got his house, Ostram House (now a youth hostel), and Thomas Wilson was able to build Taigh na Hearradh in 1901–1904, which is a fine house with outstanding views; it subsequently was acquired by the Health Board for the local doctor, and it is now the residence of a retired Lochmaddy doctor.

Wilson explained his familiarity with the Long Island to the Brand Royal Commission: "… *I have been through their homes in every district; I have travelled on foot through almost every inch of the Long Island time after time. I have been in crofters' houses and cottars' houses and houses of every description, and have been constantly among the people, and I should say that I know them as well as any man at the present day … . I have a very high opinion of the people of these islands …* " [118, p.1004–1018]

Two of the other grievances expressed by Wilson and Chisholm were that they believed that the Procurator Fiscal, as Crown Agent, ought to be able to have a house, independent of any individual land proprietor; and they also considered it grossly unjust that the Lord Advocate was acting as private counsel to Sir John Campbell-Orde and, so, could not be impartial in any complaint against Campbell-Orde.

Wilson had assisted the Congested Districts Board as far back as 1898, and a curious exchange of correspondence occurred about his remuneration for such work [119]. Wilson wrote to the Secretary for Scotland pointing out that his travel to Edinburgh for a meeting of the Board had caused him to lose 8 working days, and he sought payment instead of just expenses. He had been given £1–1–0d per night plus £5–2–6d for conveyance, while the usual professional fee would have been £3 per day. After deliberations at the highest level, the Secretary of the Congested Districts Board, R.R. MacGregor, was instructed to reply that "… *you were not invited to appear before the Board in your capacity as a lawyer but as the local Factor on an estate and as one with great local experience and interest in the crofters' welfare. The Board considers therefore that you can not be awarded more than the sum granted to witnesses before Royal Commissions or other Public Enquiries …* ". [119]

It is clear that Thomas Wilson had become an acknowledged expert on crofting law and was highly regarded by the Department of Agriculture at the Scottish Office. I believe that his bad experiences under Sir John Campbell-Orde in North Uist are likely to have influenced his opinion on landlords in general and, subsequently, on Lord Leverhulme's activities in Lewis and Harris. As mentioned in Chapter 11, some critics felt that the Scottish Office had taken too much heed of Wilson's views and that he represented the crofting interests excessively strongly to Robert Munro, Secretary for Scotland at the Scottish Office, at the time when the Scottish Office had to decide whether to take sides with the land-raiding crofters in Lewis or with Leverhulme or work towards a compromise.

At first thought it is perhaps surprising that Thomas Wilson mentioned above, having been Factor to Lord Dunmore, took sides against Lord Leverhulme when the Scottish Office sought to exercise their powers under the Small Landholders (Scotland) Act 1911 and the Land Settlement (Scotland) Act 1919 to protect the crofters. The harsh treatment of Wilson and Chisholm by Campbell-Orde had already made Wilson strongly sympathetic to the crofters' cause by the time when he gained the influential position of sub-commissioner to the Board of Agriculture (forerunner of the Department of Agriculture and Fisheries, now the Scottish Environment Protection Agency) at the Scottish Office. It is remarkable that a landed proprietor like Campbell-Orde would make life so difficult for such an important public figure and legal officer as the Procurator Fiscal, Chisholm. Hence, Campbell-Orde's activities may well have set the scene for the official reception of Lord Leverhulme's efforts in Harris and Lewis at the Scottish Office. The thorough analysis by Nigel Nicolson in *Lord of the Isles* also concluded that Wilson had been strongly influential, though it appears that Nicolson had not been aware of the great antagonism between Campbell-Orde and Wilson. Nicolson's view was that *"Robert Munro [Secretary for Scotland, later Lord Alness] ... was ill advised. Thomas Wilson was so deeply sympathetic to the raiders' cause that his counsel should have been suspected ... "* [93, p. 181]

Thomas Wilson's second wife (marriage in 1901), Christina (Kirsty) Paterson (1882–1914)[174] from Berneray, was the only lady

---

[174] She died of Scarlet Fever with septicaemia (*Scarlatina maligna*)

shareholder in the Hebridean Sporting Association. Her address then was at Luskentyre, probably Luskentyre Farm, when the first share register was drawn up in 1903. Her shareholding[175] is an intriguing mystery: were the Wilsons so keen to support the venture that they put their own money into it, did they expect to make a big capital gain[176], or were they given shares, perhaps by John Malcolm, as thanks for assistance rendered? She went on to run a Temperance Hotel ("The Coffee House") in An t-Ob which was established by Lady Dunmore to provide refreshments and some accommodation for the lobster fishermen. It also housed the South Harris Estate Office[177]. This building gained some notoriety for being haunted. When one of the maids left, the ghost ceased to appear [48, p.97–99]. Shortly afterwards, the house was burned down, and its condition in the Inland Revenue's Valuation survey (approx. 1911) was stated to be "ruinous". However, the house was rebuilt, and remains as a private dwelling.

Thomas Wilson's third marriage (1916) was to Wilhelmina Macleod (1868–1938), the sister of Sir John Lorne Macleod (1873–1946) who had been Lord Provost of Edinburgh during the First World War and who was the Chairman of the Highlands and Islands Fund[178] and Chief of the Gaelic Society of Inverness (1923–24). The Gaelic Society had been one of the bodies to complain most vociferously about Lord Leverhulme taking the title Viscount Leverhulme of the Western Isles when he was elevated to his Viscountcy in 1922. It seems inconceivable that Wilson would not have discussed the Leverhulme land issues with his brother-in-law.

It should be said, though, that Wilson was not totally opposed to Leverhulme's plans for development. Leah Leneman gave a very

---

175 She also had a holding of Preference Shares. She transferred her shares to her husband in 1913

176 Thomas Wilson (and Sir John Dewar MP) had the largest number of shares (20) in the Association, and Mrs Wilson had 15 shares. Thus the Wilsons together had the biggest investment

177 At some stage after the fire, the estate office was moved to Claremont in Tarbert

178 This had been set up to relieve hardship due to depressed conditions in the agriculture and fishing industries, and it was involved with the handing over the hereditary lands of MacLeod on Skye to the Board of Agriculture in 1920. Wilson acted as Factor for the Board of Agriculture to manage these lands

fair analysis of the Scottish Office correspondence on the matter, including quoting from an astute letter from Thomas Wilson to the Board of Agriculture which is reproduced above (page 169) [106, p.118–119]. This shows that Wilson saw the benefits of Leverhulme's schemes and realised the real need for such developments; at the same time, he knew very well the deep-rooted sentiments of the local population. He clearly envisaged that the situation could change over time with generational change.

Both Thomas Wilson and Archie Chisholm also gave influential and well-informed evidence to the Highlands and Islands Medical Service Committee in 1912, making a good case for improved medical services in the Highlands and Islands. Arising out of this, the Dewar report [120] highlighted many difficulties with service provision and promptly led to the formation of the Highlands and Islands Medical Scheme, a very successful forerunner of the National Health Service. Perhaps Wilson and Chisholm, together with Sir John Dewar, their fellow member of the Hebridean Sporting Association, deserve some credit for the ideology of the U.K. National Health Service?

Both Wilson and Chisholm worked tirelessly to assist the crofting communities. Wilson became particularly involved in government-supported land settlement schemes to the extent that he became the Department of Agriculture's Factor on Skye. His obituary in *The Scotsman* reported that: "... ... *[he] was well known throughout the Highlands and Islands in connection with land settlement schemes. He was for many years a practising solicitor at Lochmaddy North Uist, and held, at one time, practically all the local appointments in the Long Island. In 1911 he was appointed Factor and law agent under the late Congested Districts Board, and in 1912 was transferred to the Board of Agriculture for Scotland, and served as Sub-Commissioner and Senior Sub-Commissioner for Small Holdings until 1933. After his retirement, he served as temporary Senior Sub-Commissioner for Small Holdings, and Factor for the Western Island properties of the Department of Agriculture, and he continued as Factor until the end of 1925. Throughout Mr Wilson's official service, he was engaged almost entirely on land settlement schemes in the North-Western Highlands and Islands, of which he had an almost unique knowledge. An acknowledged authority on the Crofters Acts and land legislation; he was a man of great ability and outstanding personality and character, and was most devoted in all his work for the welfare of the people of the Islands, being highly regarded among the crofting community ... ."* [112]

Likewise, his headstone in Uig cemetery carries the epitaph: *"A devoted worker for land settlement in the Highlands and Islands and a friend of the people"*. At his death in 1936 he left an estate of just £142; he had already left his house in Uig, Salen Cottage, and its contents to his son, Harris Thomas Wilson.

While Thomas Wilson and Archie Chisholm were opposed to harsh landlordism and, so, were demanding land reform, there is no evidence that they sought community ownership as the present political advocates of land reform do.

CHAPTER THIRTEEN
PEOPLE INVOLVED WITH THE HEBRIDEAN SPORTING ASSOCIATION AND FINSBAY LODGE

The Lodge (with rooms for about 20 guests and with some 30 fishing boats on their numerous lochs) provided a considerable amount of employment for local people, both as domestic staff and as ghillies for the fishing. Hence, the activities of the Hebridean Sporting Association were very beneficial to the community: this may have been a key motivating factor in Thomas Wilson's involvement, though the prospect of financial gain may also have driven him. In turn, it is clear that the local community contributed enormously to the success of the venture. The following were some of the staff engaged at Finsbay Lodge:

- **Sam Morrison** (see below) as Keeper and Manager who lived in the adjacent Keeper's Cottage;
- **Christina (Kirsty) Morrison** (1864–1944), 2nd wife of Sam, the Keeper – we suppose she worked there, but her role is unknown – it is plausible that she was the Housekeeper;
- **Jane Cunningham** (1880–1951), 6 Geocrab; and her sister
- **Margaret Cunningham** (1878–1946), 1 Finsbay; and her husband
- **Donald Campbell** (1873–1951), Merchant and Postmaster, 1 Finsbay;
- **Jock (Seocam) MacKenzie** (1877–1970), fisherman, as ghillie; and his brother
- **Dugald MacKenzie** (1875–1961), fisherman, as ghillie; and his wife
- **Margaret MacAskill** (d. 1907) from Bernera;
- **Dougal MacKay** (son of Big Angus);
- **Donald Morrison**;

Fig. 13.1 Family
relationships of people
involved with Finsbay
Lodge. Names in
dotted-line boxes are
known to have worked
at, or otherwise
been closely involved
with, the Lodge. For
clarity and reasons of
space, not all family
members are shown;
also, siblings are not
necessarily shown in
order of age as would
be conventional. Dates
and addresses are
taken from statutory
Births, Deaths, and
Marriage records,
Bill Lawson's Croft
Histories [121, 122],
and various personal
communications

- **Marion MacLeod** (1894–1975)[179]
- **John MacKinnon** (1867–1945), 10 Quidinish, as ghillie;[180]
- **John MacKay** as ghillie; and
- **John MacLeod** (1885–1964) from Berneray, as steward (see below).

It is clear that many families in Harris were involved in the running of the whole venture and its success. Not surprisingly for an island community, many of the staff employed at Finsbay Lodge were related to each other – in a sense, we can see that running the Lodge was a sort of family activity.

Fig. 13.1 is a genealogy chart showing the relationships between the various families involved: those known to have been involved directly with the Lodge are shown in dotted boxes. It looks as though Sam Morrison, the Keeper and Manager, who is seen at the right of the chart, had actively recruited many relations to service Finsbay Lodge – this, of course, was of great benefit to the Hebridean Sporting Association. Sam was described in some of the Valuation Rolls as Manager, and one can suppose that Sam acted also as the equivalent of a mini-Estate Factor rather than simply as a gamekeeper.

All indications are that Finsbay Lodge and its people enjoyed a very good relationship with the community. An interesting comment made by one of the older Quidinish people with long family associations was that he had never heard a bad word said about the Lodges (both Finsbay and Horsacleit); and it is clear that some of the people associated with the Lodge, particularly Professor and Mrs Thomas Purdie were keen to relate closely with the community. Finsbay School regularly held its sports day at the Lodge, and Mrs Purdie was particularly prominent in helping the school. The school log book records that:

19 August, 1908: Professor Purdie of St Andrews University and Mrs Purdie both of whom are at present staying in Finsbay Lodge gave a nice treat to the scholars attending the school before closing for the day.

27 August 1909: School closed today for 6 weeks holidays … prizes were presented by a Paisley gentleman who was on holiday at Finsbay Lodge

---

[179] She subsequently was cook for Professor Henderson at Horsaclett, so it is possible that she was a cook at Finsbay Lodge

[180] Just possibly, John Mackinnon or John MacKay may have been Professor Irvine's ghillie, referred to in his letters to his wife in 1914

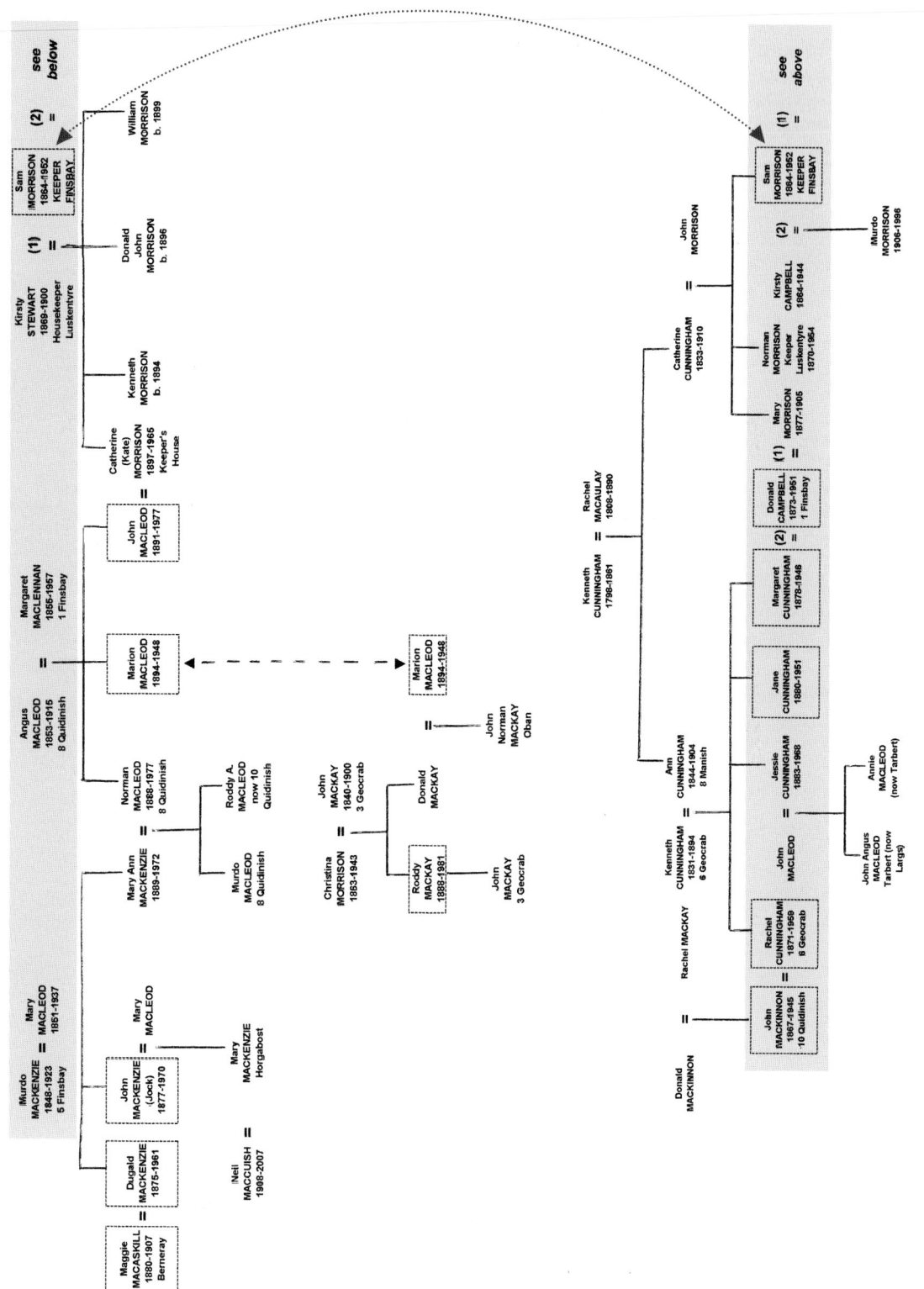

16 July 1914: … . Mrs Dr Purdie called to ask the children to a tea at the lodge

31 August 1914: The school was closed for the holiday today. Mrs Purdie and her niece Miss Rotherham called.

Fig 13.2 shows the Finsbay School sports day, pictured at Finsbay Lodge in around 1912–1914. Some of the people have been tentatively identified, and it is suspected that Mrs Purdie and her niece, Agnes Rotherham, are also present.

Fig. 13.2 Finsbay School Sports Day held at Finsbay Lodge. Reproduced by kind permission of the Harris Historical Society and John Murdo Morrison. The date is probably 1912–1914 and the identities of the numbered people are believed to be as follows:

1. DUGALD MACKENZIE (b. 1875) Crofter at 4 Finsbay and a regular ghillie over many years. Uncle (mother's brother) of Roddy A. Macleod who made the colour painting of Finsbay Lodge.

2. MORAG MACKENZIE of 4 Finsbay, Dugald's (1 above) sister; Aunt (mother's sister) of Roddy A. Macleod

3. ANNIE MACLEOD (b. 1897) of 8 Quidinish (later Mrs Alec Maclennan of 2 Finsbay); also an aunt (father's sister) of Roddy A. Macleod.

4. MAIRI MACKENZIE of 4 Finsbay, another sister of Dugald (1 above); later Mrs Kenneth Macdonald, Ardvie.

5. MAIRI MACKINNON (b. 1901) of 10 Quidinish (later Mrs John Morrison of 10 Quidinish). Her uncle, John MacKinnon of 10 Quidinish, was a ghillie and her aunt, Rachel, worked at Finsbay Lodge.

6. MORAG MACLEOD (b. 1894) of 8 Quidinish, another aunt (father's sister) of Roddy A. Macleod; later Mrs Donald Mackay.

7. DONALD JOHN MORRISON (b. 1900) Crofter at 9 Quidinish and postman for many years.

8. JOHN MORRISON (b. 1900) Crofter at 10 Quidinish.

9. (Probably) MURDO MORRISON Cottar at 9 Quidinish and cousin of Donald John Morrison (7 above).

10. DONALD MACKINNON, son of John Mackinnon crofter at 10 Quidinish and 1st cousin of Mairi Mackinnon (5 above).

11. HUGH MORRISON of 9 Quidinish, a brother of Donald John Morrison (7 above).

12. (Probably) JOHN MORRISON of Struthmore, Quidinish.

13. MARGARET ROSS (b. 1907) of 2 Ardvie (later Mrs Wilfred Leonard of Cnoc na Ba, Ardvie).

14. MARGARET MORRISON of 8 Ardvie (Station Cottage) (later Mrs Johnnie MacKenzie of 12 Quidinish).

The two ladies with elegant hats at the top right are strongly suspected to be Mrs Mary Anne Purdie and her niece Miss Agnes Rotherham.

SAMUEL (SAM) MORRISON (1864–1952) Figs. 13.3 & 13.4

Sam was the Keeper for the Hebridean Sporting Association throughout its existence. The son of a shepherd at Manish, then living at Nesebost, then Seilebost, he had been a Keeper for Lord Dunmore at Laxdale[181]. He lived from 1903 until his death in 1952 at the house built by the Association just 80 yards behind Finsbay Lodge at a cost of about £195. The house is clearly visible behind Finsbay Lodge in Archie Chisholm's postcard picture (Fig. 3.8). It blew down in a gale in 1989. One of Sam's brothers, Norman

---

[181] It is likely that he had charge of Lord Dunmore's hatching ponds at Laxdale (Figs 7.1 & 7.2)

Fig. 13.3 Sam Morrison in July 1946, ghillieing from Rodel Hotel. The happy lady angler with a 5 lb salmon is believed to be a Mrs Barbara Turnbull.

(1870–1954) was Keeper at Luskentyre[182], and Sam's first wife, Christina Stewart (1869 – 1900), a native of Grimsay, North Uist, appears to have been Housekeeper at Luskentyre Lodge. Interestingly, both Thomas Wilson and Archie Chisholm had been witnesses at the wedding in 1894, indicating their deep involvement in personal aspects of the community. The photograph in Fig. 13.5, taken by Archie Chisholm in 1894, is thought to show this wedding.

Sadly, Christina (Kirsty) died in childbirth in 1900; Sam re-married in 1904 to Christina Campbell (1866/67–1944) from Plockrapool, and we assume that this wife played a role in the running of Finsbay Lodge, probably as Housekeeper. On Sam's death the Keeper's cottage was handed down to his son-in-law, John MacLeod (b. 1891)[183]. Sam Morrison also functioned as a "truancy officer", checking the local school registers for attendances. After the Association's demise, Sam continued to work as a ghillie associated with Rodel Hotel, and the photographs of him (Figs. 13.3 & 13.4) show him in the 1940s with angling guests, almost certainly from Rodel.

Fig. 13. 4 Sam Morrison in 1948. The anglers are believed to be James and Peter Macfarlane who sent this picture as a Christmas card to Sam Morrison.

---

182 See Fig. 13.14 below
183 He was the addressee of the postcard shown above (Figs 3.8 & 3.9)

Fig. 13.5 Wedding party at Luskentyre or, more likely, Seilebost, photographed by Archie Chisholm in 1894. It is likely that this shows the marriage of Sam Morrison to Christina Stewart, at which Archie Chisholm and Thomas Wilson were witnesses, and the Minister (face in scarf) was Revd Donald McLean (Minister of Harris Parish). The location is thought to be at grid reference NG 063 971 (information from Tony Scherr, 2008), and this is probably the home of Sam's parents, John and Catherine Morrison. It is believed that this house subsequently was used as a weaving shed by Mrs Annie Kate MacCuish and was visited by H.M. The Queen in 1956 for a demonstration of the weaving of Harris tweed.
Reproduced by kind permission of Alastair Chisholm

JOHN MALCOLM JP (1858–1929)
See Fig. 13.6, also Fig. 2.3 above.

John Malcolm was one of the principal minds behind the formation of the Association, probably the key founder. He certainly was the one longest associated with it and a major financial backer of the venture – and financial loser at the end of the day. The son of a tenant farming family at Bent Neuck[184] in Dunmore, Stirlingshire, he became prominent in Glasgow business circles especially those associated with the shipping industry for which Glasgow was justly world famous at the time. Dunmore in the parish of Airth is a small

---

[184] An arable farm of 110 acres

model village originally created by the 4th Earl of Dunmore[185] for people associated with his estate and coal-mining interests there, and the Dunmore family provided the local school during the 19th century. John's father died when John was seven, and his maternal grandparents came to live at Bent Neuck. His grandfather, William Tough (~1796–1880), a native of St Ninian's Stirling, had been the renowned Innkeeper and farmer at Scourie in Sutherland, an hotel which remains a major angling centre. In 1865, Andrew Young who was Fishing Manager for Sutherland Estates wrote *"There is an excellent inn at Scourie, kept by Mr Tough, as jolly a fellow and as good a soul as ever poured mountain dew either into or out of a crystal measure ... I would advise sportsmen on their journey from one salmon river to another never to pass such mines of sport as these lochs are certain to produce ... Mr Tough, with his dog-cart, is so obliging that, for a small fee, he will set the angler down at the water's edge ... "* [125, p.16]. This is likely to be how John Malcolm was introduced to fishing.

Fig. 13.6 John Malcolm – Founding Director of the Hebridean Sporting Association. From *The Bailie* 1924, based on a Lafayette studio portrait [123

One inevitably wonders whether the young John Malcolm had been introduced to the Isle of Harris and its fishings by either the Earl of Dunmore himself or by Viscount Fincastle (who was just 12 years younger than John Malcolm) or by one of the Dunmore Estate keepers – the estate in Airth had valuable shootings, but no fishings. Though most records show William Tough as an "Innkeeper" or "Farmer", the death certificate of his daughter Mary Fergusson in 1908 describes him as "Gamekeeper". It is possible that, in his retirement at Bent Neuck, Airth, he had served as a Gamekeeper on the Dunmore Estate. John Finlayson (see p. 53–54), the keeper at Rodel, also was a native of Stirling, and other Finlaysons had been farm labourers at New Miln (which is close to Bent Neuk) in Airth.

---

185 The fine mansion, Dunmore Park, was built in 1820 for the 5th Earl and occupied by the Dunmore family from 1822 to 1911, but is now largely in disrepair [124, p.275]. A folly built as a giant pineapple in the grounds is a particular attraction, now under the stewardship of The National Trust for Scotland and available for holiday lets through the Landmark Trust.

After school at Alloa Academy, John Malcolm entered the office of Messrs Alston & Tulloch to start his career as a ship broker. This was at a time when Glasgow and the Clyde were at the forefront of the British Empire's shipping industry, and this explains the prosperity that he gained which enabled him to create the Hebridean Sporting Association and to meet some of its eventual debts. It also brought him into contact with important civic and commercial men. After 6 years with that firm, he joined Messrs Pile & Co. before working for Howard Houlder. In 1881, Howard Houlder (1858–1932), who became one of the most prominent names of the shipbroking world, had come from London to Glasgow to open a branch office of Houlder Brothers[186]. By 1885 he had decided to break away from the family shipping business and start his own shipbroking business. In 1885 Howard Houlder returned to London to form a London shipbroking office, and he left John Malcolm to run the Glasgow office. In 1888, John was made a partner and the firm became Howard Houlder, Malcolm and Co. In 1900, John Malcolm and 6 partners formed The Gifford Trading Company in order to buy and trade with the steel ship *SS Gifford*. Until his retirement he was a partner of Messrs Howard Houlder, Malcolm & Co, Shipbrokers, Glasgow, and he had been President of the Institute of Shipbrokers of the United Kingdom; also President of the Shipowners' and Shipbrokers' Benevolent Association[187] [126]. In 1920 at the time of his correspondence with Norman Robertson about the sale of Finsbay Lodge to Lord Leverhulme, his business address was at Malcolm & Eadie, shipbrokers, Glasgow. He was decorated by the King of Belgium for work to alleviate suffering in Belgium during the First World War. He was also a Director of the Shandon Hydropathic Co. Ltd[188]

---

[186] Three brothers created Houlder Brothers & Co who initially were ship and insurance brokers, but then became ship owners. Their Houlder Line was a prestigious steamship company operating from 1856 specialising in sailings to USA, New Zealand, Australia, and the Argentine. It owned the 'Grange' ships and amalgamated with the 'Shire' Line. Howard was the son of one of the partners, Alfred Houlder, and was given his first ship for his 21st birthday

[187] J.A. Roxburgh and Thomas Dunlop, two other members of the Hebridean Sporting Association, had served as Presidents

[188] The Shandon Hydropathic was the magnificent former residence of Robert Napier (1791–1876), the legendary shipbuilder, near Helensburgh. It was demolished to make way for the Faslane naval dockyard

and of the Scottish Property Trust Ltd. John had been a member and President of the West of Scotland Angling Club. He married and had 4 children, but no living descendants have been traced. At his death in 1929 his estate was worth £96,629[189]. Two sons[190] died in the First World War, and his only daughter, Margaret, a retired Red Cross officer, died in 1974. Brief biographies of his numerous activities and interests together with sketches of him were published in *The Bailie* [1, 123] which was a fashionable Glasgow weekly magazine.

ROBERT (ROBIN) DUFF BELL (1871–1942)
See Fig. 13.7

He was a whisky magnate. Robin Bell was the younger brother of Arthur K. Bell, Chairman of the eponymous Perth whisky company. In his young days, he had worked in the industry, including representing the company in Australia and New Zealand. However *"he was regarded as something of a playboy and ... once his brother had taken over the firm Robert eased himself out of the responsibilities of running a business that was getting rather beyond him ..."* Later, when his brother died suddenly, Robert *"was called from his life as a country gentleman to take over the position of managing director ..."* which he held for just one month before a successor was appointed [127].

Fig. 13.7 Robert (Robin) Duff Bell. Reproduced by kind permission of Diageo Plc

[189] It is fair to presume that much of his prosperity, which permitted the formation and existence of the Hebridean Sporting Association, had accrued from the shipbroking work for Houlder

[190] One son was named Archibald Houlder Malcolm (b. 1892) – note the connection with Howard Houlder, the shipbroker for whom John Malcolm had been Glasgow partner. He was killed in active service in France as Lieutenant with the Highland Light Infantry in 1918 (memorial at Henin Communal Cemetry extension). Another son, James Waddell Malcolm (b. 1894) was killed in active service in Gallipoli as 2nd Lieutenant in the Highland Light Infantry in 1915 (memorial at Helles)

ERSKINE BEVERIDGE LLD, FRSE, JP (1851–1920) See Fig. 13.8

Erskine Beveridge owned a major linen works in Dunfermline, Fife. Indeed, this firm, founded by his father, Erskine Beveridge Sr (1803–1864), was arguably the largest and best producer of fine damask linen in the world and a major part of Dunfermline's industrial heritage [128]. Sadly, the firm ceased operations in 1989, and the substantial works were demolished in 1990. Erskine Beveridge had two other claims to importance: he wrote several books of historical significance and he undertook "amateur", but serious, archaeological investigations. He had a holiday home at Vallay, an island reached by a causeway off the north coast of North Uist, where he bred Highland ponies. His book on the archaeology of North Uist is still the authoritative work on the subject [129]. His other books covered topics such as Scottish place names [130], Dunfermline history [131, 132], churchyard memorials in Crail [133], and antiquities on Coll and Tiree [134], also photography [135]. He was Vice-President of the Society of Antiquaries of Scotland from 1915 to 1918. Fishing was listed as one of his interests, but he also was a generous philanthropist to projects that appealed to him – these included the Episcopal Church and its new Rectory in Dunfermline (where the author's grandfather was Rector from 1908 to 1938) and other churches; as with many other shareholders, we cannot say whether his shareholding in the Hebridean Sporting Association was simply for altruism in support for a new Hebridean venture that interested him or for giving him access to its fishings. His name never appeared in *The Scotsman's* angling reports. Despite all his generous donations, his estate at death amounted to £105,787 [136].

THOMAS BINNIE Jr (1887–1937)

Thomas Binnie, a Director of the Hebridean Sporting Association from 1907, described himself as "land valuator", the equivalent of a surveyor. His father and grandfather, both named Thomas, were distinguished master builders, involved in substantial developments in Glasgow in its formative heyday. Indeed, Thomas Binnie Jr was born in Binnie Place. The family business became Thomas Binnie and Hendry at 207 Hope Street, Glasgow, but Thomas retired in 1923 due to ill-health. During the War, he had been a consultant to the government and the Admiralty in connection with property acquisitions; he also had been a referee under the Finance Act of 1909–10. He was a Director also of McAlpine's Nursing Home and of Commercial Union Assurance Co in 1919. He was a member of the Incorporation of Freemasons and was said to be involved with a number of charitable organisations.

NEILSON BIRD (1841–1925)

His family firm was a well-known firm of Glasgow Writers (Solicitors), which now remains after many amalgamations in the form of Bird Semple & Co

JOHN COLLINS (d. 1916)[191]

He was a greatly respected master at Rugby School, where he had been a pupil, for over 40 years, and Housemaster for half of that time. A First Class graduate in Classics from Cambridge, he started his teaching career at Clifton College, Bristol. In his early days he was good at football and racquets (squash), but suffered damage to a hand in a shooting accident. He was Commander of the school's Rifle Corps and was said to *"infuse into it much of his own methodical and orderly spirit ... "* [137].

---

[191] It appears that he was fishing at Finsbay Lodge when Professor Irvine stayed there in 1914

SIR JOHN ALEXANDER DEWAR MP (1856–1929) See Fig. 13.9

He was the son of John Dewar Sr who had founded the whisky firm of John Dewar & Sons of Perth and became the first Lord Forteviot. John Dewar Jr was prominent in politics, both local and national. He served as a councillor in Perth, becoming Lord Provost from 1893 to 1899, and was Liberal M.P. for Inverness-shire from 1900 to 1916. (Harris was in his constituency) He chaired two commissions of inquiry into medical conditions in the Highlands and Islands – see p. 185. In line with his interests in rural regeneration, he formed the "model village" of Forteviot in his Perthshire estate in the style of a small Dutch township. Like his fellow whisky magnate R.D. Bell (see above), Sir John was a major philanthropist, especially in the city of Perth where he restored St John's church as a War Memorial and provided a new maternity ward at the Perth Royal Infirmary [138]. Unfortunately, many of the family's papers that might have related to his membership of the Hebridean Sporting Association appear to have been discarded during the drive to re-process paper pulp during the Second World War.

Fig. 13.9 Sir John Alexander Dewar. Reproduced by kind permission of John Dewar & Sons Ltd.

JAMES STEDMAN DIXON LLD (1846–1911)

James Dixon, the son of a stockbroker, initially trained as a mining engineer but later became a coalmaster (mine owner) in Lanarkshire. He became regarded as one of the leading figures in the British mining industry and served as President of many professional bodies including the Institution of Mining Engineers of Great Britain. In 1902, he provided funds for a lectureship in mining engineering at the University of Glasgow. Subsequently he increased the endowment to pay for a professor, the James S. Dixon Chair of Mining. In 1989 these funds were reallocated to found the James S. Dixon Chair of Applied Geology, so his philanthropy is still effective.

ARTHUR JOHN CASWALL DOWDING MA (1848–1932) See Fig. 13.10

This member was born in Devizes, Wiltshire, one of 10 children; he was educated at Winchester and New College, Oxford. He became an Assistant Master at a school in Slough, then at Haileybury, and then at Fettes, Edinburgh (1876–1879) before moving to Moffat. In Moffat he, together with Rev. W.H. Churchill[192], founded in 1879, and was first Headmaster of, St Ninian's preparatory boarding school for boys[193]. Initially there were 9 pupils (see Fig. 13.10), but it soon became a fairly substantial school – the 1881 Census records 30 pupils, and the roll grew to 70 – and it was highly regarded. It closed in 1979. The building is now named Dowding House and provides sheltered housing for the R.A.F. Association. He had retired to Lansdowne Road, Wimbledon, Surrey in 1897 by the time he joined the Association.

Fig. 13.10 Arthur Dowding (in doorway, to right of Mrs Dowding) with his St. Ninian's School, Moffat in 1879, its first year. Picture kindly supplied by Moffat Museum Trust.

His three sons achieved great distinction in the Armed Services. The eldest, Hugh Caswall Tremenheere Dowding (1882–1970),

---

[192] In 1883 Churchill left to found Stone House school in Broadstairs.
[193] The only other prep school in Scotland at this time was Cargilfield. In 1923, one of the Masters at St. Ninian's went on to found Craigflower school in Fife (now closed).

educated at St. Ninian's and Winchester, served in both World Wars, and went on to become Air Chief Marshall Lord Dowding, Commander-in-Chief of Fighter Command (1936–1940). Of him, Winston Churchill eventually said *"We must regard the generalship here shown as an example of genius in the art of war"*. The second son, Vice-Admiral Sir Arthur Ninian Dowding (1886–1966) became Admiral-Superintendent of Devonport dockyard. The youngest son was Squadron Commander Kenneth [Tremenheere or Townley] Dowding (1889–1979), who became a solicitor in London.

SIR THOMAS DUNLOP (1855–1937)
See Fig. 13.11

Thomas Dunlop was Chairman of Thomas Dunlop & Sons, Shipowners, Glasgow, having succeeded his father, Thomas Dunlop (1831–1893) who founded the company. The history of the family shipping line was written by G. Rankin Taylor [140]. Thomas Jr acquired the line of Clan vessels and, later, the Queen line. He was a member of the Hebridean Sporting Association, and various angling records show him to have been a lifelong keen and successful fisherman from boyhood. He often accompanied Hugh C. Young fishing in competitions on Loch Leven; Hugh Young was a generous benefactor of John McCallum's shipping services to the Western Isles. Thomas Dunlop became Lord Provost and Lord Lieutenant of Glasgow, 1914 to 1917, and was created a baronet in 1916. In addition to his long period of civic service, he was renowned for yachting. One of his sons (Peter Mitchell Dunlop) served an apprenticeship with Howard Houlder, Shipbrokers (the firm of which John Malcolm had been a partner) before becoming a partner in the Thomas Dunlop shipping firm.

EBENEZER BROWN FLEMING (1858–1912)

The son of the Presbyterian minister in Inverkeithing, he was a Glasgow merchant specialising in supplying Turkey Red dye for fabrics. He became renowned for producing wax-prints of Dutch style for export to Ghana and other African countries, where brightly coloured National costumes are characteristic, and thus creating an innovative industry.

FORBES FRASER FRCS CBE (1871–1924)
See Fig. 13.12

Mr Fraser, a native of Arbroath, was one of the relatively few members of the Association residing in England, and he was the Chief Surgeon in Bath after whom the Royal United Hospital, newly opened by HRH The Duke of Connaught, was re-named in honour of him. He had been widely admired for his service as Consulting Surgeon to the Second Army and the Army of the Rhine, based at various Casualty Clearing Stations and at Le Touquet and Remy Siding, where he undertook valuable research into different methods of suturing wounds, [141, p.420], during the First World War. He died from septicaemia a year after being poisoned by a scratch from an infected bone during a surgical operation. Nowadays, this would be readily treatable by antibiotics. His *The Times* obituary recorded: " *... the highest standard of work ... abundantly endowed with the capacity for enjoyment, a magnetic and delightful companion, <u>a keen and finished fisherman</u>, full of fun and good fellowship, courteous and unselfish ... "* (my underlining). He had founded several clubs, including the Country Surgeons' Club and the Bath and Bristol Surgical Club, but he also was a keen sportsman (" *... He rose early and worked late, and thus found time to go hunting and to win prizes in point-to-point races ... "*) He was a good physician as well as surgeon and, outside his profession, a keen salmon angler and motorist, a witty raconteur, and a man of much charm [141, p.421]. Among his collection of books auctioned after his death there were fishing books, including Hamish Stuart's *Lochs and Loch Fishing* mentioned above as one of the few books referring to the creation of lochs in Harris.

Fig. 13.12 Mr Forbes Fraser FRCS. Reproduced from *The British Medical Journal*

Rev WILLIAM BALDWIN JACQUES (1864–1913)

He was one of only two clergymen to be shareholders of the Hebridean Sporting Association. He was Rector and Patron of Burton Latimer in Northamptonshire from 1895–1911, then moved to Orlingbury. Both he and his wife were prosperous, employing numerous staff at the rectory. Two stained glass windows and two bells were donated to the church in memory of him and his son who was killed in action in 1916.

RODERICK MACKAY (1888–1981)

His son recollects that his father's first job (he lived in Geocrab) after leaving school was involved as a labourer with building Finsbay Lodge.

JOHN MACLEOD (1885–1964)

A native of Berneray he, as mentioned above, was a steward at the Lodge. He spent the first part of his career in domestic service from an early age and then entered the church; it was said that *"… he was employed in Finsbay Lodge where he learnt the rudiments of stewarding, and in subsequent years followed this career in such establishments as "Barr and Strouds" in Glasgow, and in military messes during his war service, but mostly in ships and yachts … …* [142, p.199]. In due course, and after the death of his first wife, he trained to become a lay-missionary with the United Free Church of Scotland. His first calling was to St Kilda where, from 1926–29, he was Missionary and schoolmaster. One of his sons, Alex, became principal teacher in Gaelic and deputy headmaster at the Sir E. Scott school in Tarbert; in turn, one of Alex's daughters, Mrs MacSween, followed in his footsteps as Gaelic teacher at that school.

This makes it clear that the "hotel management" side of the enterprise was skillfully managed, e.g. with properly trained "stewards". Unfortunately, there is no similar information about the staffing of Rodel House; however, we may assume that it too was run professionally, a background that would (or should) have prepared it well for its future as an hotel.

NORMAN ROBERTSON JP, FRICS
(1882–1961) See Fig. 13.13

Although Norman Robertson was never a member of the Hebridean Sporting Association, it is appropriate to include a biographical note since he, as Factor for South Harris Estate from 1911 till 1925, was intimately involved in the leases of Rodel Lodge after 1911, in Lord Leverhulme's purchase of Finsbay Lodge in 1920 and the subsequent decisions about it, and then in the sale of the Harris Estates after Lord Leverhulme's death in 1925. He was a native of Portree, Skye, becoming assistant factor for Lady Cathcart's South Uist estate before coming to Harris to succeed Thomas Wilson in 1911. He was a highly respected man, though without the potent land reform views that dominated Thomas Wilson's attitude. Although the papers of the South Harris estate appear to have been destroyed, a consequence of the break-up of the estate in 1925, a great deal of Norman Robertson's correspondence with Lord Leverhulme has been preserved in the Unilever Archives (see Chapters 3 & 4). It is clear from this that Mr Robertson had a very detailed understanding of estate management matters and that he was greatly trusted by Lord Leverhulme. Norman Robertson went on to manage North Harris estate and to own part of the Uig estate in Lewis. It is thought that he would have made

Fig. 13.13 Norman Robertson, Factor of South Harris. Reproduced by kind permission of Mrs Daphne Carr, Norman Robertson's grand-daughter

a bid to buy South Harris as a single Lot personally if he had not been involved professionally in managing Knight, Frank & Rutley's auction in 1925. He occupied many public offices in Harris and Lewis (as his predecessor had done), served as a Justice of the Peace (JP), and he became a Director of the Harris Tweed Association (known as the Harris Tweed Authority since 1993). He represented the Western Isles on Inverness-shire County Council for the grand time of 38 years, and his experience of island governance led to him being invited to assist the Falkland Islands Government Service, though he declined as this would have taken him away from home for many months.

SIR JOHN ARCHIBALD ROXBURGH DL, LLD, JP (1854–1937)

He was another shipping member of the Hebridean Sporting Association and was chairman of Roxburgh, Colin Scott & Co Ltd, Glasgow. The family firm owned originally square riggers, then acquired the Helmsdale Steamship Company which had "shire-named" ships, including *SS Hallamshire, SS Breconshire*, etc which may have passed in due course to the Clan Line (see above under Sir Thomas Dunlop). He was Dean of Guild for Glasgow (1913–14), and was knighted in 1934. He was Colonel in the Territorial Army, commanding the 5th bn. The Cameronians (Scottish Rifles) (1906–11) and was President of the Boys' Brigade for 14 years till 1933.

CHRISTINA WILSON (née Paterson) (1882–1914)

The only lady shareholder in the Hebridean Sporting Association. She was the 2nd wife of Thomas Wilson, and she transferred her shares to him in 1913. It is open to speculation as to whether she bought the shares, a little unlikely for a lady of her means, or whether they were a gift in recognition of Thomas Wilson's help in arranging the Leases etc with Viscount Fincastle. Or was Thomas Wilson making a risky investment in the hope of a big capital gain after the deaths of the founding Directors? After moving from Luskentyre in 1908, she ran the "coffee-shop" (or Temperance Hotel, later known as Nurse Boyd's House, where the Strond road joins Ferry Road) established in An t-Ob (Leverburgh) for the lobster fishermen by Lady Dunmore. This house gained a reputation for being haunted, but was burned down around 1911[194], then rebuilt by Kenneth Campbell, the farmer at Rodel. It is still occupied. The story of its purported haunting is given by Alasdair MacGregor,

---

[194] At the time of the Inland Revenue Valuation Survey, it was described as "ruinous"

and the haunting was said to have ceased when a maid living there departed [48, p.97–99]. For some years, she and Thomas (then in Lochmaddy) acted as guardians for Mary Morrison, the first daughter of Norman Morrison (Keeper at Luskentyre and brother of Sam Morrison, Keeper at Finsbay Lodge), as Mary's mother had died in 1909 when Mary was three. Fig. 13.14 shows Norman Morrison with Mary and his second wife, Katie, together with son Dogan (Donald) and daughter Rachel.

Christina Wilson died of *scarlatina maligna* in 1914 at Lochmaddy.

The above is not intended to be a detailed biography of all associated with the Hebridean Sporting Association, but to give a snapshot of the diverse backgrounds of some of the people. Further information about the members of the Association is provided in Appendix 2.

One cannot escape the impression that most of the shareholders were very interesting characters; many had generated personal wealth through self-effort and their own enterprise and many of them had a conspicuous interest in contributing to society. While some were relatively elderly bachelors, many were young married men, so there was no obvious stereotype among the shareholders. One feels that the smoking room at Finsbay Lodge, mentioned by Sir James Irvine (p. 154), must have been the setting for much convivial discussion about matters of the day as well as the typical banter that anglers regularly exchange! Nowadays, some of these activities would be described as "professional networking", and it is likely that the atmosphere did provide opportunities for social intercourse that would ultimately impinge on real commercial and academic progress, quite apart from the happy relaxation that visitors to the Hebrides regularly enjoy. The employment opportunities for local people and the general broadening of horizons must have contributed significantly to the development of the Isle of Harris in the first two decades of the twentieth century.

APPENDIX ONE:
THE HEBRIDEAN SPORTING ASSOCIATION – PROSPECTUS ISSUED IN 1903 [2]

"This Association is formed for the purpose of acquiring, by purchase or lease, Sporting and Fishing Estates and Rights in the Hebrides or elsewhere, and providing Sport for Sportsmen, especially Anglers.

The merits of the Outer Hebrides as a Sporting Resort are well known to many Anglers, who return year after year to spend an enjoyable holiday amidst the finest of Highland scenery. Those who have not had that pleasure may be referred to the pages of Mr. Hamish Stuart's practical work on *"Lochs and Loch Fishing"*, wherein the possibilities and experiences of many fishing holidays in the Hebrides are fully described. The Sportsman's Guide may be also referred to as setting forth some of the Lochs, but those mentioned there are, comparatively, only a few, many having scarcely ever been visited by the ordinary Angler.

The Association have arranged (1) a Lease of Rodel Lodge (furnished), together with Fishings and Shootings in the Island of South Harris, Outer Hebrides, for five years from 16 June, 1903; and (2) a Lease for fifteen years from 16 June, 1903, of the Fishings (including certain rights excepted from the Rodel lease), and Shootings of nearly the whole of the Eastern half of South Harris aforesaid, divided into two sections known as Finsbay and Grosebay, with a break in favour of the Association at the end of five years.. The Rent payable under the Lease of Rodel is £350 per annum, and that payable under the Lease of Finsbay and Grosebay is £500 per annum. The Subjects let comprise over 38,000 acres

Hill and Low Ground, mostly heather, with numerous Islands and over 40 Fishing Lochs, the names and Particulars of the principal of which are given in the annexed list.

As will be seen from these particulars, the Lochs afford great variety of Sport, containing as they do, Salmon, Sea Trout, and Brown Trout, and they are capable of yielding good Sport to a large number of Anglers. The Obbe Lochs are well known and justly celebrated, and the Lochs in the other Sections also afford good Sport. The Fishings have never before been open to the public, and consequently they have not been over-fished or run out in any way.

The Shootings comprise Grouse, Snipe, Woodcock, Golden Plover, Wild Duck, Wild Geese, Rabbits, Rock Pigeons, and Seals. There are ample facilities for Canoeing, Mountain Climbing, Sea Excursions and Fishing, and Camping out.

Rodel Lodge will accommodate from 10 to 15 guests. It is situated about 4 miles from the Obbe Lochs by a good road, and while no driving, is necessary a brake will be provided if required.

It is proposed to erect a Lodge or Hotel in the Norwegian style, on Finsbay, within easy walking distance of the Lochs there, and no driving will be required. The Lodge will accommodate about 20 guests, and its erection will be gone on with at once so as to be ready by 1 July, 1903. Various estimates have been received for the erection of this house, and the cost thereof is stated approximately in the Estimate of Capital Expenditure appended hereto. At the termination of the Lease, this Lodge may be taken over by the proprietor at a valuation but, if not, it will remain the property of the Association.

An Estimate of the Capital Expenditure is appended hereto, and an Estimate of the annual Income and Expenditure has also been prepared, and can be seen at the office of the Solicitors or Secretary. These are to some extent approximate only, but those of the Income are based on the charges made in existing Hebridean Hotels and the number of visitors to the same. In certain months it is impossible to accommodate all the visitors. As illustrating the run upon those Hotels the following is an extract from an article by a well-known author, who was in the Outer Hebrides as an ordinary visitor, which appeared in the *Glasgow Evening News* of 26 August, 1901:

ENGLAND IN THE ISLANDS

The man who does not interest himself much in fishing affairs would be amazed at the number of Englishmen which the love of fishing, or the fad (whichever it may be), brings at this season to the most remote islands of our Western Sea. In some of these hotels guests have fishing privileges over many lochs in their neighbourhood, and to these the stream of Sassenachs for two or three months every year never slackens. You wonder how Tooting, or Leamington, or Chorley ever heard of Uist or Harris, and marvel that they should come to the dim sheiling on the misty island from which mountains divide them and a world of seas at the cost of so much time and money, only to slay a sea trout or two if luck is with them.

Members who take the minimum number of 10 Shares will have equal rights to all the privileges of the Association, and they will have a preference when intending visitors exceed the accommodation. It is intended to reserve Rodel Lodge, Shootings, and Fishings for Members only, except when not fully occupied by them. Any friends introduced by Members will also have a preference over the public.

The climate of Harris is healthy, the air pure and bracing, and the scenery magnificent. The mail steamer calls daily at Tarbert and Rodel (north and south ends of districts leased), and there are postal and telegraphic services convenient.

The minimum subscription upon which the Directors will proceed to allotment is forty per cent of the present issue; the preliminary expenses are estimated at £300 ; and the Articles of Association provide that the qualification of a Director shall be the holding of not less than ten Shares. Any remuneration to the Directors shall be fixed by the Members at their Annual Meetings.

The only Contracts proposed to be entered into are the Leases before referred to and a contract for the erection of the Lodge or Hotel on Finsbay. No promotion money of any kind has been or will be paid.

Prospectuses and Forms of Application for Shares may be had from the Solicitors or Secretary of the Company, and copies of the Memorandum and Articles of Association, and of the adjusted drafts of said Leases, can be seen at their Offices. Application for Shares may be made on the accompanying form. If no allotment is made the deposit will be returned in full.

A copy of the Memorandum of Association and of the Signatories thereto is annexed hereto, and is to be deemed part of this Prospectus.

Signed January 31st 1903, dated 11 February 1903

John Dempster; Jno. Malcolm;
William Fergusson; James Anderson"

SHAREHOLDERS IN THE HEBRIDEAN SPORTING ASSOCIATION, LTD

Name		Stated Profession	Address (as stated)		Pref Shares	Notes
Anderson	James	Manufacturer	4 Kingsborough Gds	Glasgow	P	**Director resigned 10/5/07**
Anderson	Robert	Manufacturer	12 Princes Sq	Glasgow		
Anstruther	Charles James	Major 17th Lancers	c/o Cox & Co, 16 Charing Cross	London		To: Executors before June 1913
Begg	Andrew Vannan	WS	14 Frederick St	Edinburgh	P	Died 1935 aet 77
Bell	Robin D		c/o Arthur Bell & Sons	Perth		Robert Duff Bell, Craigenvar, Scone. See biography
Beveridge	Erskine	Manufacturer	St Leonards Hill	Dunfermline		See biography
Binnie	Thomas (Jr)	Land Valuator	207 Hope St	Glasgow	P	**Director from 10/5/07; died 1937 aet 69.** See biography
Bird	Neilson	Writer	7 Montgomerie Quadrant	Glasgow	P	See biography
Blaine	William Fleming	Gentleman	18 St Swithins Lane	London	P	
Bond	E. Morton	Gentleman	Croylands	Surbiton		
Bond	Hubert Morton	Gentleman	Croylands	Surbiton		Law stationer's clerk; b. abt 1877
Bond	Richard Henry		Croylands	Surbiton		
Bond	Richard Shaw	Gentleman	Croylands	Surbiton		Publisher & printer; b. abt 1844

Name		Stated Profession	Address (as stated)		Pref Shares	Notes
Boyes	Thomas James Gilchrist	Solicitor	Thorton	Bonnybridge		Died 1925 aet 77
Brown	Albert Richard	Merchant	34 West George St	Glasgow		
Brown	James	Coal Merchant	135 Buchanan St	Glasgow		
Butler	Charles		115 Bathune Rd, Stamford Hill	London		
Chisholm	Archibald Alexander	Procurator Fiscal		Lochmaddy		
Clayton	Ronald Percy	Solicitor	Laurel Bank, Wavertree	Liverpool		
Cochran	Reginald Purves	Capt RN	Buntings,	Uxbridge		To: Helen Cochran, Executrix before June 1911
Collins	John	Asst Master, Rugby	1 Hillmorton Rd	Rugby		d.1916. See biography
Cook	William	Writer	77 St Vincent St	Glasgow		To: Execs before 31/12/16
Cope	John Arnold	Tobacco manufacturer	Stanley House. Halewood	Liverpool (nr)		
Corporation of Queen Victoria Clergy Fund						(legacy from estate of A.D. Yorke – see below)
Dean	Charles Yardley	Gentleman	30 Dounlenze, Stoke Bishop	Bristol		Later: Westholme, Ryders Ave, Westgate on Sea
Dempster	John	Merchant	Craigmiln, Carmunnock	Glasgow (nr)	P	**Director; died 8/1914 aet 66**
Dewar	John A.	M.P.	Murrays Hall	Scone		Later: Sir John A Dewar, Abercairney, Crieff
Dixon	James Stedman	Coalmaster	127 St Vincent St	Glasgow	P	Died 6/1911 aet 66. To: Mrs Isabella Dixon, Fairleigh, Bothwell
Douglas	John Park	Manufacturer	Rocklea	Kilmacolm	P	

Name		Stated Profession	Address (as stated)		Pref Shares	Notes
Dowding	Arthur John Caswall	Retired Schoolmaster	15 Lansdowne Rd Wimbledon	London	P	1848–1932 See biography
Dunlop	Thomas	Shipowner	70 Wellington St	Glasgow		1855–1937. See biography
Fergusson	William	Solicitor	Veremont Pk Gds N, Partick	Glasgow	P	**Director & Chairman; died 5/1916**
Fleming	Ebenezer Brown	(Manufacturer)	Lochnabrae	Garelochead	P	Died 4/1912 aet 53; To WE Fleming, below. See biog.
Fleming	WE		Millfoot Ho, Bearsden	Glasgow		from above
Fraser	Forbes	Surgeon	2 The Circus	Bath		1871–1924 See biography above
Grant	James Cameron	Colonel (Indian Army)	Law Park	St Andrews		
Greenhill	William	Ch. Accountant	6a George St	Edinburgh	P	Died 1946 aet 83; 2nd wife = Jean Inglis
Greig	Gerald Andrew	Gentleman	6 Hughenden Terr	Glasgow		
Greig	Robert Bertram Gillespie	Wine Merchant	64 Waterloo St	Glasgow	P	To: Wright & Greig Ltd before May 1907
Hislop	William	Solicitor	162 St Vincent St	Glasgow		Died 1927 aet 69
Howat	William	Bolt & Rivet Manufr	9 Parkgrove Terr	Glasgow		
Hutton	Gilbert Montgomerie	Capt RE (then Maj)	c/o Cox & Co, Charing Cross	London		To: Executors before June 1912
Inglis	George Alexander	Engineer	4 Princes Terr, Dowanhill	Glasgow	P	Died 1951 aet 76 (shipbuilding family)
Jackson	William	Engineer	6 Montague St, Kelvinside	Glasgow		
Jacques	William Baldwin	Rector	Burton Latimer Rectory	Kettering		1864–1913. See biography
Kennedy	Moses Hunter	Railway Contractor	23 Kingsborough Gdns	Glasgow	P	Died 1931 aet 68

Name		Stated Profession	Address (as stated)		Pref Shares	Notes
Kirkbride	Isaac	Gentleman	2 Broad St	Nottingham		To: Executors before June 1912
MacLeod	Dugald Brodie	Retired Clothier	11 Belhaven Terrace	Glasgow		Died 1928 aet 86
MacLeod	Thomas Calder	Merchant	53 Bothwell St	Glasgow		Died 1912 aet 58; retd iron merchant
Malcolm	John	Ship Broker	70 Wellington St	Glasgow	P	**Founding Director; died 1929 aet 70**
Manning	John Westley	Barrister	21 Redcliff Gardens	London		
McCallum Jr	Robert	Property Agent	69 Union St	Glasgow		
Mitchell	James	Bank Agent	Auchengray	Caldercruix		
Morton	George	Stockbroker	104 West George St	Glasgow		
Murray	Charles R	Merchant	Woodbank, Partickhill	Glasgow		To: Execs before Sept 1918
Nevill	Hugh	JP	4 Corbert Ct, Gracechurch St	London		
Reid	William Loudon	Physician	7 Royal Crescent	Glasgow	P	Died 1931 aet 86 To: Mrs Josephine Reid
Roberton	John Stewart	Solicitor	176 St Vincent St	Glasgow	P	
Roxburgh	John Archibald	Ship Owner	3 Royal Exchange Sq	Glasgow		1854–1937. See biography
Russell	Thomas	Solicitor	7 High St	Paisley		
Sloan	James Robert	Gentleman	Southfield, Crosshill	Glasgow		Retd cotton & woolen mfr, died 1928 aet 78
Stevenson	Samuel	Timber Merchant	Polmadie Sawmills, Rutherglen Rd	Glasgow	P	**Became Director Feb 1918; died 1935 aet 64**
Stirling	George Duke	Ch. Accountant	154 St Vincent St	Glasgow		**Comp. Secy. Died 7/1913 aet 58**
Strathie	David	Ch. Accountant	162 St Vincent St	Glasgow	P	**Auditor**

Name	Stated Profession	Address (as stated)		Pref Shares	Notes
Thompson Rev Peter	Clergyman	Annfield, 48 Well St, Hackney	London		
Verel Alphonso Anthony	Merchant	179 West George St	Glasgow	P	Died 1911 aet 55
Vickery George	Architect	Harrowlands, Tower Hill	Dorking		b. 1847
Walker G. Chapman		Army & Navy Club, Pall Mall	London	P	71 Linden Gds, Notting Hill Gate
Waring Holburt Jacob	Surgeon	37 Wimpole St	London		
Wilson John	Ch. Accountant	154 St Vincent St	Glasgow		
Wilson Mrs Christina		Luskentyre, Harris	Harris	P	Shares later transferred to Thomas Wilson, Lochmaddy
Wilson Thomas	Solicitor		Lochmaddy	P	
Wood James	Coal Master	Bathville House	Armadale		
Wright John Moncrieff	Gentleman	c/o Rev John Wright	Kinross		
Wright & Greig Ltd (legacy from RBG Greig – see above)					
Wyndham Percy	Civil Servant	Indian Civil Service, Mirzapur	India	P	c/o Bank, Cockermouth
Yorke Arthur Dudley	(? Oilshop keeper)	16 Grosvenor St	London	P	To: Executors pre 6/1911; to Corpn Q Victoria Clergy

P is this column indicates that Preference Shares, up to 5, were subsequently taken up

HEBRIDEAN SPORTING ASSOCIATION LTD - EXTRACTS FROM THE COMPANY'S ANNUAL ACCOUNTS

	Year to December 1906	Year to December 1907	Year to December 1908	Year to December 1909
ASSETS [all at cost price]				
Finsbay Lodge, buildings	£2,893-16-7d	£2,893-16-7d	£2,893-16-7d	£2,893-16-7d
Finsbay Lodge Foundations	£502-2-2d	£502-2-2d	£502-2-2d	£502-2-2d
Garden, roads, piers, fences etc	£382-14-6d	£382-14-6d	£382-14-6d	£382-14-6d
Finsbay Lodge water supply	£604-4-0d	£604-4-0d	£604-4-0d	£604-4-0d
Total for Finsbay Lodge	£4,382-17-3d	£4,382-17-3d	£4,382-17-3d	£4,382-17-3d
Keeper's House, & hut at Grosebay	£196-10-5d	£196-10-5d	£196-10-5d	£196-10-5d
Rodel House alterations	£16-4-0d	£16-4-0d	£16-4-0d	£16-4-0d
Furnishings, Finsbay Lodge		£1,197-15-0d	£1,197-15-0d	£1,197-15-0d
Furnishings, Rodel House		£241-13-3d	£241-13-3d	£241-13-3d
Furnishings, total	£1431-9-6d	£1439-8-3d	£1439-8-3d	£1439-8-3d
Improvements of lochs	£393-9-1d	£412-0-4d	£412-0-4d	£412-0-4d
Carriages, tools, guns, boats etc	£396-17-1d	£396-17-1d	£394-17-1d	£394-17-1d
Preliminary expenses	£314-17-4	£314-17-4d	£314-17-4d	£314-17-4d
Stores on hand	£175-14-0d	£22-13-1d	£19-2-0d	£19-0-9d
Stock of picture post-cards				
Sundry debtors	£10-15-0d	£137-2-10.5d	£111-3-0d	£118-15-4d
Cash on hand	£15-9-3d			

Year to December 1910	Year to December 1911	Year to December 1912	Year to December 1913	Year to December 1914	Year to December 1915	Year to December 1916
		No data			[see note 1]	
£2,893-16-7d	£2,893-16-7d		£2,893-16-7d	£2,893-16-7d	£2,893-16-7d	£2,893-16-7d
£502-2-2d	£502-2-2d		£502-2-2d	£502-2-2d	£502-2-2d	£502-2-2d
£382-14-6d	£382-14-6d		£382-14-6d	£382-14-6d	£382-14-6d	£382-14-6d
£604-4-0d	£604-4-0d		£604-4-0d	£604-4-0d	£604-4-0d	£604-4-0d
£4,382-17-3d	£4,382-17-3d		£4,382-17-3d	£4,382-17-3d	£4,382-17-3d	£4,382-17-3d
£196-10-5d	£196-10-5d		£196-10-5d	£196-10-5d	£196-10-5d	£196-10-5d
£16-4-0d	£16-4-0d		£16-4-0d	£16-4-0d		
£1,197-15-0d	£1,197-15-0d		£1,197-15-0d	£1,197-15-0d	£1,197-15-0d	£1,197-15-0d
£241-13-3d	£241-13-3d		£241-13-3d	£241-13-3d		
£1439-8-3d	£1439-8-3d		£1439-8-3d	£1439-8-3d	£1,197-15-0d	£1,197-15-0d
£412-0-4d	£412-0-4d		£412-0-4d	£412-0-4d	£412-0-4d	£412-0-4d
£394-17-1d	£394-17-1d		£394-17-1d	£394-17-1d	£222-11-4d	£222-11-4d
£314-17-4d	£314-17-4d		£314-17-4d	£314-17-4d	£314-17-4d	£314-17-4d
£9-1-0d	£9-1-0d		£8-3-0d	£8-3-0d		
						£8-3-0d
£137-10-9d	£64-8-11d		£41-15-4d	£180-19-3d	£1-0-0d	£1-0-0d

	Year to December 1906	Year to December 1907	Year to December 1908	Year to December 1909
Debenture interest waived by Holders				
Year's balance	**-£669-14-11d**	**-£508-5-2.5d**	**-£244-11-5d**	**-£184-15-4.5d**
Cumulative loss at end of year	**£3,087-14-9d**	**£3,595-19-11.5d**	**£3,840-4-11d**	**£4,025-0-3.5d**

Note 1 - 1915 was the year when the expenses of giving up Rodel Lodge were incurred

LIABILITIES				
NOMINAL CAPITAL [£13,000]	£13,000	£13,000	£13,000	£13,000
300 5% Cum. Preference Shares				
1000 Ordinary shares				
ISSUED CAPITAL				
115 Preference Shares, fully paid				
less calls in arrears		£1100-0-0d	£1100-0-0d	£1100-0-0d
755 Ordinary Shares, fully paid				
less calls in arrears		£7535-0-0d	£7535-0-0d	£7535-0-0d
Debentures		£840	£840	£890
SUNDRY CREDITORS:				
Rent	£288-10-0d	£275-0-0d	£275-0-0d	£275-0-0d
Taxes	£218-18-7d	£242-8-3d	£219-15-0d	£326-9-8.5d
Bank overdraft with interest to date	£712-12-0d	£395-1-4d	£507-11-10d	£482-9-0d
Loan account [note 2]	£300-0-0d	£300-0-0d	£300-0-0d	£300-0-0d
Trade creditors & others	£418-15-10d	£227-1-0d	£349-17-9d	£410-12-4d
John Malcolm [note3]				
Thomas Wilson				
David Strathie & Co [auditors]				

Year to December 1910	Year to December 1911	Year to December 1912	Year to December 1913	Year to December 1914	Year to December 1915	Year to December 1916
	£143-8-2d					
-£45-3-2d	£26-6-9d	£41-6-3d	£20-11-5.5d	-£43-17-4d	-£643-18-1.5d	-£280-6-7d
£4,070-3-5.5d	£3,900-8-6.5d	£3,859-2-3.5d	£3,838-10-10d	£3,838-10-10d	£4,526-6-3.5d	£4,806-12-10.5d
		No data			[see note 1]	
£13,000	£13,000		£13,000	£13,000	£13,000	£13,000
£1100-0-d	£1100-0-d		£1100-0-d	£1100-0-d	£1100-0-d	£1100-0-d
£7535-0-0d	£7535-0-0d		£7535-0-0d	£7535-0-0d	£7535-0-0d	£7535-0-0d
£890	£890		£890	£890	£890	£890
£275-0-0d	£275-0-0d		£275-0-0d	£400-0-0d*	£162-0-11d#	£167-1-3d#
£359-5-9d	£201-16-1d		£148-4-0d	£182-2-7d		
£517-14-3d	£501-17-4d		£507-5-0d	£418-12-0d		£519-19-6d
£300-0-0d	£300-0-0d		£300-0-0d	£450-0-0d		
£416-9-10.5d	£326-19-8.5d		£289-14-10d	£252-10-6d		
					£311-6-7d	£517-5-10d
					£184-19-11d	£194-4-11
					£31-4-0d	£35-8-0d

	Year to December 1906	Year to December 1907	Year to December 1908	Year to December 1909
Boyes & Fergusson [solicitors]				
Interest on loan, GD Stirling's Executry				
Directors' Guarantee a/c				
LOANS:				
GD Stirling's Executry				
John Malcolm				
John Dempster, Guaranteed				
Thomas Binnie				
Mr Fergusson's Representatives				

Note 1 - 1915 was the year when the expenses of giving up Rodel Lodge were incurred
Note 2 - Loan account probably represents loans from GD Stirling & John Dempster; these were itemised invidually in 1915 & 1916
Note 3 - This sum probably represents payment of rent & taxes made personally by John Malcolm on behalf of the Company; personal debts were listed individually in 1915 & 1916
* - "as adjusted" [sic]
# - including taxes and insurance

	Year to December 1906	Year to December 1907	Year to December 1908	Year to December 1909
PROFIT & LOSS ACCOUNT:				
Expenditure				
Food etc	£865-7-3d	£312-11-0.5d	£144-16-7d	£161-2-3d
Fuel	£73-10-4d	£56-4-6d	£9-9-6d	£16-13-5d
Garden	£37-5-8d	£20-7-2d		
Printing & stationery	£4-13-6d	6-2d	£8-16-11d	£5-19-2d
Rents, taxes, insurance [notes 4 & 5]	£673-9-2d	£603-8-5d	£688-3-11.5d	£681-102.5d

Year to December 1910	Year to December 1911	Year to December 1912	Year to December 1913	Year to December 1914	Year to December 1915	Year to December 1916
					£68-10-5.5d	£97-2-10.5d
					£33-18-2d	£45-10-8d
					£7-18-9d	£7-18-9d
					£300	£300
					£50	£50
					£150	£150
					£50	£50
					£50	£50

Year to December 1910	Year to December 1911	Year to Dec. 1912	Year to December 1913	Year to December 1914	Year to December 1915	Year to December 1916
		No data			[see note 1]	
£4-7-9d	[note 6]				£98-14-7.5d	£80-14-9.5d
£5-0-0d	[note 6]				£18-10-0d	
£3-18-9d	£1-16-6d		£1-13-3d	£1-14-0d	£3-8-6d	
£686-9-1d	£689-11-8d		£719-3-5d	£603-18-3d	£162-0-11d	£167-1-3d

	Year to December 1906	Year to December 1907	Year to December 1908	Year to December 1909
Wages & salaries	£404-6-4d	£207-5-4.5d	£132-6-7d	£113-17-7d
Provender & stabling	£55-6-5d	£36-11-6d		
Tobacco & cigars		£1-17-8d		
Advertising & commission	£37-16-4d	£19-2-8d	£24-15-6d	£10-8-0d
Repairs & house expenses	£48-12-0d	£52-13-0d	£15-0-0.5d	£46-0-4.5d
Interest	£53-11-5d	£79-18-6d		£84-6-6d
General charges	£30-3-9d	£27-4-5d	£15-2-6d	£14-6-11d
Maintenance of lochs	£18-16-0d	£12-6-2d	£12-13-3d	£9-2-6d
Fishing tackle		16-10d		
Picture postcards		£1-0-10d		
Legal expenses				
TOTAL	£2302-18-2d	£1431-14-3d	£1132-16-5d	£1143-6-11d
Income				
Board & lodging receipts + Rodel Angling Club	£1633-3-3d	£923-9-0.5d	£888-11-5.5d	£958-11-6.5d
Debenture interest waived by holders				
Surplus for year				
Deficit for year	£669-14-11d	£508-5-2.5d	£244-4-11.5d	£184-15-4.5d
CUMULATIVE DEFICIT	£3,087-14-9d	£3,595-19-11.5d	£3,840-4-11d	£4,025-0-3.5d

Note 1 - 1915 was the year when the expenses, recorded as a book loss of £299-3-9d, of giving up Rodel Lodge were incurred

Note 4 - The Company was £550 in arrears of rent at March 1915 when they were summonsed in the Court of Session, Edinburgh, by The Earl of Dunmore

Note 5 - Rent specified in the 1903 Leases was £850 [being £500 pa for Finsbay + £350 for Rodel]; this was reduced by 1906 (new lease was probably in March 1906 with loss of Horsacleit/Grosebay fishings)

Note 6 - Food & fuel costs are now apparently being allocated to the Rodel and Finsbay angling club accounts instead of the Association's accounts

Year to December 1910	Year to December 1911	Year to December 1912	Year to December 1913	Year to December 1914	Year to December 1915	Year to December 1916
£41-0-7d	£27-4-0d		£14-14-0d	£14-14-0d	£104-19-9d	£105-19-9d
£19-15-0d						
£74-7-8d					£6-13-11d	£6-6-0d
£92-3-10d	£90-14-2d		£55-15-0d	£51-2-8d	£47-5-2d	£48-10-11d
£7-13-4d	£1-9-6d		£3-3-11.5d	£2-8-5d	£17-7-3d	£20-7-10.5d
					£18-5-1d	
£934-16-0d	£837-2-7d		£815-1-1d	£673-17-4d	£661-18-0.5d	£280-6-7d
£889-12-10d	£795-4-0d		£815-1-1d	£630-0-0d	£128-15-10d	£167-3-1d
	£41-18-7d					
	£26-6-9d	£41-6-3d	£20-11-5.5d			
£45-3-2d				£43-17-4d	£643-18-1.5d	£280-6-7d
£4,070-3-5.5d	£3,900-8-6.5d	£3,859-2-3.5d	£3,838-10-10d	£3,838-10-10d	£4,526-6-3.5d	£4,806-12-10.5d

APPENDIX FOUR

EXTRACTS FROM FISHING RESULTS REPORTED IN THE SCOTSMAN NEWSPAPER FOR THE HEBRIDEAN SPORTING ASSOCIATION

Date of report	Catch for	SEA TROUT				SALMON			No. of rods with reported catch
		No.	Weight	Average weight	Heaviest	No.	Weight		
8-Aug-1903	5 days	244	from 0.5 to 2 lb		..	..	..	Rodel	6 rods
22-Sep-1904	1 week	245	total 126 lb	8 oz	2lb 14 oz	1	5 lb		
19-Aug-1905	16-Aug	27	14 lb	8 oz	..	..	..		
	17-Aug	12	9 lb 14 oz	13 oz	2 lb	1	4 lb 14 oz	Finsbay	6 rods
13-Sep-1905	8-Sep	21	12 lb	9 oz	..	..	..	Rodel	6 rods
	8-Sep	23	11 lb 11 oz	8 oz	..	..	..	Finsbay	4 rods
19-Sep-1905	14-Sep	31	23 lb 10 oz	12 oz	..	..	..	Rodel	5 rods
	14-Sep	37	25 lb 4 oz	11 oz	2 lb 8 oz	..	..	Finsbay	6 rods
21-Sep-1905	16-Sep	12	10 lb 8 oz	14 oz	..	1	6 lb 4 oz	Rodel	3 rods
3-Apr-1906	28-Mar	23	16 lb	11 oz	2 lb	..	..	Rodel/Obbe	1 rod
	29-Mar	13	16 lb	1 lb 4 oz	4 lb 3 oz	..	..	Rodel/Obbe	1 rod

Date of report	Catch for	SEA TROUT				SALMON				No. of rods with reported catch
		No.	Weight	Average weight	Heaviest		No.	Weight		
2-May-1906	27-Apr	14	11 lb 8 oz	13 oz	3 lb 4 oz	:			: Rodel	2 rods
	30-Apr	33	26 lb	13 oz		:			:	2 rods
9-May-1906	4-May	31	24 lb 8 oz	13 oz	2 lb	:			: Rodel	2 rods
18-May-1906	3 days	15	7 lb	7 oz	2 lb 8 oz	:			: Rodel	1 rod
	2 days	11	5 lb	7 oz		:			: Finsbay	1 rod
9-Jul-1906	5-Jul					:	1	7 lb	: Rodel	
	4 days	8			4 lb	:			: Finsbay	
17-Aug-2007	13-Aug	21	9 lb 13 oz	7 oz		:			: Rodel	3 rods
	14-Aug	5	5 lb 6 oz	1 lb 1 oz	2 lb 10 oz	:			: Rodel	2 rods
6-Sep-1906	week	95	69 lb	12 oz	5 lb 12 oz	:	1	3 lb 8 oz	: Rodel	
6-Aug-1907	3 days	48			2 lb 4 oz	:	5	22 lb 14 oz	: Rodel	
	1-Aug		22 lb 4 oz			:			: Finsbay	2 rods
13-Aug-1907	9-Aug	2			5 lb 12 oz	:			: Obbe	1 rod
	8-Aug	50				:			: Finsbay	7 rods
22-Aug-1907	15-Aug	18	9 lb 12 oz	9 oz		:			: Rodel	1 rod
	16-Aug	24	19 lb 8 oz	13 oz	4 lb	:	1	5 lb 4 oz	: Rodel	4 rods
	17-Aug	3	1 lb 8 oz	8 oz		:	1	4 lb 4 oz	: Finsbay	2 rods

Date of report	Catch for	SEA TROUT					SALMON				No. of rods with reported catch
		No.	Weight	Average weight	Heaviest		No.	Weight			
	17-Aug	37	22 lb 10 oz	10 oz		:			:	Finsbay	7 rods
30-Aug-1907	26-Aug	30	16 lbs	9 oz		:	2	7 lb 12 oz	:	Rodel	3 rods
	26-Aug	9	8 lb 14 oz	1 lb	2 lb 1 oz	:			:	Finsbay	7 rods
7-Sep-1907	31-Aug	14	12 lb 5 oz	14 oz	3 lb	:			:	Finsbay	2 rods
	2-Sep	11	11 lb 1 oz	1 lb 1 oz		:			:	Finsbay	2 rods
12-Oct-1907	5 days	56	40 lb 4 oz	12 oz		:			:	Rodel	3 rods
17-Oct-1907	4 days	59	42 lb 13 oz	12 oz	2 lb 4 oz	:			:	Rodel	3 rods
27-Jul-1909	22-Jul	7			1 lb 7 oz	:	1	5 lb 4 oz	:	Rodel	2 rods
17-Aug-1909		7			1 lb 11 oz	:	1	4 lb 4 oz	:	Rodel	4 rods
	few days	161			2 lb 7 oz	:			:	Finsbay	
25-Aug-1909	24-Aug	55			4 lb 8 oz	:	2		:	Rodel	4 rods
	24-Aug	29			2 lb 10 oz	:	1	6 lb	:	Finsbay	5 rods
						:			:		
19-Aug-1910	16-Aug	6			3 lb	:			:		
	17-Aug	1	4 lb 4 oz		4 lb 4 oz	:	1	6 lb 12 oz	:	Rodel	1 rod
25-Aug-1910	23-Aug					:	2	12 lb	:	Rodel	1 rod
5-Sep-1910		22			4 lb 8 oz	:			:	Rodel	5 rods

Date of report	Catch for	SEA TROUT				SALMON			No. of rods with reported catch
		No.	Weight	Average weight	Heaviest	No.	Weight		
27-Apr-1911	21-Apr	11			1 lb 10 oz			: Rodel	1 rod
	22-Apr	8			3 lb 12 oz			: Rodel	1 rod
2-May-1911	4 days	58			2 lb 12 oz			: Rodel	1 rod
9-Sep-1912	6-Sep	13			4 lb	2	14 lb 8 oz	: Rodel	3 rods
14-Sep-1912	10-Sep	48			2 lb 4 oz			: Rodel	4 rods
26-Sep-1912	1 day	8			1 lb 8 oz	2	21 lb 8 oz	: Rodel	2 rods
30-Sep-1912	27-Sep					3	18 lb 12 oz	: Rodel	3 rods
30-Jul-1913	1 day	6	5 lb 5 oz	14 oz		2	12 lb	: Rodel	2 rods
4-Aug-1913	29-Jul	3			1 lb 8 oz	1	5 lb 4 oz	: Rodel	1 rod
	30-Jul	13			2 lb 8 oz			: Rodel	1 rod
15-Aug-1913	11-Aug	11			3 lb 4 oz			: Rodel	3 rods
19-Sep-1913	12-Sep	27	20 lb	12 oz	2 lb 12 oz			: Rodel	
	13-Sep	19	14 lb 8 oz	12 oz	2 lb 8 oz			: Rodel	
	15-Sep	17	12 lb	11 oz	3 lb 8 oz			: Rodel	

Date of report	Catch for	SEA TROUT				SALMON		Location	No. of rods with reported catch
		No.	Weight	Average weight	Heaviest	No.	Weight		
11-Apr-1914	1 week	35			2 lb	1	4 lb 12 oz	Rodel	1 rod
26-Aug-1914	1 day	10				1	18 lb	Rodel	1 rod
17-Jul-1930	8 days	50			1 lb 12 oz			Rodel	
	3 days	55			3 lb			Rodel	
OVERALL		Average about 18 sea trout per day			max 5 lb 12 oz	Average about 0.32 salmon per day			

BIBLIOGRAPHY

1. **The Bailie** (26 February 1913) *Men You Know. No. 2016*: Glasgow. p. 1–3.
2. **National Archives of Scotland** Hebridean Sporting Association, Ltd. **BT2/5276**.
3. **Stuart, Hamish** (1899) *Lochs and Loch Fishing*. London: Chapman & Hall.
4. **National Archives of Scotland** (1917) Inventory of the personal estate of William Fergusson. **SC/36/48/274/93**.
5. **National Archives of Scotland** (1915) Earl of Dunmore *vs* Hebridean Sporting Association Ltd. *Court of Session*, **CS256/512/1**.
6. **National Archives of Scotland** (8 November 1916) Feu Charter by Alexander Edward, Earl of Dunmore to the Hebridean Sporting Association Ltd. **GRS/103/436 190–196**.
7. **Calderwood, W.L.** (1909) *The Salmon Rivers and Lochs of Scotland*. 1st ed. London: Edward Arnold.
8. **Calderwood, W.L.** (1921) *The Salmon Rivers and Lochs of Scotland*. 2nd ed. London: Edward Arnold.
9. **Wigan, Michael** (2000) *Grimersta: the Story of a Great Fishery*: (Privately published).
10. **Lawson, Bill** (2002) *Harris in History and Legend*. Edinburgh: John Donald.
11. **Macdonald, Emily** (1965) *Twenty Years of Hebridean Memories*. 2nd ed.
12. **Macdonald, Donald** (2004) *Tales and Traditions of the Lews*. Edinburgh: Birlinn.
13. **Charnley, Bob** (1993) *The Western Isles: A Postcard Tour. 2 – Harris and Lewis*. Portree: Maclean Press.
14. **Charnley, Bob** (1992) *The Western Isles: A Postcard Tour. 1 – Barra to North Uist*. Portree: Maclean Press.
15. **Stuart, Hamish** (1917) *The Book of the Sea Trout, with some Chapters on Salmon*. London: Martin Secker.
16. **Cattanach to Leverhulme** (16 October 1923) *Unilever Archives*, **Box 120**.
17. **National Archives of Scotland** (approx 1911) Inland Revenue (Scotland) Field Books – Inverness-shire. **IRS 68/4/57**.
18. **Leverhulme to Robertson** (23 September 1919) *Unilever Archives*, **Box 101**.

19. **Robertson to Leverhulme** (25 June 1920) *Unilever Archives,* **Box 110.**
20. **Malcolm to Robertson** (22 June 1920) *Unilever Archives,* **Box 101.**
21. **Leverhulme to Robertson** (8 September 1920) *Unilever Archives,* **Box 101.**
22. **Robertson to Leverhulme** (1 July 1920) *Unilever Archives,* **Box 101.**
23. **Robertson to Leverhulme** (2 February 1921) *Unilever Archives,* **Box 101.**
24. **Leverhulme to Robertson** (7 February 1921) *Unilever Archives,* **Box 101.**
25. **Leverhulme to Cattanach** (3 September 1923) *Unilever Archives,* **Box 120.**
26. **Wilkinson, Peter & Astley, Joan Bright** (1997) *Gubbins & SOE.* Barnsley: Pen & Sword.
27. **The Scotsman** (2 September 1876) *Inverness-shire: Magnificent sporting estate for sale.*
28. **Robertson to Sanders** (27 March 1923) *Unilever Archives,* **Box 115.**
29. **Robertson to Sanders** (7 May 1923) *Unilever Archives,* **Box 115.**
30. **Robertson to Sanders** (5 December 1921) *Unilever Archives,* **Box 115.**
31. **Brown, J. Crichton** (3 September 1921) *Unilever Archives,* **Box 115.**
32. **Robertson to Sanders** (13 September 1922) *Unilever Archives,* **Box 115.**
33. **Robertson to Sanders** (13 February 1922) *Unilever Archives,* **Box 115.**
34. **Sanders to Robertson** (17 February 1922) *Unilever Archives,* **Box 115.**
35. **Sanders to Robertson** (17 March 1922) *Unilever Archives,* **Box 115.**
36. **Robertson to Sanders** (7 March 1923) *Unilever Archives,* **Box 115.**
37. **Robertson to Sanders** (27 March 1923) *Unilever Archives,* **Box 115.**
38. **Robertson to Leverhulme** (28 April 1923) *Unilever Archives,* **Box 115.**
39. **Shepherd & Wedderburn to Sanders** (23 June 1924) *Unilever Archives,* **Box 89.**
40. **Bridgett, R.C.** (1929) *Sea-Trout Fishing.* London: Herbert Jenkins.
41. **Mundle, C.W.K.** (1978) *Game Fishing: Methods and Memories.* London: Barrie and Jenkins.
42. **Headley, Stan.** (2005) *The Loch Fisher's Bible.* London: Robert Hale.
43. **Maitland, P.S. & Campbell, R.N.** (1992) *Freshwater Fishes.* The New Naturalist. London: Harper Collins.
44. **Leverhulme to Robertson** (16 April 1923) *Unilever Archives,* **Box 102.**
45. **Robertson to Leverhulme** (6 July 1923) *Unilever Archives,* **Box 102.**
46. **Gardner, M.L.G.** (1976) A review of factors which may influence the sea-age and maturation of Atlantic salmon, *Salmo salar L. Journal of Fish Biology,* **9**: p. 289–327.
47. **Rawlings, Bill** (2002) *The Great Salmon and Sea Trout Loughs of Ireland.* Shrewsbury: Swan Hill Press.
48. **MacGregor, Alasdair Alpin** (1933) *Searching the Hebrides with a Camera.* London: George Harrap.

49. **Adams, Rev. Joseph ["Corrigeen"]** (1938) *Fifty Years Angling in England, Scotland, The Hebrides, Ireland, Holland, Switzerland and Canada.* London: Hutchinson.

50. **Stirling, John** (1929) *Fifty Years with the Rod.* London: Philip Allan.

51. **Jones, David S.D.** (2008) *The Sporting Estates of the Outer Hebrides, Past and Present.* Fovant: Polraen Publications.

52. **Harris, G. & Milner, N.** editors (2006) *Sea Trout: Biology, Conservation and Management. Proceedings of the First International Sea Trout Symposium, Cardiff, July 2004.* Blackwell: Oxford.

53. **Nall, G.H.** (1930) *The Life of the Sea Trout, especially in Scottish Waters; with chapters on the reading & measuring of scales.* London: Sealey, Service & Co.

54. **Nall, G.H.** (1934 No. IV) *Sea trout of Lewis and Harris: Further notes on collections of scales from this district,* in *Fisheries Scotland, Salmon Fish.* H.M.S.O.: Edinburgh.

55. **Fahy, Edward** (1985) *Child of the Tides: A Sea Trout Handbook.* Dun Laoghaire: Glendale Press.

56. **Fahy, E.** (1978) Variation in some biological characteristics of British sea trout, *Salmo trutta* L. *Journal of Fish Biology,* **13**: p. 123–138.

57. **Maisse, G., Mourot, B., Breton, B., Fostier, A., Marcuzzi, O., Le Bail, P.Y., Bagliniere, J.L., Richard, A.** (1991) Sexual maturity in sea trout, *Salmo trutta* L., running up the River Calonne (Normandy, France) at the "finnock" stage. *Journal of Fish Biology,* **39**: p. 705–715.

58. **Henzell, H.P.** (1949) *Fishing for Sea Trout.* London: Adam & Charles Black.

59. **Fahy, E.** (1985) Protecting finnock as a sea trout conservation measure. *Salmon and Trout Magazine,* **230**: p. 66–69.

60. **Menzies, W.J.M.** (1936) *Sea Trout and Trout.* London: Edward Arnold.

61. **Campbell, R.N.** (1971) The growth of Brown Trout, *Salmo trutta L.,* in northern Scotland with special reference to the improvement of fisheries. *Journal of Fish Biology,* **3**: p. 1–28.

62. **Harris, G.** (2006) A review of the statutory regulations to conserve sea trout stocks in England and Wales., in *Sea Trout: Biology, Conservation and Management,* Harris, G. & Milner, N., editors. Blackwell: Oxford. p. 441–456.

63. **Poole, E., Dillane, M., DeEyto, E., Rogan, G., McGinty, P., Whelan, K.** (2006) Characteristics of the Burrishole sea trout population: Census, marine survival, enhancement and stock-recruitment relationship, 1971–2003., in *Sea Trout: Biology, Conservation and Management,* Harris, G. & Milner, N., editors. Blackwell: Oxford. p. 279–306.

64. **Butler, J.R.A., Walker, A.F.** (2006) Characteristics of the sea trout *Salmo trutta* (L.) stock collapse in the River Ewe (Wester Ross, Scotland), in 1998–2001, in *Sea Trout: Biology, Conservation and Management,* Harris, G. & Milner, N., editors. Blackwell: Oxford. p. 45–59.

65. **Milner, N.J., Harris, G.S., Gargan, P., Beveridge, M., Pawson, M.G., Walker, A., Whelan, K.** (2006) Perspectives on sea trout science and management, in *Sea Trout Biology, Conservation and Management*, Harris G, & Milner, N., editors. Blackwell: Oxford. p. 480–490.

66. **Evans, R., Greest, V.** (2006) The rod and net sea trout fisheries of England and Wales., in *Sea Trout: Biology, Conservation and Management.*, Harris, G. & Milner, N., editors. Blackwell: Oxford. p. 107–114.

67. **Gargan, P.G., Poole, W.R., Forde, G.P.** (2006) A review of the status of Irish sea trout stocks, in *Sea Trout: Biology, Conservation and Management*, Harris, G. & Milner, N., editors. Blackwell: Oxford. p. 25–44.

68. **Gargan, P.G., Roche, W.K., Forde, G.P., Ferguson, A.** (2006) Characteristics of the sea trout (*Salmo trutta L.*) stocks from the Owengowla and Invermore fisheries, Connemara, Western Ireland, and recent trends in marine survival., in *Sea Trout: Biology, Conservation and Management*, Harris, G. & Milner, N., editors. Blackwell: Oxford. p. 60–75.

69. **Hatton-Ellis, M., Hay, D.W., Walker, A.F., Northcott, S.J.** (2006) Sea lice *Lepeophtheirus salmonis* infestations of post-smolt sea trout in Loch Shieldaig, Wester Ross, 1999–2003, in *Sea Trout: Biology, Conservation and Management*, Harris, G. & Milner, N., editors. Blackwell: Oxford. p. 372–376.

70. **National Archives of Scotland** (1936) Land settlement: Estates of Luskentyre and Borve. *Department of Agriculture*, **E824/614**.

71. **Campbell, Patrick** (2005) *Tunnel Tigers: A first hand account of a hydro boy in the Highlands.* Edinburgh: Luath Press.

72. **Hall, Robert** (1885) *The Highland Sportsman and Tourist.* London: Simpkin, Marshall & Co.

73. **Hunter, Janet** (2001) *The Islanders and the Orb: the History of the Harris Tweed Industry 1835–1995.* Stornoway: Acair.

74. **The Scotsman** (28 April 1923) *Rodel.*

75. **Young, Archibald** (1886) *Fourth Annual Report of the Fishery Board for Scotland.* H.M.S.O.: Edinburgh. p. 283.

76. **The Scotsman** (2 September 1876) *Inverness-shire: Magnificent sporting estate for sale.*

77. **Shearer, W.M.** (1992) *The Atlantic Salmon. Natural History, Exploitation and Future Management.* Oxford: Fishing News Books.

78. **"Sixty-one" [Rev. George Hely-Hutchinson]** (1875) *Reminiscences of the Lews or Twenty Years' Wild Sport in the Hebrides.* 3rd ed. London: Bickers & Son.

79. **Shetland News** (28 July 1900) *S. Magnus Hotel, Hillswick.*

80. **Shetland Times** (28 July 1900) *Opening of St Magnus Hotel, Hillswick.*

81. **Robertson to Leverhulme** (29 January 1921) *Unilever Archives*, **Box 101**.

82. **Irvine, J.C.** (2004) *George Gerald Henderson*, in *Oxford Dictionary of National Biography*: Oxford.

83. **Jones, David S.D.** (2007) *Game on Lewis and Harris – Past and Present.* Port of Ness: The Islands Book Trust.

84. **Scott to Leverhulme** (October 1919) *Unilever Archives,* **Box 97**.

85. **Dott, N.** (1956) Obituary: E. Norman Jamieson OBE, FRCSEd. *British Medical Journal,* **1**: p. 1431.

86. **Anon. (J.C.R-G.)** (1956) Obituary: Edward Norman Jamieson OBE, FRCSE, LDS. *The Lancet,* **1**: p. 970.

87. **National Archives of Scotland** (1906–07) Congested Districts Board: Proposed tri-weekly steamer call at Stockinish and Finsbay on the northward journey of the Dunvegan Mail Steamer. **AF 42/3515**.

88. **National Archives of Scotland** (1908) Congested Districts Board: Transmitting resolution of Harris Parish Council pointing out necessity for a steamer call at Finsbay as well as Stockinish. **AF 42/4506**.

89. **National Archives of Scotland** (1903) Congested Districts Board: Telegraph extension to Finsbay & Rodel. **AF 42/1706**.

90. **Robins, N.S. & Meek, D.E.** (2006) *The Kingdom of MacBrayne.* Edinburgh: Birlinn.

91. **Leverhulme to Lissenden** (15 January 1919) *Unilever Archives,* **Box 101**.

92. **Leverhulme to Robertson** (6 October 1923) *Unilever Archives,* **Box 102**.

93. **Nicolson, Nigel** (1960) *Lord of the Isles.* London: Weidenfeld and Nicolson.

94. **Irvine, Mabel V.** (1970) *The Avenue of Years: A Memoir of Sir James Irvine, Principal and Vice-Chancellor of the University of St. Andrews 1921–1952 by his Wife.* Edinburgh: Blackwood.

95. **Irvine, J.C.** (1917) Thomas Purdie. *Journal of the Chemical Society,* **111**: p. 359–369.

96. **P.F.F.** (1922) Thomas Purdie 1843–1916. *Proceedings of the Royal Society, Series A,* **101**: p. iv-xiv.

97. **Read, John** (1953) James Colquhoun Irvine, 1877–1952. *Obituary Notices of Fellows of The Royal Society,* **8**: p. 458–489.

98. **Leverhulme, Lord** (1927) *Viscount Leverhulme by his Son.* London: George Allen & Unwin.

99. **Hutchinson, Roger** (2003) *The Soapman: Lewis, Harris and Lord Leverhulme.* Edinburgh: Birlinn.

100. **Jolly, W.P.** (1976) *Lord Leverhulme: A Biography.* London: Constable.

101. **Williams, Harley** (1948) *Men of Stress.* London: Jonathan Cape.

102. **Leverhulme to Hope** (11 July 1913): Unilever Archives.

103. **Mawson, T.H.** (1926) *The Art & Craft of Garden Making.* 5th ed. London: Batsford.

104. **Leverhulme to Robertson** (July 1921) *Unilever Archives,* **Box 101**.

105. **Leverhulme to Robertson** (10 January 1922) *Unilever Archives,* **Box 101**.

106. **Leneman, Leah** (1989) *Fit for Heroes? Land Settlement in Scotland after World War I.* Aberdeen: Aberdeen University Press.

107. **MacDonald, Colin** (1943) *Highland Journey or Suil Air Ais.* Edinburgh: The Moray Press.

108. **National Archives of Scotland** (1914–1921) Board of Agriculture: Orinsay and Stimerray, Lewis. Proposals, including general correspondence on land settlement in Lewis. **AF83/354**.

109. **Anderson, Iain F.** (1937) *Across Hebridean Seas.* London: Chatto and Windus.

110. **Lumley & Dowell** (1915) *The Isle of Lewis: Shootings & Fishings to be Let under a New Regime.* Lumley & Dowell (letting agents): London.

111. **Leverhulme** (1921) *Unilever Archives,* **Box 86**.

112. **The Scotsman** (7 September 1936) *Late Mr Thomas Wilson: Solicitor's Work on Land Settlement Schemes in Highlands and Islands.*

113. **Transactions of the Inverness Scientific Society.** 13 December 1921.

114. **Transactions of the Inverness Scientific Society.** 13 March 1923.

115. **Transactions of the Inverness Scientific Society.** 12 December 1916.

116. **Highland Council Archive Service** (1908–1929) Inverness Field Club Minute Book (11 January 1927). **HRA/030/A4**.

117. **Stewart, K.** (October 2004) A journal they can call their own. *The Scots Magazine*: p. 418–421.

118. **Royal Commission (Highlands and Islands, 1892)** (1895) *Minutes of evidence taken before the Royal Commission (Highlands and Islands, 1892).* H.M.S.O.: Edinburgh.

119. **National Archives of Scotland** (1898) Congested Districts Board: Thomas Wilson, Lochmaddy requesting allowance for time engaged by him in traveling to and from Harris and attending meeting of C.D.B. **AF 42/168**.

120. **Dewar, Sir John** (1912) *Highlands and Islands Medical Service Committee: Report to Lords Commissioners of His Majesty's Treasury* H.M.S.O.: Edinburgh.

121. **Lawson, Bill** (1994) *Croft History: Isle of Harris, volume 1.* Northton, Isle of Harris: Bill Lawson.

122. **Lawson, Bill** (2002) *Croft History: Isle of Harris, volume 3.* Northton, Isle of Harris: Bill Lawson.

123. **The Bailie** (24 December 1924) *Men You Know. No. 2724*: Glasgow. p. 3.

124. **Scott, Ian** (2006) *Falkirk: A History.* Edinburgh: Birlinn.

125. **Young, Andrew** (1865) *The Angler's Guide to the Rivers and Lakes in the North of Scotland.* Edinburgh: Adam & Charles Black.

126. **Glasgow Herald** (22 January 1929) *Glasgow Shipowner's Death.*

127. **House, Jack** (1984) *Pride of Perth.* London: Hutchinson Benham.

128. **Walker, Hugh** (1991) *Dunfermline Linen: The Story of Erskine Beveridge and St. Leonard's Works 1833–1989.* Dunfermline: Carnegie Dunfermline Trust.

129. **Beveridge, Erskine** (2001) *North Uist: Its Archaeology and Topography. (Reprinted from 1911 edition).* Edinburgh: Birlinn.

130. **Beveridge, Erskine** (1923) *The 'Abers' and 'Invers' of Scotland.* Edinburgh: William Brown.
131. **Beveridge, Erskine** (1901) *A Bibliography of Works relating to Dunfermline and West Fife.* Dunfermline: William Clark.
132. **Beveridge, Erskine** (1917) *The Burgh Records of Dunfermline 1488–1584.* Edinburgh: William Brown.
133. **Beveridge, Erskine** (1893) *The Churchyard Memorials of Crail.* Edinburgh: T & A. Constable.
134. **Beveridge, Erskine** (1903) *Coll and Tiree, their Prehistoric Forts and Eclesiastical Antiquities.* Edinburgh: T & A Constable.
135. **Beveridge, Erskine** (1922) *Wanderings with a Camera.* Edinburgh: William Brown.
136. **Neale, C.** (2004) *Erskine Beveridge 1851–1920,* in *Oxford Dictionary of National Biography*: Oxford.
137. **Anon.** (1916) In Memoriam: John Collins. *The Meteor,* (5 June): p. 59.
138. **Weir, R.B.** (2004) *John Alexander Dewar, First Baron Forteviot (1856–1929),* in *Oxford Dictionary of National Biography.* Oxford University Press: Oxford. p. 1000–1002.
139. **Taylor, G. Rankin** (1951) *Thomas Dunlop & Sons, Shipowners 1851–1951.* Glasgow: Thomas Dunlop.
140. **Taylor, G. Rankin** (1951) *Thomas Dunlop & Sons, Shipowners.* Glasgow: (Privately published).
141. **Power, D'Arcy** (1930) *Plarr's Lives of the Fellows of the Royal College of Surgeons of England.* Bristol: John Wright (for The Royal College of Surgeons).
142. **Quine, D.A.** (1998) *St. Kilda Portraits.* Ambleside: David Quine.

References from Leverhulme Business Correspondence Archive Collection cited with kind permission of Unilever.

BIBLIOGRAPHY 237

Seann Loidse Ghrinn Fhionnasbhaigh

Eadar Ròineabhal aosda is Loch seasgair Fhionnasbhaigh
laigh rùn-diomhair fuadain, seann Loidse eireachdail
Fhionnasbhaigh.
Thainig fir Ghlaschu, agus thogadh an Loidse air a' Ghroba
Dubh.
Chruthaicheadh lochan, rinneadh obair—cosnaidh, ghlacadh
iasg, is chaitheadh airgead.
Ochòin, thraoigh na cistean—airgid, chaidh am màl gun
phàigheadh, is dh'fhalbh na daoine.
Bha an Loidse bhochd gun iarrtas oirre, is dh'eug i.
Chaidh na pìosan breagha fiodha do thaighean elle anns na
Hearadh.
Tha na daoine js an gillean 's an searbhantan air siubhal.
Tha ceòthan Tim an dèidh cur am falach gach cuimhneachan
de'n t-seann Loidse ghrinn
agus, na clachan aosda an sud fhathast chan innis a chaoidh
na sgeòil-ruin.

[Translation by John Angus Macleod]

The Fine Old Lodge of Finsbay

Between ancient Roneval and the sheltered Loch Finsbay
There lay a fugitive mystery, the fine old Lodge of Finsbay.
The men of Glasgow came, and the Lodge was born at the
Groba Dubh.
Lochs were made, jobs were given, fish were caught, and
money was spent.
Alas, the coffers dried up, and the men went away.
The poor Lodge was unwanted, and it passed away.
The fine wooden bits went to other homes in Harris.
The men and their ghillies and maids have passed away.
The mists of time have hidden the memories of the fine old
Lodge,
And the old stones still there will never tell the secrets.

[MLGG]

INDEX